THE
HISTORY OF
CAMBODIA

ADVISORY BOARD

THE HISTORY OF CAMBODIA

Justin Corfield

959.6
C797h

The Greenwood Histories of the Modern Nations
Frank W. Thackeray and John E. Findling, Series Editors

1/10

GREENWOOD PRESS
An Imprint of ABC-CLIO, LLC

A B C ⬥ C L I O

Santa Barbara, California • Denver, Colorado • Oxford, England

Copyright 2009 by Justin Corfield

All rights reserved. No part of this publication may be reproduced,
stored in a retrieval system, or transmitted, in any form or by any means,
electronic, mechanical, photocopying, recording, or otherwise,
except for the inclusion of brief quotations in a review, without
prior permission in writing from the publisher.

Library of Congress Cataloging-in-Publication Data

Corfield, Justin J.
   The history of Cambodia / Justin Corfield.
       p. cm.—(The Greenwood histories of the modern nations)
   Includes bibliographical references and index.
   ISBN 978-0-313-35722-0 (paper : alk. paper)—ISBN 978-0-313-35723-7
(ebook)   1. Cambodia—History.   I. Title.
   DS554.5.C67   2009
   959.6—dc22   2009028948

13   12   11   10   09   1   2   3   4   5

This book is also available on the World Wide Web as an eBook.
Visit www.abc-clio.com for details.

ABC-CLIO, LLC
130 Cremona Drive, P.O. Box 1911
Santa Barbara, California 93116-1911

This book is printed on acid-free paper ∞
Manufactured in the United States of America

Contents

A photo essay follows page 66

Series Foreword

The Greenwood Histories of the Modern Nations series is intended to provide students and interested laypeople with up-to-date, concise, and analytical histories of many of the nations of the contemporary world. Not since the 1960s has there been a systematic attempt to publish a series of national histories, and as series advisors, we believe that this series will prove to be a valuable contribution to our understanding of other countries in our increasingly interdependent world.

Some 40 years ago, at the end of the 1960s, the Cold War was an accepted reality of global politics. The process of decolonization was still in progress, the idea of a unified Europe with a single currency was unheard of, the United States was mired in a war in Vietnam, and the economic boom in Asia was still years in the future. Richard Nixon was president of the United States, Mao Tse-tung (not yet Mao Zedong) ruled China, Leonid Brezhnev guided the Soviet Union, and Harold Wilson was prime minister of the United Kingdom. Authoritarian dictators still controlled most of Latin America, the Middle East was reeling in the wake of the Six-Day War, and Shah Mohammad Reza Pahlavi was at the height of his power in Iran.

Since then, the Cold War has ended, the Soviet Union has vanished, leaving 15 independent republics in its wake, the advent of the computer age has radically transformed global communications, the rising demand for oil makes

the Middle East still a dangerous flashpoint, and the rise of new economic powers like the People's Republic of China and India threatens to bring about a new
world order. All of these developments have had a dramatic impact on the recent history of every nation of the world.

For this series, which was launched in 1998, we first selected nations whose
political, economic, and socio-cultural affairs marked them as among the most
important of our time. For each nation, we found an author who was recognized
as a specialist in the history of that nation. These authors worked cooperatively
with us and with Greenwood Press to produce volumes that reflected current
research on their nations and that are interesting and informative to their readers. In the first decade of the series, more than 40 volumes were published,
and as of 2008, some are moving into second editions.

The success of the series has encouraged us to broaden our scope to include
additional nations, whose histories have had significant effects on their regions,
if not on the entire world. In addition, geopolitical changes have elevated other
nations into positions of greater importance in world affairs and, so, we have
chosen to include them in this series as well. The importance of a series such
as this cannot be underestimated. As a superpower whose influence is felt all
over the world, the United States can claim a "special" relationship with almost
every other nation. Yet many Americans know very little about the histories of
nations with which the United States relates. How did they get to be the way
they are? What kind of political systems have evolved there? What kind of
influence do they have on their own regions? What are the dominant political,
religious, and cultural forces that move their leaders? These and many other
questions are answered in the volumes of this series.

The authors who contribute to this series write comprehensive histories of
their nations, dating back, in some instances, to prehistoric times. Each of them,
however, has devoted a significant portion of their book to events of the past
40 years because the modern era has contributed the most to contemporary
issues that have an impact on U.S. policy. Authors make every effort to be as
up-to-date as possible so that readers can benefit from discussion and analysis
of recent events.

In addition to the historical narrative, each volume contains an introductory
chapter giving an overview of that country's geography, political institutions,
economic structure, and cultural attributes. This is meant to give readers a snap-
shot of the nation as it exists in the contemporary world. Each history also includes supplementary information following the narrative, which may include
a timeline that represents a succinct chronology of the nation's historical evo-
lution, biographical sketches of the nation's most important historical figures,
and a glossary of important terms or concepts that are usually expressed in a
foreign language. Finally, each author prepares a comprehensive bibliography
for readers who wish to pursue the subject further.

Readers of these volumes will find them fascinating and well written. More importantly, they will come away with a better understanding of the contemporary world and the nations that comprise it. As series advisors, we hope that this series will contribute to a heightened sense of global understanding as we move through the early years of the twenty-first century.

Frank W. Thackeray and John E. Findling
Indiana University Southeast

Preface

This book derives from an interest in Cambodia dating back to my school days, when I became fascinated by Angkor, which my parents had visited many years earlier, in 1963. When I was 11, I had to present a talk at school, and I chose Angkor as my topic, using photographs my parents had taken of the temples as visual aids. This eventually led to my studies at the University of Hull, and then at Monash University, Australia, where I completed my doctoral thesis on the Cambodian government during the period from 1970 until 1975. Since then, I have been teaching and over this time, I have incurred many debts. A large number of Cambodian politicians and their families have granted interviews, and helped provide me an abundance of information that is not available elsewhere, as have academics, former diplomats, and others connected with Cambodia, whose knowledge, ideas, advice, and insight have been invaluable.

My first thanks must be to the Cambodians who have helped me understand their country. Piphal Engly and her husband Than Hin have been family friends for many years, and my thanks to both of them must be recorded; and also to Sok Pirun, another close friend over a long period of time, who died just before I finished this manuscript. I have enjoyed my discussions with the late Chhean Vam, Douc Rasy, Roland Eng, Ieng Mouly, Keat Sukun, Khau

Meng Hean, the late Kol Touch, Kong Korm, Prince Samyl Monipong, Prince Ravivaddhana Monipong, Nhek Bun Chhay, Prince Norodom Ranariddh, Prince Norodom Sirivudh, Oeur Hunly, Sam Rainsy, the late Son Sann, Son Soubert, Mme Suon Kaset, the late Thach Reng, Saumaura Tioulong, Truong Mealy, Australian diplomat Noel Deschamps, British diplomats John Powell-Jones and Richard Tallboys, and Geraldine Cox, as well as so many other Cambodians and people who have lived in Cambodia. During my research for this thesis, the late Keo Ann sent me a great deal of information, as have His Majesty The King Father, Norodom Sihanouk, and his brother-in-law Oum Mannorine. I am indebted to them for their help. I must also mention and acknowledge many others whom I have spoken to, or corresponded with over the many years of following Cambodian history, including Cham Prasidh, Chan Ven, Dam Ry, Keo Amphan, Uch Kiman, and, very briefly, Hun Sen.

This book could not have been written without the availability of so much already published scholarship on the country; I have used the works of Clive Christie, Claude Jacques, Ben Kiernan, Jefferson Lee, Marie Alexandrine Martin, Jacques Nepote, Milton Osborne, Philip Short, Serge Thion, John Tully, and, most of all, David Chandler, with whom I have discussed so many aspects of Cambodian history over the years.

For simplicity's sake, and to avoid confusion, I have used the regnal names of the kings even before they assumed the throne, and have standardized many other names. I have also necessarily had to simplify some of the contorted incidents and scandals in Cambodia, and some of the ideas expressed by other authors; I offer my apologies for these simplifications.

In recent years, a number of Cambodians visiting Australia have been generous enough to talk to myself and my students, and I must acknowledge their generosity: Kong Korm, Nhek Bun Chhay, Saumara Tioulong, Serei Kosal, Truong Mealy, Ung Bun Ang, and, of course, the indefatigable Sam Rainsy on so many occasions. Questions from my students over my 16 years at Corio have helped me refine many of my views, and I trust that this is reflected in the current work. Andrew Boyle asked me to acknowledge the students of Allen House, in which some of this book was written. Mention should also be made of "The Cambodia Council," a fundraising group established at our school in 2008 to raise money for housing for the poor of Cambodia, the initiative of Alex Millington, who was aided by Sam Aull, Andy Hsiao, Jian Jen, Lauren Simpson, and Sabrina Teh—the latter five, along with my colleague Zaiqin Sun, traveled to Cambodia in January 2009, where we built two houses near Phnom Penh with Habitat for Humanity. Our trip was not without incident, and I must acknowledge Samdech Krom Preah Norodom Ranariddh, Chap Nhalyvoud, General Nhek Bun Chhay, Phan Sothy, Sam Rainsy, Saumara Tioulong, Kong Korm, and Son Chhay for sparing us so much of their time during our visit, and for their generosity toward me and toward my students.

I must also thank my uncle Jacky Yeo for looking after me during so many visits to the Institute of Southeast Asian Studies in Singapore, over so many years. His daughter is now researching for her doctoral thesis on Cambodia in the United States. Lastly, I must thank my parents, especially my father, Robin Corfield, for his many thoughtful contributions to this book. Without his help, this book could never have been completed.

Cambodia. [Cartography by Bookcomp, Inc.]

Introduction

The symbol of Angkor Wat has dominated Cambodian consciousness since its construction in the 12th century, appearing on all Cambodian flags after the country achieved independence: Royalist, Republican, or Communist. It has been that temple that has drawn—and continues to draw—visitors and tourists from all over the world, and that has often caused people to become interested in the country.

In both politics and academia, there have been many controversies connected to the temple, and whether King Suryavarman I should receive the glory for his vision, or whether that in return goes to the tens of thousands of people who toiled in its construction. Although Cambodian history clearly runs much deeper than one temple, the debates over Angkor Wat mirror the disputes in mainstream Cambodian historiography, and indeed in the study of history elsewhere. History is certainly both the story of the rulers and the ruled.

Since the time of the earliest Chinese records of Funan, the land ruled by "Cambodian" kings has changed, so the history of Cambodia is also a history of the Cambodian people, as well as the land within the current territorial boundaries of the Kingdom of Cambodia. Thus, the history of Cambodia certainly includes Funan—wherever it was located—and the Khmer Krom in southern Vietnam, as well as the Cambodian exiles and diaspora overseas.

During the Vietnam War, Cambodia appeared in the consciousness of Western nations as a neutral country on the brink of being dragged into the conflict, which, of course, it was in 1970. This fighting engulfed the entire country and made it inaccessible to most foreigners until the late 1980s, when tourists again began to return to a country that had been devastated by the fighting and the killings that had been undertaken in the late 1970s. These deaths gained international attention in the 1984 film *The Killing Fields*, which alerted a new generation of people to Cambodia, as happened again with the 2001 film *Lara Croft: Tomb Raider*. The tourists came not only for the temples, but also for the climate, the hospitality they received, and the lifestyle that was on offer.

As so many writers have commented, the two faces of Cambodia show a happy and welcoming aspect, but also a desperately dark side. Politics remain a part of everyday life, with so many households proudly declaring their support for one or other political party with plaques outside their homes or at the entrances to their villages. Some see this as the optimism of the emerging pluralist society—but others view it as the intrusion of political parties into people's everyday lives, including within the Cambodian diaspora, where politics divide communities as much as they do in the country itself. Many of the best and the brightest in Cambodia experienced the benefits that foreign countries had to provide in terms of education, work experience, lifestyle, and wealth, returning home to play their part in the rebuilding of their country.

Until recently, few visitors to the country saw much more than Phnom Penh, Siemreap, and the temples. They experienced a bustling, multicultural, and easy-going capital, and an area geared for the tourist trade. But more and more people have been visiting the countryside, which is becoming increasingly safer and more accessible. This has led to more reflective accounts of Cambodia and Cambodians, and life away from the machinations of politics in Phnom Penh.

For most people in Cambodia, wages are meager, with a GDP per capita of $818, and with Cambodia appearing 151st of 163 on the list of countries as defined as corrupt by Transparency International. This has resulted in many hardships, which so many have stoically endured for long periods of time. The global economic crisis from 2008 has certainly affected Cambodia, and will continue to affect the country in terms of a reduction in demand for goods made in the country, as well as a decline in tourists. The recent discovery of oil off the coast of Cambodia may provide benefits for the country as a whole, but there are worries that the wealth could end up in the hands of corrupt government officials unless there are greater efforts to benefit all the people of Cambodia. Certainly, the despoiling of the countryside in massive illegal logging, and other environmentally disastrous projects, only benefited some members of the government and the ruling party, and this does not bode well for the future.

The periods of Cambodian confrontations with neighbors have also ended. For too long since medieval times, the energies of the Cambodian peoples have been occupied in wars with Siam/Thailand, Vietnam, and other regional powers. The neutrality of Cambodia in the late 1950s and early 1960s was successful from a foreign policy perspective, although it did have significant detrimental effects on the economy. But these effects paled into insignificance with the outbreak of war in 1970, when a new government tried to take on many of the problems that Sihanouk had sidestepped. It managed to reenergize the nationalism of the people, though often with horrific results, and it did lead to ultimate defeat and a long period of rule by Communists. Cambodia's membership in the Association of Southeast Asian Nations (ASEAN) from 1999, and its heavier reliance on international trade and tourism have been forces for good.

However, through all the travails and troubles that have faced Cambodia, the Cambodian Royal Family has been the one single institution to have survived with its dignity intact. Not even Buddhism, the national religion practiced by most of the population, has had the same broad appeal. Members of the same family have ruled Cambodia since the *devaraja* cult was formed at the start of the ninth century. This makes the Cambodian Royal Family much older than any others in the region, and one of the oldest in the world. Although there have been weak rulers who became too influenced by one or another neighbor, or by a particular problem, the kings and queens who have ruled the country have provided a sense of national identity that even various factions of the Communist parties have tried to utilize to their benefit. Recent developments in Cambodia have certainly strengthened the role of the monarchy and it is hoped that over time, there will be more to unite the Cambodian people than to divide them.

Abbreviations

AKP	Agence Khmère de Presse
ANKI	National Army for an Independent Kampuchea
ANS	Armée Nationale Sihanoukienne
ARVN	Army of the Republic of Vietnam
ASEAN	Association of Southeast Asian Nations
BLDP	Buddhist Liberal Democratic Party
CEDOREK	Centre de Documentation et de Recherche sur la Civilisation Khmère
CGDK	Coalition Government of Democratic Kampuchea
CIA	U.S. Central Intelligence Agency
COSVN	Central Office of South Vietnam
CPAF	Cambodian People's Armed Forces
CPK	Communist Party of Kampuchea
CPP	Cambodian People's Party
DK	Democratic Kampuchea
EFEO	École Française d'Extrême-Orient (French Far Eastern School)

FANK   Forces Armées Nationales Khmères (Khmer National
                Armed Forces)

FARK   Forces Armées Royales Khmères (Royal Cambodian
                Armed Forces)

FTUWKC   Free Trade Union of Workers of the Kingdom of Cambodia

FUNCINPEC   Front Uni National Pour Un Cambodge Indépendant,
                Neutre, Pacifique et Coopératif (National United Front
                for an Independent, Neutral, Peaceful, and Cooperative
                Cambodia)

FUNK   National United Front of Kampuchea

GRUNK   Gouvernement Royal d'Union Nationale du Kampuchea
                (Royal Government of National Union of Kampuchea)

ICORC   International Committee for the Reconstruction
                of Cambodia

ICP   Indochina Communist Party

ICSC   International Commission for Supervision and Control

KNP   Khmer Nation Party

KPNLAF   Khmer People's National Liberation Armed Forces

KPNLF   Khmer People's National Liberation Front

KPRP   Khmer People's Revolutionary Party (1951–1960)

LDP   Liberal Democratic Party

MOLINAKA   Mouvement de Liberation Nationale du Kampuchea
                (National Movement for the Liberation of Kampuchea)

NADK   National Army of Democratic Kampuchea

NCR   Non-Communist Resistance

NFL   National Front for the Liberation of South Vietnam

NGO   Non-Government Organization

PDK   Party of Democratic Kampuchea

PGUNUWBK   Provisional Government of National Union
                and Well-Being of Kampuchea

PRK   People's Republic of Kampuchea

PRPK	People's Revolutionary Party of Kampuchea (1981–1991)
PSR	Socio-Republican Party
RCAF	Royal Cambodian Armed Forces
SEATO	Southeast Asia Treaty Organization
SNC	Supreme National Council
SOC	State of Cambodia
SRP	Sam Rainsy Party
UFNSK	United Front for the National Salvation of Kampuchea
UNTAC	United Nations Transitional Authority in Cambodia
WPK	Workers' Party of Kampuchea

Timeline of Historical Events

1145   Khmers defeat Champa in battle

1177–1178   Chams launch surprise attack on Angkor

1181   King Jayavarman VII crowned

1190   Jayavarman VII defeats the Chams and introduces Buddhism

1220   Khmer armies driven from Champa

1296–1297   Chinese emissary Zhou Daguan visits Angkor

1432   Capture and destruction of the city of Angkor by the Siamese

1434   Legendary date for the founding of the city of Phnom Penh

1512–1513   Portuguese writer Tomé Pires writes the earliest surviving
              European account of Cambodia

1623   King Chey Chettha II allows the establishment of a Vietnamese
              customs post at Prey Nokor (modern-day Ho Chi Minh City)

1651–1656   British East India Company establish a factory at Oudong

1749   King Chettha V cedes lands in the Lower Mekong to Vietnam

1772   Siamese invade Cambodia and oust Phnom Penh

1779   Ang Eng, age seven, is made king of Cambodia by the Siamese

1811–1812   Siamese and Vietnamese fight in Cambodia

1835–1840   Vietnam occupies Cambodia

1848   Coronation of Ang Duong as King of Cambodia; he makes
              contact with the British and then the French

1860   King Ang Duong dies; his oldest son becomes King Norodom

1863   King Norodom agrees to the establishment of a French
              protectorate

1865   The Cambodian capital moved from Oudong to Phnom Penh

1866   Poukombo Revolt against French rule

1876   Prince Si Votha starts a guerilla campaign against the French

1898   Thiounn becomes Minister of the Palace, remaining in power
              until 1941

1900   Crown Prince Yukanthor goes to France to criticize the French
              colonial administration and is sent into exile

1906   King Sisowath goes to France for Paris Exhibition

1911   Establishment of Collège Sisowath, which becomes Lycée Sisowath
        in 1936

1916   Peasants revolt against high taxes imposed during World War I

1920   Opening of the Albert Sarraut Museum, later the National Museum
        of Cambodia

1925   French *résident* Félix Bardez murdered

1927   Death of King Sisowath; succeeded by his son Sisowath Monivong

1930   Formation of the Indochina Communist Party

1936   Publication of *Nagara Vatta*, the first Khmer-language newspaper

1939   Start of World War II

1940   Thailand attacks Cambodia, sparking short Franco-Thai War

1941   Death of King Sisowath Monivong, who was succeeded by his
        grandson, Prince Norodom Sihanouk; Japanese soldiers arrive in
        Cambodia

1942   Umbrella Revolt against the French; organizers jailed in massive
        crackdown with Cambodian nationalist Son Ngoc Thanh fleeing
        to Japan

1943   French try to romanize the Khmer alphabet, leading to protests
        from Buddhists

1945   Japanese force King Sihanouk to proclaim independence; return
        of Son Ngoc Thanh who becomes Prime Minister; return of the
        French

1946   France grants internal autonomy to Cambodia; establishment of
        political parties, notably the Democrat Party, which wins the
        elections for the Constituent Assembly

1947   Death of Prince Sisowath Youtevong; elections to the first National
        Assembly

1949   Yem Sambaur becomes prime minister; dissolution of the National
        Assembly; France grants Cambodia semi-independence

1950   Assassination of Democrat politician Ieu Koeus

1951   Elections to the second National Assembly; Son Ngoc Thanh returns
        from France

1952   Son Ngoc Thanh leaves for the Dangrek Mountains; start of the Royal Crusade for Independence; sacking of the Huy Kanthoul government

1953   France grants independence to Cambodia

1954   Geneva Accords end Indochina War; Cambodian independence recognized by international community

1955   Sihanouk wins referendum on popularity; Sihanouk abdicates in favor of his father Suramarit; elections to the third National Assembly won by the newly established Sangkum Reastr Niyum

1958   Elections to the fourth National Assembly, with women voting for the first time; Cambodia establishes diplomatic relations with the People's Republic of China

1959   Sihanouk denounces "Bangkok Plot," with Sam Sary fleeing Cambodia; Dap Chhuon plot ends with death of Dap Chhuon; assassination attempt on Royal Family

1960   Death of King Suramarit; National Assembly elects Sihanouk as head of state; referendum approves Sihanouk's rule

1962   First census of Cambodia; elections to the fifth National Assembly; World Court awards Preah Vihear Temple to Cambodia; Saloth Sar (Pol Pot) becomes acting secretary of the Khmer People's Revolutionary Party, which is renamed the Workers' Party of Kampuchea

1963   Pol Pot confirmed as secretary of the Workers' Party of Kampuchea, then flees Phnom Penh; Chinese President Liu Shaoqi visits Phnom Penh; Sihanouk names Prince Naradipo as his heir; overthrow of Ngo Dinh Diem in South Vietnam

1964   Nationalization of banks in Cambodia; execution of Preap In

1965   Cambodia breaks diplomatic relations with the United States

1966   French President Charles de Gaulle visits Phnom Penh; elections to the sixth National Assembly; Lon Nol becomes prime minister

1967   Outbreak of Samlaut rebellion in Battambang; pro-Communist parliamentarians Khieu Samphan, Hou You, and, later, Hu Nim flee to the jungle; Lon Nol government collapses

1968   Increase in tensions along the Cambodian-South Vietnamese border; schoolboy Hun Sen also flees to the jungle

1969   Lon Nol returns as prime minister; Prince Sirik Matak becomes deputy prime minister

1970   Sihanouk leaves for France; demonstrations are held in Phnom Penh against the presence of Vietnamese Communists on Cambodian territory; Sihanouk ousted by the National Assembly; first civil war starts with Sihanouk proclaiming the National United Front of Kampuchea, later known as the Royal Government of National Union (GRUNK); U.S.-South Vietnamese soldiers "invade" Cambodia; proclamation of the Khmer Republic

1971   Lon Nol launches Operation Chenla II, the last Republican military offensive

1972   Keo Ann criticizes official corruption, leading to student demonstrations; Lon Nol appoints himself president and Son Ngoc Thanh as prime minister; presidential elections held; elections held for the National Assembly and the Senate

1973   Lon Nol proclaims a "State of Siege"; Sihanouk tours liberated areas of the country; formation of the High Political Council to run Khmer Republic; Long Boret becomes prime minister

1974   Assassination of Keo Sangkim sparks more demonstrations in Phnom Penh

1975   Lon Nol leaves for Hawaii; U.S. evacuation with Operation Eagle Pull; Sak Suthsakhan becomes head of state; GRUNK forces take control of Phnom Penh and begin forced evacuation of all urban areas in the country; establishment of Democratic Kampuchea; Prince Sihanouk returns to Phnom Penh

1976   The Constitution of Democratic Kampuchea promulgated; "elections" held for Assembly of People's Representatives; Pol Pot becomes prime minister

1977   Disputes along Cambodian-Vietnamese border

1978   Radio Hanoi broadcasts Khmer-language appeal for uprising in Democratic Kampuchea; border dispute escalates; Vietnam invades Cambodia

1979   Vietnamese soldiers capture Phnom Penh; proclamation of the People's Republic of Kampuchea (PRK); China invades Vietnam; several hundred thousand refugees head to Thailand; formation of the Khmer People's National Liberation Front (KPNLF)

1980   Reintroduction of money and postal services into Cambodia;
                heavy fighting along Thai-Cambodian border

1981   Prince Sihanouk establishes the National United Front for an
                Independent, Neutral, Peaceful, and Cooperative Cambodia
                (FUNCINPEC); elections held for a National Assembly in
                the PRK

1982   Establishment of the Coalition Government of Democratic
                Kampuchea (CGDK) by FUNCINPEC, the KPNLF, and the
                Party of Democratic Kampuchea (PDK); CGDK gets
                Cambodia's seat at the United Nations

1983–1984   Fighting intensifies on Thai-Cambodian border

1985   Hun Sen becomes prime minister

1987   Hun Sen meets Prince Sihanouk in France

1988   First Jakarta Informal Meeting held

1989   Second Jakarta Informal Meeting; PRK transforms into the
                State of Cambodia, with Buddhism as the state religion and
                the right to own private property restored; Vietnam
                announces the withdrawal of its soldiers from Cambodia

1990   Third Jakarta Informal Meeting; establishment of the
                Supreme National Council

1991   People's Revolutionary Party of Kampuchea transforms
                itself into the Cambodian People's Party; signing of Paris
                Agreements; near-lynching of Khieu Samphan during his
                return to Phnom Penh

1992   Yasushi Akashi arrives to head the United Nations
                Transitional Authority in Cambodia; the PDK decides to
                pull out of the electoral process

1993   FUNCINPEC wins elections; CPP refuses to accept defeat
                and after secession attempt by some CPP supporters, forces
                itself into coalition government with Prince Ranariddh as
                first prime minister, and Hun Sen as second prime minister;
                new constitution approved; restoration of the constitutional
                monarchy

1994   Political strike with Prince Chakrapong and Sin Son
                attempting another coup; finance minister Sam Rainsy

	ousted after trying to push through an anti-corruption drive; Prince Sirivudh, foreign minister, resigns in protest
1995	Sam Rainsy is expelled from FUNCINPEC and forms the Khmer Nation Party; Prince Sirivudh hounded from Phnom Penh by Hun Sen
1996	FUNCINPEC decides to form electoral alliance with Sam Rainsy and some of the remaining PDK members; Khmer Rouge officially splits
1997	Hand grenade attack on Sam Rainsy kills 16, which is blamed on the CPP by the FBI; Son Sen murdered on orders from Pol Pot, who is then arrested by Ta Mok; Hun Sen launches coup d'état against Prince Ranariddh; interior minister Ho Sok murdered; Royalists regroup at O'Smach; U.S. journalist Nate Thayer witnesses trial of Pol Pot at Anlong Veng
1998	Prince Ranariddh returns to Phnom Penh; death of Pol Pot; elections to the National Assembly won by the CPP, with many claims of irregularities in the vote counting procedures; last remaining Khmer Rouge surrender
1999	Formation of the Senate; arrest of Khmer Rouge security chief "Duch"; Cambodia joins the Association of Southeast Asian Nations; murder of actress Piseth Pilika
2000–2002	Law and order crisis, with increases in politically motivated assassinations; conservation groups condemn the clearing of the forests
2003	National Assembly elections results in victory for CPP, with Sam Rainsy's Sam Rainsy Party (SRP) coming in second, ahead of FUNCINPEC; major political crisis as opposition refuse to take part in a new government
2004	King Sihanouk abdicates; Throne Council convenes and elects Prince Sihamoni as the new king
2005	Hun Sen hounds Sam Rainsy out of the country after the opposition leader accuses Hun Sen of being behind the 1997 assassination attempt; FUNCINPEC ousts Prince Norodom Ranariddh
2006	Trial of former Khmer Rouge continues facing procedural problems

2007   Formation of the Human Rights Party

2008   Border dispute between Cambodia and Thailand over Preah Vihear
         Temple; National Assembly elections, which are held amidst massive
         voting irregularities and a divided opposition, sees the CPP win 72
         of the 123 seats; Sam Rainsy emerges as the main opposition leader
         in the country

1

Funan, Chenla, and Angkor

In the absence of any major prehistoric remains or significant evidence of set-tlement, archaeologists, anthropologists, historians, linguists, and politicians have long debated the origins of Cambodia. Remains dating back to 4200 B.C.E. have been found in northwestern Cambodia and they point to a people who lived in caves, while archaeologists working in other caves along the southern coast have uncovered remains dating to 3000 B.C.E. Many more remains from about 1500 B.C.E. have been found at Samrong Sen in northwest Cambodia, and there are also much earlier traces of a Hoa Binh culture in Battambang.

At some stage, the people living in Cambodia left the caves and started growing crops and keeping domesticated animals. They utilized swidden cul-tivation, a technique best known as "slash and burn," by which people would take over an area of forest, clear it of trees, and then burn the undergrowth, with the ashes providing nutrients for the soil for several years, and the timber being used for housing and firewood. After a few years, the soil would degen-erate, and people would move on. After 50 years, the jungle vegetation would regrow, and the original site would be unrecognizable. This is the method by which the *Khmer Loeu*, or Upper (or Highland) Khmers, still live, although they are now running out of forest, not because of their slash-and-burn system, but, rather, owing to excessive (and usually illegal) logging.

From the 1960s forward, some writers sought to demonstrate that the *Khmer Loeu* were the original Khmer people. The Cambodian Communists certainly felt that this was the case, and the Communist leadership in the 1970s believed that these were the "original Khmers," who were untainted by the corrupting influence of the city lifestyle, the Vietnamese and Chinese ways of life, and beliefs in either Hinduism or Buddhism, which would come to characterize Funan, Chenla, and Angkor. Numbering around 200,000 today, the *Khmer Loeu* scratch out a somewhat miserable existence—both geographically and socially—on the fringes of mainstream Cambodian society.

Folklore ascribes the founding of Cambodia to an Indian prince, Kaundinya. He was sailing in the South China Sea when, as he approached the Cambodian shore, his ship was intercepted by a canoe belonging to Queen Willowleaf, the ruler of the land, and the daughter of the many-headed Naga god. The two fell in love, and they established a kingdom with a largely Indian ruling class and local subjects, which constituted the origin of the Khmer people, who were heavily influenced by India, with actual (and spiritual) descent from the Nagas. Variations of this story have been told in Cambodian schools, monasteries, and homes for at least 200 years, if not longer.

THE EMPIRE OF FUNAN

The Cambodian Royalist tradition perceives the origins of Cambodia to be quite different. They hark back not to the caves at Samrong Sen, but to the Empire of Funan. The Chinese referred to it as an "empire" and to the rulers as "kings"; indeed, most historians see Cambodia as a kingdom, or even a principality or collection of principalities. It operated along the coast and Chinese chroniclers refer to the first king, who ruled in about 200 C.E., as Fan Shih-Man, a name that is clearly a Chinese transliteration. He went to war against a neighboring land, bringing back many slaves, but was killed in battle and succeeded by another king, Fan Chan. Fan Chan sent an embassy with expensive gifts and musical accompaniment to China in 243. This embassy received a very positive reception in China, and the representatives stayed longer than they had planned. By the time they returned to Funan, the king had died and Fan Hsun ruled Cambodia.

Fan Hsun wanted to emulate Fan Shih-Man and also to keep his army busy outside Funan. He formed an alliance with Fan Hsiung, the King of Champa, located to the north of Funan, and the two sent soldiers to attack Tonkin in northern Vietnam. It was not until 503 that a second embassy was sent to China and, in return, the King of Funan, Jayavarman, was confirmed by the Chinese Emperor as General of the South Pacific and King of Funan. By this time, Funan had started to decline, although another embassy to China in 539 brought with it a live rhinoceros and also a long piece of hair from the head of Lord Buddha. The last embassy to China was in 649, by which time Funan no longer had the wealth that had characterized it several centuries earlier.

The Chinese wrote about the capital of Funan as a wealthy trading port. A Chinese embassy to Funan in 245 noted: "The king rides mounted on an elephant. His subjects are ugly and black; their hair is frizzy; they wear neither clothing nor shoes." The Chinese claimed that they urged the locals to wear loincloths, and the idea caught on. They note that the city had a library, as well as canals in which many crocodiles lurked.

Historians have long been puzzled about the exact location of the capital of Funan, and in the late 1930s, the French archaeologist Louis Malleret, working at a site called Oc-Eo, uncovered the remains of a major port city. These remains date from the correct period to be from Funan, and the site is linked to the Bassac River by a canal. Overall, the city covered some 450 hectares (1.74 square miles), and was laid out in a complicated geometrical manner, suggesting that its design was centrally planned. The whole site is crisscrossed by a number of canals that link the city to the sea. Excavations there have uncovered many tantalizing finds, including two Roman coins, one from the reign of Antoninus Pius, dated 152, and the other from the reign of Marcus Aurelius (161–180). This does not prove that there was direct trade with the Roman Empire, but it does show that there may have been indirect trade between Europe and Oc-Eo, and no other site that has been found in the region can qualify as the capital of Funan. The only problem for many nationalists is that Oc-Eo is not in modern-day Cambodia; it is in southern Vietnam.

Some Cambodian nationalists have wished to deny that the political origins of Cambodia, through Funan, could be in modern-day Vietnam. Other, even more ardent Cambodian nationalists actually claim southern Vietnam; for them, the existence of Oc-Eo proves that the land was originally theirs. As there is a great paucity of written records about Funan, it is not hard to merge the three themes, the *Khmer Loeu*, Kaundinya, and Oc-Eo, through a simple comparison with Britain in the Dark Ages, where the original Celtic peoples were driven to the west and north of the lands they held there by the more militaristic Anglo-Saxons, who often had Germanic origins. Some of these Anglo-Saxons married local chiefs, while others killed them. The English language is said to come from Friesland in modern-day Netherlands. Perhaps the *Khmer Loeu* occupied most of the region within the present boundaries of Cambodia some 2,000 years ago. Funan, with its wealth and military, might have expanded westwards. By the time Angkor existed, the *Khmer Loeu* were living on the fringes of the area they had once occupied. Over time, the Vietnamese people, moving southwards, came to occupy what became southern Vietnam, swamping the remaining Cambodians living there, and making them a minority in a land that had once been theirs—and which some Cambodians claim should still be theirs. This has transpired in Kosovo in Europe, so its occurrence in early medieval South-East Asia is entirely feasible.

THE KINGDOM OF CHENLA

With the decline of Funan, another kingdom called Chenla (or Zhenla) emerged. This was the name given in Chinese accounts of an entity that sent tributes to the Chinese emperors. Archaeologists and historians have estimated that Chenla extended from the fourth century to the early eighth century.

By the time Funan emerged, archaeological evidence shows that the settlement at Oc-Eo was in decline, while another settlement at Angkor Borei, near the present-day Cambodian city of Takeo, south of Phnom Penh, was beginning to thrive. The reason for Funan's decline is unknown, but its gradual fading suggests that it was not destroyed in a military campaign, as Angkor would be in 1432. Its location near the marshes of the Mekong Delta, and its canals, which might have become stagnant, suggest that the cause of its demise might have been malaria, the bane of so many ancient and medieval (and even modern) societies.

So, what exactly was this entity called Chenla, which emerged as Funan came to decline? There is one theory that there were two kingdoms, both of which were called Chenla, with one ruling the land along the sea, and another dominating the inland area. There are some theorists who feel that Chenla was, in fact, in northern Cambodia, in what is now Champassac, the southern part of Laos. The Chinese noted that there was a king called Bhavavarman who lived in the sixth century, and the French historian Georges Coèdes felt that he was probably the descendant of the Funanese royal family that had married into the family of a Khmer ruler, moving the focus of Funan from Oc-Eo inland to Angkor Borei. This would mean that Chenla was originally an extension of Funan, but with a different geographical focus, in the same way that the Anglo-Saxons in early medieval Britain moved their administrative headquarters from Winchester, the then-capital of Wessex, to London.

There is also another theory that seems just as plausible. The historian Michael Vickery felt that there was possibly a range of small principalities in the region, accounting for the massive increase in surviving stone inscriptions in the seventh century, with the earliest dating back to 612 at Angkor Borei, and that Chenla could have been comprised of a number of principalities that emerged from within Funan, as its central power ebbed.

JAYAVARMAN II AND THE GOD-KINGS

In 802, an event took place that led to King Jayavarman II establishing a line of *devarajas*, or "god-kings." This created a Royal Family that ruled on account of its descent from the gods—by divine right, or with the "Mandate of Heaven," to quote the English and Chinese equivalents. At Phnom Kulen, north of the Angkor site, Jayavarman II established a system of rule that would continue to the present day. Indeed, the present king, King Norodom Sihamoni, is a descendant of Jayavarman II, and Georges Coedès traces the ancestry of Jayavarman II from his great-great-great-great grandfather Baladitya to the Kings of Funan.

Little is actually known about Jayavarman II's life, unlike those of many of his successors, but he was clearly able to unite the various small kingdoms and principalities under a unified government, probably through military campaigns as much as through diplomacy, leading him to become their overlord.

In Jayavarman's name, the suffix "-varman" means "king." The French expert on Angkor, Claude Jacques, felt that the evidence points to Jayavarman returning from a place called Java in about 770, when he was about twenty. Whether Java is the modern island bearing that name, or that of a kingdom located elsewhere in the region, is still debated and, as historian David Chandler has always argued, information about Jayavarman II's life and the events of 802 comes from an inscription dating back to 1050, which was many years later, and some of the genealogies listed are clearly exaggerated at best or, at worst, invented. It might be as accurate as the British Roll of Battle Abbey that was first published in 1577 to describe who was present at the Battle of Hastings in 1066. Although he may have come from Java, we are left with little doubt that Jayavarman ensured that Cambodia would not be controlled from there, and as a result, he is recognized as the first truly independent monarch of any substantial entity situated in what is now Cambodia.

Jayavarman II also shifted the focus of the rule of Chenla, Funan, and all the other states and principalities to an area near the great lake, the Tonle Sap. This reduced the pressure from invaders who could easily attack Funan from the sea. The move may also have been undertaken for largely religious reasons, as Mount Meru in the region is said to have been imbued with great spiritual potency. The capital was soon to become the city of Angkor.

When Jayavarman II died after a reign of 48 years, his son, Jayavarman III, became the new king. He was an elephant hunter and a wise ruler. When he died, the next ruler was his first cousin, Indravarman. This raises an interesting issue regarding kingship in medieval Angkor. Although most writers feel that the descent of the Royal Family in Angkor was through the male line, a few historians have argued in favor of a matrilineal line of descent by which kings were the husbands of women from a Royal Family. Indravarman's father was the brother of Jayavarman III's mother, but Indravarman's parents were their first cousins, meaning that the source of his descent could have been his mother. This historical mystery has obsessed genealogists for at least a century, with most observers feeling that Indravarman took over because

Jayavarman III had no heir, or because he was a member of the Royal Family, who merely usurped the throne. This argument for a matrilineal line could also have been an excuse for minor members of the Royal Family to occasionally usurp the throne in medieval times.

Indravarman was certainly involved in extending the irrigation systems and establishing reservoirs for rainwater, as stated on his inscriptions. This has been cited as evidence of a significant rise in the region's population, an assumption that is probably correct. He married into a noble family that also claimed to be descended from the Kings of Funan, with his wife also being his fourth cousin.

THE FOUNDING OF ANGKOR

Indravarman reigned for only 12 years before his death and was succeeded by his son Yasovarman I, who reigned for 11 years. His wife was said to be of Funanese royal descent, once again tying Angkor back to Funan. Extravagant, an extrovert, and ruthless, Yasovarman I established the city of Yasodharapura, which was about 16 square kilometers and would serve as the site of what became known as Angkor, a massive city that was even larger than Rome. Yasovarman I was a powerful ruler, and his inscriptions note that he was "a giant capable of wrestling with elephants and slaying tigers with his bare hands." One surviving poem has the God Creator of the Universe complaining, "Why did I create a rival for myself in this king?"

The city of Yasodharapura was built around a natural hill, Phnom Bakheng, and dedicated to the Hindu god, Siva. According to tradition, the hill represented Mount Meru, and the 1,000 ornamental ponds built around it served as natural mirrors for the buildings being constructed nearby. Yasovarman I died in 900 and was succeeded by his older son, Harshavarman I, and then by his younger son, Isanavarman II (Isanavarman I having been the King of Chenla from 616 until about 635). While Harshavarman reigned for about 22 years and was able to build on the work of his father, his younger brother's reign was barely a year long, cut short by the usurper Jayavarman IV, who moved the capital to Koh Ker. Jayavarman IV's mother was the daughter of Indravarman I, and his claim through his wife certainly muddied the waters in disputes between those who believe descent extends through the paternal line, and those who feel it emanates from the maternal line. Jayavarman IV managed to maintain control for 14 years, and his son, Harshavarman II, ruled for another 2 years. After his death in 944, Rajendravarman, a nephew of Yasovarman, returned the capital to Angkor, where it would remain for nearly 500 years.

The move back to Angkor allowed Rajendravarman to begin a major building program made possible by an early military strike at Champa, and his diplomatic skill enabled him to prevent any possible war with that kingdom. The many temples that Rajendravarman built included Banteai Srei, arguably the most beautiful of any of the surviving structures, and the one that captivated the British writer Sacheverell Sitwell when he visited the region from 1960 to 1961. With its great wealth, Angkor started to attract musicians, dancers, poets, and architects. Rajendravarman's son and successor, Jayavarman V, introduced an advisory body resembling the British Privy Council, and allowed women to join. These were Royal appointees and the chief of the body effectively exercised the power of Prime Minister. Jayavarman V's reign, lasting 33 years, also reflected the growing influence of Brahman astrologers. However, when he died, his son, Udayadityavarman I, became king, but was overthrown after a few months, as was his successor Jayaviriavarman (of unknown ancestry), who also only survived for a few months.

Suryavarman I took over in 1006. He was a successful general, and had also descended from the mother of Indravarman I, marrying a descendant of Harshavarman I, although this was not his claim to the throne. With a power base in the northeast of the Kingdom of Angkor—the same area where Jayavarman II had generated much of his support in the 790s—he marched on the capital with his supporters and seized it by force. Scores of rulers in the ancient and medieval worlds have come to power in this manner and then married into the existing royal family, with Horemheb in Ancient Egypt probably being the most famous ruler to do so. Temple inscriptions describe the great power exerted by both Horemheb and Suryavarman I. Suryavarman I changed the monasteries that received Royal patronage, rewarding those that had supported his bid for the kingdom, and punishing those that had not. He expanded the area ruled over by Angkor, annexing parts of modern-day Thailand, and enacted massive building projects to reenergize the capital, which had seen its population depleted in the war that brought him to the throne. There is also clear evidence that overseas trade increased during the reign of Suryavarman I, who died in 1050. After his death, his son, Udayadityavarman II, ruled for 16 years, followed by another one of his sons, Harshavarman III, who ruled for 14 years. This period of continuity and peace led Angkor to become one of the great cities of the medieval world.

SURYAVARMAN II AND ANGKOR WAT

Harshavarman III's death in 1080 led Jayavarman VI to become king. He was another usurper, but this time, the usurper seems to have made no pretense of being a member of the Royal Family. He may have come to power with the assassination of his predecessor—an event that he may have played some part in—but his reign was long and peaceful, and he was a patron of many temples, such as that at Preah Vihear, which would become famous during the border dispute that erupted in the 1950s, and again in 2008, between Cambodia and Thailand. Jayavarman VI was then succeeded by his brother Dharanindravarman I, who reigned for six years. In what might have been an attempt to seek legitimacy, his young grandson, Dharanindravarman II, later married the daughter of Harshavarman III. Whether this ended the rift between the two families, or merely papered over some of the cracks, is not known because it was not this young Dharanindravarman who initially became king, but his cousin, Suryavarman II.

In 1113, when Suryavarman started his reign, which was to last for 35 years, his name echoed that of Suryavarman I, who had also taken over in a time of strife. He seems to have decided on a major building project that would transform Angkor, one that indeed subsequently transformed Cambodia's national identity. Suryavarman II commenced the construction of Angkor Wat. Dedicated to the Indian deity Vishnu, the temple complex was enclosed in an outer wall that was about one square kilometer. Built around a hill, the central tower was to symbolize Mount Meru, with four towers around it. When viewed from the front, three towers are visible, and when viewed at an angle, five can be seen. The inner walls of Angkor Wat are carved with bas-reliefs depicting events described in the Ramayana, as well as the life of Krishna, with floral images and representations of the *apsaras*, or celestial dancers, on the outside walls. Each figure is different, and it is possible that they—like the Terracotta soldiers in China—actually represented different individuals.

Suryavarman possibly envisaged the temple as a tomb to himself and it was certainly completed and dedicated just before his death. Recent aerial imaging of the area has shown that it was built on the site of another temple complex. By the time it was finished, Angkor Wat had become the largest religious complex in the world. Popular with tourists since being rediscovered by the French writer Henri Mouhot in the 1850s, representations of the complex have appeared on all of the country's national flags since it achieved independence, with most depicting the view of three towers, although the People's Republic of Kampuchea designed one bearing all five towers.

The wealth utilized to build the temple certainly came from taxation and foreign conquest—King Suryavarman II was also the first ruler of Angkor to establish diplomatic relations with China, and this probably led to increased trade. Suryavarman II was the first ruler to govern a unified Cambodia since the death of Udayadityavarman II in 1066. Marxist writers have also pointed to what became known as the Asiatic Mode of Production, which revolved around a central authority figure, and others, such as Jan Myrdal, have noted the heavy use of slaves. These problems have never, however, prevented the Cambodian Communists from harking back to the imagery of Angkor, although the more intellectual ones see it as the work of the people, rather than as the vision of the king. But it has not only fascinated Cambodians—it has fascinated people all over the world. One writer, Eleanor Mannikka, managed to measure the whole site in *hat*, a Cambodian measurement that is equivalent to 1.3 feet (0.4 meter). This showed that the distance from the entrance to the central tower was 1,728 *hat*, which corresponded to the legendary golden age of 1,728,000 years in Indian mythology. Measuring the other parts of the temple revealed that there was a strong correlation with the next three global ages, introducing the concept of a secret "code" in the building design.

KING JAYAVARMAN VII AND THE DEMISE OF ANGKOR

Following the death of Suryavarman II in 1150, his cousin, Dharanindravarman II, became the new king. Very little is known about the next 30 years, as there is only one surviving inscription for this period. It appears that a king, Yasovarman II, usurped the throne, and reigned for 15 years before he was overthrown in a palace coup d'état. Tribhuvanadityavarman then reigned for about 15 years, with the Chams, the enemies of the Khmers, invading in 1178. Around that year, Dharanindravarman II's son, Jayavarman VII, became king, with his rule consecrated in 1181. Dharanindravarman was a fervent Buddhist, and this was certainly reflected in the role adopted by this new king, who had studied Mahayana Buddhism in depth.

The Buddhist concept of a monarch, which was introduced by Jayavarman VII, was very different from that of a Hindu ruler. The latter was to be a fierce warrior, and a leader of his people in battle. His main role was to defend the honor and territory of his country from attack. Occasionally, the construction of an irrigation system demonstrated his love for his people, but he ruled because of his right so to do, and because of military might, not owing to the support of the populace. The Buddhist concept, similar to some Confucian precepts, that Jayavarman VII was to introduce, and that his successors were to display, involved the king ruling very much at the behest of the people, as the guardian of the population of the country, and with the very best interests of the populace at heart. For this reason, after independence was achieved in 1953, Jayavarman VII became celebrated in Cambodian history books, with Prince Norodom Sihanouk very much championing the role played by his great predecessor and ancestor.

Although political change was the most symbolic part of Jayavarman VII's reign, his construction work at the Bayon in Angkor Thom is certainly the greatest architectural feat of this period. The 54 towers at the Bayon each have four massive faces, with some seeing them as representing the *bodhisatva*

Avalokitesvara and demonstrating the omnipotence and piety of Jayavarman VII. The four faces, each looking in a different direction, took on great symbolic meaning.

In 1190, Jayavarman VII led the armies of Angkor to battle against the Chams, defeating them and occupying much of Champa. His reign signified the last high point of the Kingdom of Angkor and two years after his death in 1218, the Cham armies were able to rally their forces and retake many of their lands. Jayavarman VII had been succeeded by his son Indravarman III, and, in turn, his son, Jayavarman VIII. He only had a daughter, so his son-in-law, Indravarman III, became the next king.

In 1296, the Chinese emissary Zhou Daguan (Chou Ta-kuan) visited the city of Angkor after being sent there by the newly installed Yuan (Mongol) government of Kublai Khan, who had died two years earlier. The new Chinese government was anxious to know about Angkor, and Zhou Daguan's descriptions of the city provide the historian's greatest insight into everyday life in Angkor. He noted that the Cambodians banned the export of beans and wheat because of the demand for these products, and because there was no local gold or silver, Chinese gold and silver coins and ingots were heavily valued. Daguan noted that there were rhinoceroses and elephants, as well as "mountain horses" and massive rats, and that families respected their water buffalos after death, never eating them, as they regarded them as having rendered a great family service during their lifetimes. He also mentioned the *Khmer Loeu*, who, he notes, were often captured and sold as slaves. He provides a classical image of Angkor, but it was a city in decline.

The reason for this gradual decline may be the spread of malaria, the disease which might have been responsible for the end of Funan. In addition, a number of outlying states that had previously paid tribute to Angkor had begun to break away and came to support the Siamese, who were extending their empire from their capital of Ayuthia. The decline was probably the result of both of these causes, and Angkor certainly ceased to have the wealth that had characterized it before. Historians have also argued that the process of temple building sapped the country's energy, as the building of Versailles did to the French economy in the early 18th century. In 1431, the Siamese launched a major attack on the city, and in the following year, they destroyed it, taking away many of its inhabitants as slaves. They may also have wrecked some of the irrigation canals to ensure the city never emerged as a threat again. This was the traditional method of ruining a city after its capture, and it was reminiscent of some of the events that transpired in April 1975, when the Cambodian Communists took Phnom Penh.

2

From the Fall of Angkor
to the French Protectorate
(1432–1863)

The capture and sacking of the city of Angkor by the Siamese in 1432 was a major turning point in the history of Cambodia. According to traditional accounts of the country's history, the attack was sudden and unexpected, and afterward, Angkor was abandoned and the new king, Ponhea Yat, moved the capital to Phnom Penh, a site that could be better protected from invaders.

What actually happened is a little more complicated. There were 21 missions from Angkor to China between 1371 and 1432, the age of the Ming emperors, and this tends to suggest that the kings of Angkor realized they were under threat and were anxious to arrange an alliance with China. After the defeat of Angkor, Ponhea Yat first moved the capital to Srei Santhor, before it was moved to Phnom Penh. The closer ties that were sought with China—both for political and military reasons, and for trade—dictated the location of the new capital. Phnom Penh was situated on a bend in the Mekong River, further from the Siamese and the possibility of Siamese raids, with much easier boat access to China. There might also have been dynastic reasons, with Ponhea Yat or his successors drawing support and patronage ties from the area around Phnom Penh.

The official date for the establishment of Phnom Penh as the capital of the country was 1434, although there was a settlement on the site at least a century earlier. By tradition, a pious woman called Penh, living in a village at the site of the present city, saw an image of the Buddha floating in the river, and she pulled it to the shore and then built a shrine (Wat Phnom) to house it, and from this, Phnom Penh gained its name. The temple of Wat Phnom survives—albeit, with the present temple being a more recent construction.

However, Claude Jacques has demonstrated that the city of Angkor was not totally abandoned after 1432. He has found evidence of habitation throughout much of the 15th century, and people may have continued to live there into the 16th century. There are also accounts by Portuguese adventurers that have survived in the archives in Lisbon, where they were uncovered by the British academic Charles Boxer. In 1556, Gaspar da Cruz, a Portuguese missionary, went to see the Cambodian Court, which was located at the town of Lovek. He spent about a year there, but was unable to make any converts, and does not mention anything about Angkor in his writings. However, Diego do Couto, writing in 1599 about his visit to Cambodia, mentioned that a Cambodian king had, while on an elephant hunt, discovered the ruins of a temple. This coincides with some inscriptions that have been found at Angkor and date back to the 1560s.

THE ARRIVAL OF THE EUROPEANS

Although the location of the new city made it easier for the Chinese merchants to come and go, they were not the only traders who visited Phnom Penh. As already mentioned, Gaspar da Cruz arrived in 1556 in search of converts to Roman Catholicism, and Diego de Couto came in 1599, but these were not the only Portuguese who arrived in the country, or, by any means, the only two Europeans. The first mention of Cambodia in Western literature was made, however, by Tomé Pires in the *Suma Oriental*.

The Portuguese had plans to conquer parts of South-East Asia to add to the possessions they already held, namely Malacca (modern-day Melaka, Malaysia); and Timor (modern-day East Timor, or Timor Leste). Diogo Veloso from Portugal settled in Cambodia in 1583, and is reported to have married a Cambodian princess; another Portuguese called Blaz Ruiz also arrived. This occurred during the period after the Battle of the Three Kings in Morocco in 1578, which led, 18 months later, to the thrones of Portugal and Spain being united under a single ruler, which reduced friction among some of the early voyagers. These Spanish and Portuguese "conquistadors," as John Tully has called them, might have been able to annex the region by relying on small armies utilizing gunpowder and cannons, but they did not. Instead, they settled in the country, and some took on positions at the Royal Court, where they remained in important positions, especially those in charge of the Cambodian royal artillery. A few families, such as that of Delopez, continued to be influential up to the end of the monarchy in 1970. There were also Spanish from the Philippines who were encouraged to trade with Cambodia, and evidence of this connection with the Iberian Peninsula has been found by linguists. There are some words that derive from the Portuguese, with *riel*, denoting a unit of Cambodian currency, and *kradas* from *carta* (paper) being the most obvious examples.

Although the Portuguese were the first Europeans to arrive in Cambodia, it was not long before others followed. The Dutch East India Company (Vereenigde Oost-indische Compagnie: VOC) had established major bases in the East Indies, and during the early 17th century, they became keen on expanding their colonial empire, which was, as it was for the Spanish and Portuguese, a source of great wealth. In July 1639, the VOC recorded that it had purchased 125,000 deerskins from Cambodia for export to Japan. However, the trade was disrupted by Court intrigue. The Dutch were keen to challenge the role of the Portuguese in the region, and in 1641, they managed to capture the main Portuguese base at Malacca. This encouraged them in their efforts in Cambodia. However, in two separate incidents in 1643 and 1644, Dutch ships in the Mekong River were attacked and 156 Dutch men, and about 1,000 Cambodians, were killed in the fighting that resulted. Two Dutch ships and 50 Dutch sailors were captured by the Cambodians, and although the Dutch East India Company continued trading with Cambodia, it was far more cautious and was not that concerned when their new rivals, the English, became involved.

The English East India Company established a factory—a trading station—at Phnom Penh, and the work conducted by the British historian David Bassett revealed a great deal about this trading station. It faced innumerable problems, and never had more than a handful of staff during the time of its trade— from 1651 to 1656. Some 45 years later, in 1701, a British merchant called Charles Lister was planning to settle in Cambodia. He had a basic knowledge of medicine, or certainly claimed that he did, and by chance, he managed to cure the Cambodian king, Chettha IV. This led to Lister being appointed as the Court physician, a position that was subsequently filled by his descendants, who were still in the same position in 1822. In 1702, the year after Lister arrived, a British trader named Allan Ketchpole established an East India Company trading post on the island of Poulo Condore, which was then a part of Cambodia.

Around the same time that Lister and Ketchpole arrived in Cambodia, the Scottish seafarer Alexander Hamilton was sailing around the region, with his description of the ports subsequently published in his *A New Voyage to the East Indies* in 1727. In this book, Hamilton mentions traveling to Cupangsoap (Kompong Som, now Sihanoukville), where he could buy elephant teeth (ivory) and "gum Cambodge." He noted that Phnom Penh, which he described as the "City of Cambodia," produced gold, raw silk, and ivory, with meat and fish being available at low prices.

VILLAGE LIFE

For most of Cambodia's rural population, the arrival of the Europeans did not have much of an effect on everyday life. The vast majority lived in isolated villages scattered through the country. Their daily life was dictated by the agricultural cycle, and they paid taxes to a government they rarely encountered, signaling their obedience to a king most of them had never seen. Some of them might have visited Angkor, Phnom Penh, Lovek, or Udong, the various capitals, during this period, but many never left their villages. Their contact with the rest of the country was through monks who lived in the temples and monasteries found throughout the country, and moved around these institutions.

For these villagers, the central part of the community was the temple, and their main role was as farmers who used their buffalo to plough the fields, planted and then harvested the rice, caught fish, raised chickens and ducks, and looked after their families. Disease, especially malaria, and occasional periods of want kept down the population size, and with the exception of when armies ravaged the land, or there were natural disasters, there seems to be little evidence of starvation. In the evenings, village elders would tell stories about Buddha or Hindu mythology, famous Khmers who fought the Vietnamese or Siamese, or the Chams, as well as the era during which the Khmer people ruled the whole region. This practice continued through the period of French colonization, and is still evident in certain parts of the country today in the form of folk songs.

As shown by the work of anthropologist May Ebihara, the villagers enjoyed a similar status to the villeins in feudal Europe. They were not slaves—although slavery did exist—but nevertheless were powerless, being part of an elaborate patronage system in which their loyalty was to a landowner, who was sometimes, but not always, a member of the Royal Family. As in feudal Europe, the king also held land (and thereby villages) in his own right, and he would occasionally visit these areas. This led to the establishment of what were to become large royal land-holdings in particular parts of the country, especially in the provinces of Kampong Cham and Battambang. The traditions of this client relationship remained strong and were evident as late as 1993, when the Royalist party, FUNCINPEC, won a large number of seats from these provinces during the country's first contested elections in 21 years, as the party also did in the capital and in Kandal, around the Phnom Penh, the center of Royalist power for so many centuries.

In medieval times, as in later Cambodian periods, the main threat to the country came from neighboring Vietnam. As with Cambodia's past being traced to settlements in southern Vietnam, the political history of Vietnam was derived from parts of southern China, with the Vietnamese people coming south as the Han Chinese people gradually expanded their control of what is now the People's Republic of China. By the time Angkor was established, the Vietnamese were living in a prosperous agricultural society around Hanoi, as evidenced by the Temple of Literature and other surviving institutions from medieval Vietnam. They gradually expanded southwards, and this led to their conflict with the Chams, who they defeated in battle on many occasions. By 1213, Champa was effectively controlled by Vietnam, although it had regained its independence in 1326. By 1471, the Vietnamese had conquered all of Champa and the Vietnamese people were moving southwards, bringing them into contact, and then conflict, with the Khmers. In 1623, the Cambodian king, Chey Chettha II, allowed the Vietnamese to establish a small customs post and garrison at a place called Prey Nokor. It was said that Chey Chettha II was influenced by his wife, who was Vietnamese. This settlement was to become the town, and later the city, of Saigon (modern-day Ho Chi Minh City).

In 1717, a Siamese fleet burned the Cambodian port of Kompong Som, and it became clear that the Cambodians were now located between two much more powerful, and much wealthier, neighbors. The Siamese capital, Ayuthia, was at its most resplendent, and the Vietnamese were encroaching further into the Mekong delta region such that in 1749, the Cambodian king, Chetta V, had to cede the lower Mekong area to Vietnam. What might have granted the Cambodians a reprieve was the Burmese invasion of Siam, which led to the siege and overthrow of Ayuthia in 1767. However, all it resulted in was a lull in the Siamese attacks. The Siamese regrouped around a man who became known as Taksin "the Great," and the capital was established on Thonburi on the coast, and Taksin's successor, King Rama I, moved the capital across the river to Bangkok, where it has remained since then.

Historians marvel at how quickly Taksin was able to lead the Siamese armies into battle against the Burmese after their crushing defeat in 1767. It has been suggested that the Siamese armies were otherwise engaged when Ayuthia fell, but the length of the siege makes this theory less tenable. Certainly, Taksin managed to gather a large army and not only drove out, and kept out, the Burmese in Siam, but also, in 1772, turned eastwards and attacked Phnom Penh, burning it to the ground. In 1779, Taksin made Ang Eng, a seven-year-old member of the Cambodian Royal Family, the King of Cambodia, with the Cambodian rulers essentially owing fealty to the kings of Thailand. Cambodian princes were then taken to Bangkok, where they were educated. In 1782, Taksin was executed by his successor, Rama I, a famous general who had secured his reputation fighting in Cambodia, and who, indeed, was fighting there at the time of Taksin's overthrow, which propelled him to power.

The overall result of these changes in Thailand was that many members of the Cambodian Royal Family were educated in Thailand, and Thai customs came to permeate their court system. The most noticeable manifestations of this influence were dress and court dancing, which were much more similar to the Thai style than that of the *apsaras* depicted on Angkor Wat. In the 1960s, Cambodia's leader, Prince Sihanouk, told a story about how, in 1432, when Angkor was overthrown, the dancing troupe was captured and taken to Siam, leading to changes in their costuming and mannerisms. This telescopes the events of 300 years into an instance, but the symbolism of the story is certainly relevant, given that the Cambodian Court came to resemble the style adopted by its Thai neighbor.

There was a reprieve from total annexation owing to the events that occurred in Siam, but at that time, Cambodia's other neighbor, Vietnam, was being rocked by the Tay Son Rebellion and the emergence of the Nguyen Lords. This resulted in the establishment of the Nguyen Dynasty in 1802 and the beginning of Emperor Gia Long's reign. Initially, Gia Long had to deal with the problems of taking over a new country, and providing firm leadership after a civil war. On the other hand, in Siam, it seems that the foreign invasion by Burma had helped unite the people—and certainly the politicians—behind Taksin, that is, until his execution, and the coronation of Rama I. However, the fighting in Vietnam had a very different effect, with the country essentially plunged into a civil war. There was a period of necessary reconstruction, but it did not last long.

There was also a struggle for the monarchy in Cambodia, and King Ang Chan II found himself in trouble. As mentioned earlier, his father, King Ang Eng, came to the throne at the age of seven. He was crowned King of Cambodia, but the ceremony took place in Bangkok and he had then returned to Cambodia, where he built a new capital of Udong (Oudong). However, he died in 1796 or early 1797, from an overdose of herbs while being treated for an illness. Although he was only 23 when he died, he had already taken four wives, and had fathered six children. His first wife, Ut, is best known as the founder of the temple known as the Dhann Te Wat. Their son was to become Ang Chan II. His younger full brother was Prince Ang Snguon. Ang Eng had two children with his second wife Khe. One of these, Prince Ang Bhim, who died at age five, and the other, Princess Meatuccha, died childless. With his third wife, Rat, he had a son, Prince Ang Em, and with his fourth wife, Ros, he had a son named Ang Duong, who was born around the time of his father's death. Such a situation was bound to cause problems.

As King of Cambodia, Ang Chan II was certainly pro-Vietnamese in his policies. He seems to have personally hated Rama I, but the exact reasons for this hatred are not known. It may be that Ang Chan resented the influence of the Siamese in general over Cambodia, or he may have disliked how Rama I came to power: by executing Taksin. Kings tend to hate regicides, even if (or especially if) the latter elevate themselves to the monarchy in the immediate aftermath. Either way, Ang Chan II refused to attend the cremation of Rama I in 1809, and executed two Cambodian officials who did attend, seeing them as too pro-Siamese.

By this time, the Siamese had garnered some important influence at the Cambodian Royal Court. Ang Chan's first wife was Tep, the daughter of the Governor of Battambang, who was known as Baen. Baen was a prominent supporter of the Siamese, and ruled Battambang as a semi-autonomous province that was associated with both Siam and Cambodia. Just as importantly, Siam had also acquired the friendship of Prince Ang Snguon, the full brother of Ang Chan II. In 1811, when Ang Chan was about 19, and Ang Snguon was about 17, the 2 brothers had a falling out and the Siamese indicated that they would support Ang Snguon, who had fled to Bangkok for safety and was probably accompanied by his half-brother, Prince Ang Em, as the two teenagers were about the same age. Ang Chan II, who had surrounded himself with Vietnamese bodyguards, immediately called on the Vietnamese for help. In 1811, the Vietnamese armies of Emperor Gia Long invaded Cambodia, and for the next two years, they were involved in battles against Cambodians and the Siamese armies of Rama II, who had taken over Siam after the death of his father, Rama I.

In 1812, Ang Chan II moved the Cambodian capital from his father's capital of Udong back to Phnom Penh, and twice a month, he paid his respects to a tablet bearing the name of the Emperor of Vietnam at a Vietnamese temple near Phnom Penh to show his thanks for the Vietnamese managing to win the war. However, the victory was never complete, as Siam had been able to occupy much of the country's western region and have Ang Snguon and Ang Em declared Co-Regents of Cambodia until 1813. Thailand's occupation of Battambang led to, essentially, the establishment of boundaries that would be resurrected in 1940. Ang Snguon died in Bangkok in 1822. By this time, owing to the events unfolding in Vietnam, many Chams had moved to Cambodia and there was a significant Cham presence in Phnom Penh. Their mosque, the Noor Al-Ihsan—"Light of Beneficence"—was built in 1813 in the Cambodian capital, and they proved to be loyal allies of the Cambodian Crown.

Under Ang Chan II, Court support for the Vietnamese was not observed by many Cambodians . In 1816, a Cambodian army marched into the northeastern part of the country against the Vietnamese, and was the last Cambodian army to go on the offensive against foreign forces until 1970. Around 1820, the Vietnamese also forced many Cambodians to take part in the construction of the Vinh Te Canal. The use of Cambodians as slave labor was to become a major component of stories about the antipathy of the two ethnic groups. This conflict and general discontent led to an anti-Vietnamese uprising in the southeast portion of the country, which started around Ba Phnom, the site where Jayavarman II had become the first "God-King" of Angkor. Ethnic Cambodians in the Lower Mekong, the area ceded to Vietnam and by then known as the Khmer Krom, were also involved in disturbances.

Ang Chan II continued to rule Cambodia until 1834. Surprisingly, Siamese court documents show that he sent an annual tribute to Bangkok, so he was probably sitting on the proverbial fence. Before Ang Chan II's death in 1832, the Vietnamese troops in Cambodia had been controlled by Le Van Duyet, a general whom the Vietnamese Emperor Minh Mang distrusted. Under Rama II, the Siamese were sent in to attack Phnom Penh and the Vietnamese there, realizing that they could not defend the city, withdrew, taking Ang Chan II with them. However, the Siamese forces also had to withdraw, and Ang Chan returned to his capital in 1834 with a large Vietnamese force. Then, in Phnom Penh, the Vietnamese placed the king under strict control, and quickly started to distrust him. The King died in Phnom Penh in early 1835 on board a royal barge that had been moored opposite his ruined palace. Curiously, this was to be the location where Lon Nol would hold his Royalist prisoners from 1970 to 1973—he deemed them pro-Vietnamese. Tradition and superstition certainly influenced many of Lon Nol's decisions, but this overlap was probably a coincidence.

The eldest daughter of Ang Chan II, Princess Ang Baen, was too pro-Thai for the Vietnamese. They arrested her, and she died two years later. The King's second daughter, Ang Mey, became the first ruling Queen in modern Cambodian history, and possibly the first ever in Cambodia, if one discounts the legendary Princess Willowleaf. Ang Mey, who became known as Princess Khieu ("Blue"), had been openly pro-Vietnamese, following in the tradition of her father. At this stage, Siam's rulers were more concerned with developments in the Malay peninsula, and were content when Prince Ang Em, the Queen's uncle, was appointed as Governor of Battambang, a post he would hold until 1844.

The period from 1835 through 1840 in Cambodian history was characterized by the first Vietnamese occupation of the country. The coronation of Ang Mey had resounded with Vietnamese symbolism, and a large Vietnamese garrison was sent over to Cambodia to enforce her rule. More importantly, the Vietnamese Emperor decided that there should be an effective colonization of Cambodia, and large numbers of Vietnamese migrants were sent into the country. This caused many problems, leading to the danger that Cambodia's identity would be overtaken by that of Vietnam. Gradually, the system of local government was overhauled and replaced with a Vietnamese method and Vietnamese titles.

Siam's rulers were wary of these developments, as well as the location of Prince Ang Duong, the youngest child of King Ang Eng. They felt that the Vietnamese were trying to lure him to Phnom Penh, where he could be used as a pawn. He was arrested and brought back to Bangkok, with the Thais still believing that Prince Ang Em, Duong's older brother, would be a better ruler. Prince Ang Duong was governor of Battambang when, in September 1840, a rebellion against the Vietnamese broke out in Cambodia. It lasted until early 1841, when it collapsed as the Vietnamese sent in large numbers of soldiers, and the Siamese refused to commit their own soldiers to help the rebels.

In August 1841, Queen Ang Mey and her two sisters seem to have been intoxicated by the Vietnamese during a Vietnamese opera and then lured on board a barge and taken off to Vietnam. Although the actual rebellion did not last, the Vietnamese soldiers in Cambodia were worn down by Cambodian guerillas, and the death of the Vietnamese Emperor Minh Mang led his son, Emperor Thieu Tri, to call the soldiers back to Vietnam; he had more pressing problems at home. This was yet another instance of Cambodia managing to escape occupation owing to a civil war that was occurring in a neighboring country.

It was now the Siamese who invaded Cambodia, with the Siamese army once again led by Chaophraya Bodin. His involvement in Cambodia at this time was brief and by 1844, he had pulled his troops back to Udong, allowing the Vietnamese to reinstate Queen Ang Mey in Phnom Penh. The Vietnamese managed to take Prince Ang Em with them to southern Vietnam, where he died in 1844. Although he never managed to become king, some of his descendants would be crucial players in the establishment of the Democrat Party in 1946.

KING ANG DUONG

Finally, to end the war, which was draining the coffers of both Siam and Vietnam, with Siam possessing a strong military advantage, in June 1847, the Vietnamese returned the Cambodian royal regalia that had taken Queen Ang Mey in 1841, and released the members of the Cambodian Royal Family in their custody. The Vietnamese then withdrew all of their soldiers from Cambodia. By early 1848, there were no Vietnamese soldiers in Cambodia, the first time this was the case since 1811.

In April 1848, King Ang Duong was enthroned at Udong in a traditional Cambodian ceremony, surrounded by his supporters and some Thai political advisers. He was 52, had been in Bangkok for many years, and had even been the Governor of the Siamese province of Mongkolborey in 1834. He was also the last surviving son of King Ang Eng, and the most senior male member of the Royal House. Particularly keen on extending the royal Cambodian line, he had many wives, and 18 legitimate children, 7 sons, and 11 daughters.

In addition to looking after his family—when he died, it was claimed that his body was cremated in the presence of hundreds of his descendants—Ang Duong was a keen poet and historian, and would oversee the enactment of a new legal code. However, he saw his main aim as ensuring that Cambodia remained a separate entity and was not annexed by either Siam or Vietnam. To try to achieve this goal, he sent Ros de Monteiro to Singapore to enlist first British, and then French, help. Ros de Monteiro was a Portuguese adventurer who had recently arrived in the country, and had become a valued figure in the Court. In 1853, Ang Duong sent a tribute to the French Consul in Singapore to be passed on to Emperor Napoleon III, but the Siamese were angered by this action, and the Cambodian King decided to act more cautiously. When he died in 1860, he had presided over 12 years of peace. However, he left a difficult inheritance to his oldest son, Prince Ang Vodey, who became King Norodom I.

KING NORODOM I

King Norodom I was 26 when he became King in 1860, and although he had only been at the Cambodian Royal Court for two years before he acceded to the throne, he quickly demonstrated that he was a reasonably astute operator, but nowhere near as devious as his younger brother (and successor) Sisowath.

Norodom had been born in February 1834 at Angkor Borey, and had trained as a Buddhist monk from the age of 13. However, his *noviciate* was interrupted after a year and he was taken off to Bangkok. Curiously, this occurred at the same time that Ang Duong became King, and there is every reason to believe that the Siamese were keen on grooming Ang Duong's successor. Indeed, Norodom was only allowed to return to the Royal Court in 1858, in time to meet up with his father for a few years before his death.

King Norodom was eager to prevent the Vietnamese from becoming too closely involved in the country again; his father had sought help from the French for this reason. With the Vietnamese and Siamese on either side of Cambodia, the urgent priority for the Cambodian kings—Ang Duong and Norodom—was to ensure that they allied their country with a country that was more powerful than either of its neighbors. Indeed, this was to comprise a tradition in Cambodian foreign policy until 1979. Norodom and his successors felt that the French were the only people capable of restraining the Vietnamese and holding back the Siamese. After Cambodia gained independence in 1953, Norodom Sihanouk was to continue the alliance with France, and also ally himself with China; Lon Nol was to ally himself with the United States;

and Pol Pot was to return to the alliance with China. In spite of all of these alliances, however, Vietnamese influence could not be constrained. Under French colonial rule, Vietnamese bureaucrats and plantation workers arrived in large numbers. Sihanouk was able to restrain the Vietnamese; Lon Nol relied too heavily on the military support of South Vietnam; and Pol Pot was to invite invasion by Vietnam. But this would all occur in the future. In 1863, when King Norodom I signed the agreement that would establish the French Protectorate, he did genuinely believe this was in the best interests of his people and in many cases, he was probably right.

3

The French Protectorate (1863–1941)

In August 1863, French naval officers arrived in Udong, then the Cambodian capital. On August 11, they signed the agreement that would establish the French Protectorate over Cambodia—a "Treaty of Friendship, Trade, and French Protection." This move by King Norodom came at the end of an exasperating start to his reign, which had seen a number of rebels gain the support of the Chams—descendants of the Kingdom of Champa who had settled in eastern Cambodia to escape the Vietnamese—and many others from the eastern part of the country in staging a minor rebellion that had caused the King to flee to Bangkok. There, he had been angered by the Siamese, and had then resumed his negotiations with the French.

The French officer who signed the agreement with King Norodom was Admiral Pierre de la Grandière. By this time, there were a number of French missionaries in the country, the most important of which was undoubtedly Jean-Claude Miche, who had originally come to the Mekong delta region in 1836 and moved to Battambang in 1839. Worried about the persecution of the Roman Catholics by the Vietnamese, King Norodom then relocated to Phnom Penh and was the Vicar Apostolic there until 1864. When the Protectorate Agreement was signed, he was one of the intermediaries who helped in the negotiations, and as a result, the Catholic Church was able to gain special privileges.

The rest of the agreement was fairly standard for European powers at the time; the French would appoint an adviser, known as the *Résident*, to the Royal Court at the rank of mandarin, and the French and French companies would be able to trade freely throughout the Kingdom of Cambodia. However, the agreement allowed the Cambodians to maintain a representative in the Mekong delta region at Saigon, with Buddhism remaining the state religion.

Emperor Tu Duc in Vietnam was too preoccupied with trying to keep the French out of his own country—they had already taken over the Saigon region in 1862. King Rama IV (Mongkut) of Siam was furious, and Norodom tried to placate him by signing a secret treaty in December 1863, which opposed the terms of the agreement he had signed with the French. Norodom also told the Siamese that he had not been able to read the Khmer language agreement before being bullied into signing it. He even offered to have his coronation in Bangkok, and in March 1864, the French had to prevent the Cambodian King from trying to leave Udong. On March 3, 1864, Norodom was formally crowned at Udong, and in June 1864, another ceremony was held, attended by the French and Siamese, to confirm Norodom as King of Cambodia.

On August 20, 1864, the Singapore newspaper, *Straits Times*, published details of the secret Cambodian-Thai treaty of December 1863. The French were angered and never trusted Norodom again. However, they had begun their *mission civilisatrice* with the aim of civilizing Cambodia by changing it to reflect European values. Slavery—there were about 150,000 slaves in Cambodia, of a total population of 900,000—was to be abolished, and decisions about expenditure were usurped from royal officials and delegated to bureaucrats who were mainly French, but also Vietnamese.

The first French *Résident* was Ernest Doudart de Lagrée, a naval officer who was particularly keen on using the Mekong River as a way of transporting goods into southern China. However, the Mekong Expedition of 1866–1868 demonstrated how difficult that was, putting an end to those plans. Thus, the French had to quickly turn their attention to the issue of establishing a tax base for the country. This, as it did in Europe, revolved around a land tax. The problem was that in Cambodia, land was essentially owned by the King, and people worked it "at his pleasure." If land was uncultivated or unoccupied for three years, it was free for anybody to use. The French therefore privatized the ownership of land, establishing a cadastral office in Phnom Penh. Its immediate effect was obvious, and resulted in much of the land being parceled out to peasant farmers. Thus, unlike in many other parts of Asia, most of the peasants owned their own land, leading to less problems with rapacious landlords until the situation changed, as the future Communist leader, Khieu Samphan, was to illustrate in his university thesis in the 1950s. Privatization also had the consequence of large amounts of land ending up in the hands of the Royal Family, although much of this land was gradually sold. In time, the largest landowners were King Norodom, his brother, Sisowath, and, by 1906, Prince Sisowath Essaravong, an astute son of Sisowath whose grandson, Prince Sisowath Sirik Matak, would become Prime Minister in 1972.

THE POUKOMBO REBELLION

Norodom never stood up to the French openly. He preferred to agree with them and then, through intrigue, do everything he could to oppose what he felt he had been forced into agreeing to. It may seem like an odd tactic, but he could look to nearby rulers who had tried to stand up to the French and other European powers The Kings of Burma, who were closely connected to Cambodians through religion and ethnicity, were gradually losing large parts of their country; in 1860, the Chinese and their large army had been crushed by an Anglo-French force that had entered Beijing and seized the Chinese Imperial Summer Palace. Norodom undoubtedly felt that open resistance to the French was unlikely to succeed. However, there were Cambodians who did feel that rebellion might work, and some people rallied around a man called Assoa, who led a campaign against the French from 1862 to August 1866. He claimed to be a son of Prince Ang Em, but this seems unlikely.

Then there was another pretender. King Ang Chan II had had a son and four daughters, the second of whom had become Queen Ang Mey. His son, Prince Poukombo, had died in infancy. However, in 1866, a monk in central Cambodia claimed that he was, in fact, Prince Poukombo and had survived and in doing so, was therefore the rightful king of the country. Seemingly not privy to Court developments and what the King actually thought, Poukombo claimed that Norodom had betrayed the country and called on his supporters and the Royal Army to attack the French. In outlining the history of the French Protectorate, John Tully felt that Poukombo was from the Kui people and was a Highland Khmer, or a Montagnard, as the French called them. Poukombo was certainly charismatic and in June 1866, a French administrator was killed at Tayninh in Cochinchina (as southern Vietnam had come to be known) and rebels started marching on Phnom Penh.

The French had 700 infantry in Phnom Penh, but did not dare to leave it, as the rebels destroyed a Royal Army in October 1866, killing the Cambodian Minister of the Navy, who commanded the soldiers. It was not until January 1867 that, with the start of the dry season, the French army could go on the offensive. They managed to easily defeat the rebels, and Poukombo fled to Laos. In December 1868, he returned to Cambodia and was captured and killed near a pagoda in Kompong Svay in the province of Kompong Cham to the northeast of Phnom Penh.

Although the actual revolt had ended, the problems it caused, and the hatreds it engendered, would prove to be significant in Cambodian history. Two of Poukombo's leading lieutenants were to escape and continue resistance against the French for another 20 years, and the rebellion would live on in the hearts of some local people. In 1925, a family near Kompong Svay had a son who, as a small child, heard stories about the events that had occurred 60 years earlier. He was Saloth Sar, better known to the world as Pol Pot.

PHNOM PENH

In 1866, King Norodom had moved his court back to Phnom Penh, which would serve as the country's capital from then until the present day. Although it had been possible for the Royal Courts to move backwards and forwards from Lovek, Udong, and Phnom Penh since the defeat of Angkor in 1432, the 12 years of peace under Ang Duong and the French bureaucracy would come to ensure that it would be impossible to move the location of the capital again.

The Royal Family and their retainers included as many as 1,500 people. King Norodom had at least 60 children with 37 wives, and undoubtedly had other concubines and relatives in the court—his brother Sisowath would father 24 children by 19 wives. This was certainly not as many as the kings of Siam and Vietnam during the 19th century, but both of those countries were far richer. Étienne Aymonier, the acting French *Résident* from 1879 until 1881, claimed that a large part of the country's wealth was being frittered away by these people and in 1913, the French scholar Adhémard Léclère attempted to work out, genealogically, who was who, but even he came across relatives and cousins who were a little uncertain of how they were related to whom, but still drew government pensions. Some were likely concubines or descendants of princes that had long since died.

The construction of the present Royal Palace in Phnom Penh began in 1866. The Palace was oriented to the east, unlike the Royal Palace in Bangkok, which it resembles in some ways, despite the Bangkok Palace's orientation to the north. Most of the major building work in Phnom Penh took place in the 1890s, after the Si Votha Rebellion. The French community in the country at this time was still small, and the French colonial society mixed relatively well with the wealthier Cambodians and the elite. Of course, there were exceptions, such as the notorious Thomas Caraman, who became the subject of Gregor Muller's book *Colonial Cambodia's 'Bad Frenchmen.'* Some exploited the local population, and spent their spare time in opium dens or with prostitutes. Others studied the country and ended up with a great love of Cambodian culture. Their scholarship has been crucial to our modern understanding of the country.

Because maintaining the Cambodian Court, as well as running the country itself, was costly, the French wanted to revise (or update) the 1863 Protectorate Agreement. They were establishing what was to become French Indochina, with Cochinchina, the southern part of Vietnam, based around Saigon as a

French colony, the rest of Vietnam divided into Tonkin and Annam, and Cambodia and, much later, Laos as Protectorates. In March 1884, the French told Norodom that this new agreement had to be approved by him, and he started to prevaricate. Finally, on June 14, 1884, French marines and Annamese (Vietnamese) riflemen arrived on a gunboat, and in true colonial style, the French Governor of Indochina, Charles Thomson, stormed into the Royal Palace and dragged King Norodom from his slumbers the following morning. Thomson told the King that he had to sign the agreement or he would be forced to abdicate. Never one to stand up to pressure, Norodom caved in and signed the new agreement.

THE SI VOTHA REBELLION

The signing of the 1884 agreement led some French, including Thomson, to suggest that it would be easier to completely annex Cambodia and run it as a colony, as they were doing in Cochinchina. However, any plans to do this were shelved when, in January 1885, Cambodians started attacking isolated French posts around the country. While both Assoa and Poukombo claimed to be members of the Royal Family, and were almost certainly pretenders, the leader of this rebellion was undoubtedly one of the most senior members of the Royal Family.

Si Votha had been born in 1841, as the eighth child and third son of King Ang Duong. When he was 19, he started engaging in actions against the French, who he could see were about to become the colonial power within the country. He then moved to Siam and in 1885, he decided to launch a large insurrection that has been dubbed the "Great Rebellion" by historian John Tully. Duong had the active or passive support of some members of the Royal Family who were still in Phnom Penh, and the rebels were able to enlist some ethnic Chinese and ethnic Vietnamese.

The war was essentially a guerilla campaign, with the Cambodians attacking the French and then withdrawing when faced with larger troop numbers. The French quickly realized that they would not be able to defeat the Cambodian rebels militarily and raised the idea of a negotiated settlement, but it was clear that the rebels were so confident of victory that they were not prepared to compromise. The French also had to consider their broader position. The disturbances in Cambodia came at a very difficult point for the French. In July 1885, they had deposed Emperor Ham Nghi in Vietnam, and he had launched what became known as the Can Vuong Movement to fight against the French, which tied them down there fighting until 1887.

In the Cambodian countryside, the French resorted to burning villages, launching reprisal attacks, and enacting massive retribution against those who supported the rebels. Gradually, they started taking the offensive, especially with the support of the Cambodian Army, which was placed under the control of Norodom's younger brother, Sisowath. Eventually, Norodom claimed that he might be able to restore order and toured the countryside, urging rebels to lay down their arms. His actions were successful, but Si Votha was forced to remain in the jungles until his death in 1890. By then, Cambodia was at peace, but the official population statistics show that the country's population had fallen from 945,000 in 1879 to 750,000 in 1888. Some portion of this decline could have been the result of more accurate records, but it also seems clear that many people must have fled the country or, at any rate, fled the known settlements, or died from starvation and disease.

YUKANTHOR AND THE DEATH
OF KING NORODOM

After the Si Votha Rebellion, the French decided to do as much as they could to change the nature of Cambodia, modernizing it, especially Phnom Penh, so that the people—or at least the elite—could appreciate the benefits of contact with France. This reform led to the emergence of a Cambodian middle class.

Prior to the late 1890s, there was little in the way of a middle class in Cambodia, with the King, the Court, and the elite ruling the country either in name or, after the formation of the Protectorate, with the French; there were also large numbers of peasants. When the French arrived, they brought many low-level Vietnamese bureaucrats with them, which had created additional tensions, as had the arrival of Chinese businessmen and middle-men.

The emergence of this new middle class led some members of the Royal Family to worry that they were going to lose control. Prince Duong Chakr, the 11th child of King Norodom, had gone to France in the early 1890s. There, he complained to the authorities, and for his troubles, he found himself deported to French Algeria in 1893, and died in the remote Algerian town of Djelfa some four years later. In 1901, the eldest son of King Norodom, Prince Aruna Yukanthor, decided to make a direct appeal to the French to prevent the colonial bureaucracy from not passing on messages, or distorting what he had to say. This led him to travel to Paris, where he soon became a major figure in Parisian society. He was invited to parties and dinners, and subsequently spread his criticisms of French colonial rule. This became known as the "Yukanthor Affair" and as a result, the French barred him from returning to Cambodia; he was to spend the rest of his days in Siam.

The extent to which Cambodia was an integral part of the French Empire in the early 1900s can be illustrated by the French administrative system, the postal system, and the minting of coins used in the country. But one tantalizing source provides an interesting and novel perspective. On May 8, 1902, a volcano had erupted on the French Caribbean island of Martinique and had killed everybody in the town of St. Pierre, except one prisoner, who was confined in a cell with a small window facing out toward the sea. This was an event that caused shockwaves all around the world, not the least of which, it seems, reverberated in Cambodia. People throughout the world raised vast sums for the victims, with President Theodore Roosevelt, on behalf of the U.S. government, giving $250,000, and Tsar Nicholas II of Russia giving $25,000. Even President Paul Kruger of the Transvaal, having just lost the Boer War, gave $80. People also raised money throughout the French Empire. In Cambodia, collections were made in every province and the list of donors shows the campaign's effect not only on the French, but also on Cambodian interpreters, secretaries, and schoolboys. The French *Résident-Supérieur* (the *Résident* title had been changed in 1889), Léon Jules Pol Boulloche, gave $25, but a businessman, Dupuy, the manager of Dumarest et Fils, topped Cambodia's donor list with $30. The collectors also went to many villages. The village of Banteay Chey in Kompong Chhnang raised 85 cents, while in Krang Lieu, the peasants scraped together 70 cents. What should be noted here is that not a single member of the Royal Family is listed as a donor, and King Norodom certainly did not send any money.

King Norodom had been heartbroken by what had happened to Yukanthor and Duong Chakr, and Prince Sisowath had already gained the agreement of the French that he would succeed his brother as king. Norodom retired to the Royal Palace in Phnom Penh and lived there in his last years, which were tinged with bitterness and ill health. He gradually became more and more angry at what the French had managed to do. He died on April 24, 1904, from facial cancer, and he was cremated in January 1906.

KING SISOWATH AND THE "MISSION CIVILISATRICE"

King Sisowath was very different than his brother Norodom, and he was also totally different than their other brother, Si Votha. He had been born in Battambang on September 7, 1840, which made him 63 when he became King. He had been educated in Bangkok, and was only allowed to return to Cambodia after Norodom was crowned. In exchange for his support of the French, they had promised him the throne, and he set about ruling Cambodia and helping the French bring the advantages of French culture to the country through the "Mission Civilisatrice," as it was called at the time. To this end, the crown was placed on Sisowath's head on April 26, 1904, by Paul Beau, the Governor-General of French Indochina "in the name of the government of the Republic of France."

King Norodom was not on the list of donors to the Martinique Appeal of 1902, and neither was Thiounn, an emerging Palace official of humble origins who, in 1898, had been appointed Minister of the Palace, a position he held until 1941. Under Sisowath, Thiounn became one of the most important and wealthiest non-Royals in the country, and was closely related to two other families: those of Poc, the minister of justice, and Bunchhan. Together, these three families and their relatives would play an important role in Cambodian politics, dominating it until the early 1940s, and then acquiring senior positions, with four of Thiounn's grandsons becoming very important in the Cambodian Communist movement of the 1960s.

For Sisowath, the collection for the volcanic eruption in the West Indies had symbolized that some Cambodians were now seeing themselves as part of the wider world, but it was nowhere near what he had wanted. In 1906, King Sisowath felt sufficiently confident to leave Phnom Penh and go to France, taking many of his children with him. They were going to Paris to see the Great Exhibition being held in the French capital. Many postcards were produced showing King Sisowath and his family at the Exhibition, and they certainly depicted him, dressed in a black tail coat, with a top hat, very much as a "father figure" for his country. He was greeted by tens of thousands of people, giving away lottery tickets to school children and attending the Bastille Day Parade.

Five years later, in 1911, Sisowath founded the Collège Sisowath, a secondary school that became a *lycée* for all students up to the 12th grade (year 12) in 1934. Students were taught in the French language, and the school had a dormitory for boys from country areas to allow them to study—girls would gradually be allowed to attend the school. The alumni would come to dominate Cambodian politics until 1979.

With the outbreak of World War I in 1914, there was no doubt that Cambodia would do its part for the French Empire. About 2,000 Cambodians enlisted as light infantrymen in the French forces, with Prince Sisowath Monivong, the eldest surviving son of the King, serving, as well. Several hundred were killed, including one member of the Royal Family, Prince Sisowath Leng. In addition, many other Cambodians served in labor corps or worked in munitions factories in France.

Historians have debated what King Sisowath received in return for his support for France. Certainly, he was made King in preference to any other member of the Royal Support. The boundaries between Cambodia and Siam were renegotiated a number of times and in 1904, the towns of Battambang and Siem Reap once again became part of Cambodia, although the boundaries shifted again in 1907. Sisowath must have hoped that the Cambodians would be able to win back Battambang and Siem Reap, which had been ceded to Siam in 1907. However, the hope of Siam's return ended in 1917, when that country also joined the war. By 1917, however, Siam was the least of Sisowath's problems.

Many local people were unhappy about King Sisowath's enthusiasm for Cambodian involvement in World War I, and in 1916, large numbers of peasants—perhaps as many as the 100,000 recorded in some reports—stormed into Phnom Penh, where, for the most part, they peacefully demonstrated about the high rates of taxes. Because these taxes were all collected by Cambodians on behalf of the French, the peasants now drew no distinction between the Cambodian middle class and the French. Their anger and resentment were directed toward both of these groups. The French *Résident Supérieur*, François Marius Baudouin, perhaps seeing himself in the role of the Roman general and politician from whom he took his middle name, ordered a violent crackdown on the demonstrators. Many were tracked down and thrown in prison. Baudouin admitted that 21 agitators were killed, but it is likely that the number was far higher.

When the Cambodian veterans returned to Phnom Penh, there was a brief ceremony and then they were all paid off and sent home. No veterans association for the Cambodian veterans was allowed to be established, although there was later one formed for French veterans. The French did not want hundreds of local men trained in European battle tactics and how to handle weaponry to gather on a regular basis. A victory gate was erected at the entrance to the Royal Palace in 1918, but the only time that the veterans did form a group again was when they met for the unveiling of the World War I Memorial, which showed a Cambodian and French soldier arm-in-arm, and, for the last time, when Field Marshal Joseph-Jacques-Césaire Joffre came from France in the early 1920s.

RUBBER AND REBELLION

By the 1920s, the French were keen on enlarging their rubber industry in the country, and rubber plantations were established along the Cambodian-Vietnamese border. This brought wealth for French businesses, particularly the Compagnie du Cambodge, which quickly came to dominate the local rubber industry. As in Vietnam, colonialism meant that privately owned French companies benefitted significantly, often making large profits at the expense of the French taxpayer, who had to pay for the maintenance of law and order in the colonies.

The first trouble after World War I again originated with Baudouin, who remained the *Résident Supérieur* from 1914 until 1927. He decided to build a hill resort between Phnom Penh and the riverside town of Kampot. The French in Saigon had access to Dalat, while the British in Burma had access to Maymyo, Simla in India, and the Cameron Highlands in Malaya. Baudouin felt that it was good to have a grand hotel at a place called Bokor. Its location at the top of a mountain meant that French fruit and vegetables could be grown there, and that malaria would be less prevalent than in the swampy lowlands. In spite of criticisms in the Saigon press about the cost of the project, and the number of laborers who died, Baudouin pushed ahead with the construction, which included a special bungalow for himself. The novelist Marguerite Duras later wrote that her mother, a settler in Cambodia at the time, was disgusted by the manner in which the workers were treated.

As the demand for taxes to pay for Bokor and the general administration rose, there were occasional attacks on officials. Cambodia, as Chandler showed, was more peaceable than Vietnam, and seemingly as a result, had the highest level of taxation levied on its peasant farmers. One of the attacks that occurred in 1925 involved a French tax collector who was the *Résident* in Kompong Chhnang, Félix-Louis Bardez. On April 28, 1925, in the village of Krang Leav, Bardez was murdered. The French were astounded by this, and research by David Chandler has revealed the depth of feeling in local society about the events at the time. Fifteen villagers were found guilty, and three were sentenced to death and executed. André Malraux, a French radical who was in Phnom Penh at the time, tried to help in their defense, arguing that the taxes being levied were excessive. Malraux was critical of the manner in which defense witnesses were barred from giving evidence, as well as the obvious bias of the judge in his rulings, and an attempt to poison the defense lawyer. King Sisowath bypassed making any pronouncement, except that the villagers were clearly guilty of lèse-majesté. This event subsequently became one of the great causes of the Cambodian nationalists, who saw the actions of the French as unjust and heavy-handed.

WORLDWIDE INTEREST IN ANGKOR

The initial antiquarian interest in Cambodia came from the French. Although people had visited Angkor since 1432, Henri Mouhot's book, *Travels in the Central Parts of Indo-China During the Years 1856, 1859, and 1860*, published posthumously in English in 1864, generated renewed interest in the country. Two of the early *Résidents*, Jean Moura and Étienne Aymonier, both wrote serious books about Cambodian history—*Le Royaume du Cambodge* (1883) and *Le Cambodge* (1901–1903), respectively, and this interest even encouraged the Palace official Thiounn to record the details in a Court chronicle that, not surprisingly, reflected his point of view, and served to justify his actions. Curiously, the first novelist to set a story in Cambodia—or, more specifically, just off the shore of Cambodia—was not a French or Cambodian author. The Polish/British writer Joseph Conrad set his short story, *The Secret Sharer* (1910), in a boat just off the coast of what he called "Gambodge." In the following year, the British colonial official Hugh Clifford set his *The Downfall of the Gods* in medieval Cambodia.

As a result of these and other books, interest in the country began to surface outside Cambodia, and tourists started to visit. Most wanted to go to Angkor Wat, and it was already easier to gain access to the monuments from Bangkok.

This led some writers to associate Angkor Wat, and indeed the other ruins at Angkor, with Siamese civilization, something that Thai ultra-nationalists did little to contradict. The French travel writer Pierre Loti used a section on Angkor, including a picture of Angkor Wat, as the frontispiece of his book, *Siam,* which was published in London in 1913. There is still a model of Angkor Wat inside the Royal Palace in Bangkok and it is often shown, without comment, to tourists to the Thai capital, leading some to feel that there is a historical link between the two. However, Cambodian nationalists resent the connection, and this resentment resurfaces from time to time, with rioting in Cambodia in 2003 aimed at Thai property after it was claimed that Suvanant Kongying, a Thai actress, had said that Cambodia had stolen Angkor Wat, and that it should be returned to Thailand.

Most people, however, recognized that the Angkor temple complex predated the rise of Ayuthia, and from the 1920s forward, parties of tourists went in search of Angkor. In *Angkor the Magnificent* (1925), RMS *Titanic* Survivor Helen Churchill Candee linked Angkor to Mu, the great "lost civilization" of the Pacific, which was given prominence in the works of James Churchward that came soon afterwards. Robert Casey wrote about Cambodia in *Four Faces of Siva: The Detective Story of a Vanished Race* (1929); W. Somerset Maugham set his *The Gentleman in the Parlour* (1930) in Cambodia; and Osbert Sitwell's *Escape with Me!: An Oriental Sketchbook* (1939) explained Cambodia to a British audience. Lance Colam's *The Death Treasure of the Khmers: Amazing Travels & Adventures in Search of Fabulous Treasure in Indo-China* (1939) led readers through a presumably fictional account wherein the author found and then lost the treasure hidden in Angkor. For Americans, Harry L. Foster's *A Beachcomber in the Orient* (1923), and Harry A. Franck's *East of Siam* (1939) described Phnom Penh as a rather sleepy backwater. Another book set in Cambodia and written by an American was Edgar Rice Burroughs's *Jungle Girl* (1939), which followed his success with the "Tarzan" books set in Africa. Angkor had been covered for the first time in the *National Geographic Magazine* in 1912; and the American journalist John Gunther, usually so detailed in his description of countries and people, had devoted just two lines to Cambodia in *Inside Asia* (1939). He wrote that the main item of note about the country was that it was ruled by "a native king with a nice name Sisowathmonibong (sic)."

KING SISOWATH MONIVONG

When King Sisowath died in 1929, his oldest surviving son, Prince Sisowath Monivong, became the next king. Monivong had been born on December 27, 1875, in Phnom Penh, and was in Paris at the École Coloniale when his father arrived in 1906 for the Paris Great Exhibition. He then trained at the École d'Infanterie de Saint-Marxient, and was commissioned as a sub-lieutenant, serving in World War I, by which time he was already the heir to the Cambodian throne. Monivong worked with his father for a long period of time and learned what was required to help run the country. Soon after his coronation, which took place on July 22, 1928, he would be ably assisted by his older sons, Prince Monireth and Prince Monipong. In 1927, the two boys had both gone to Nice, where they attended the local lycée, and were to be trained and receive commissions in the French Army.

By then, though, there was another crisis. The Great Depression of the 1930s affected many people across the world, and this included the Cambodians. As the demand for rubber fell, the French rubber plantations started laying off their workers, but these were mainly Vietnamese, so initially, this decline in demand did not have much of an impact on the Cambodians. However, when the price of rice in the world markets collapsed, falling to a third of its price in the 1920s, many families reduced the amount of rice that they planted. Many local administrators had to start listing regular rent arrears, and additional problems surfaced as others went into debt to money-lenders, most of whom were Chinese.

As Ben Kiernan discovered when he set out to research the origins of Cambodian Communism, a Cambodian called Ben Krahom ("Red" Ben) was arrested on July 31, 1930, after giving out pro-Communist leaflets on the streets of Phnom Penh. Events in China in the 1920s had led the Chinese community to become politicized with local branches of the Kuomintang and the Chinese Communist Party. There were also Vietnamese involved in radical politics, but Ben Krahom was the first ethnic Khmer to be involved in protests. Some Cambodian nationalists see this lack of interest as an ominous portent of what was to follow. In 1930, Ho Chi Minh founded the Indochina Communist Party, and its early members from Cambodia were all either ethnic Chinese or Vietnamese. The lack of Khmer participation at this early stage would go some way toward explaining the xenophobic upsurge of the 1970s, when the Cambodians finally took over the Communist movement from the Vietnamese and set about implementing policies far more radical than the Vietnamese would ever have considered.

King Sisowath Monivong, however, was largely unconcerned with the start of Cambodian Communism. He was more interested in courting his wives, concubines, and girlfriends. In a curious quirk of history, one of them was Long Meak, and another was her first cousin, Loth Saroeung. It was through this Palace connection that Loth Saroeung's brother, Loth Suong, and his wife, Chea Samay, came to work at the Royal Palace, with the latter becoming one of the foremost teachers of Cambodian royal ballet. They were later joined by Loth Suong's younger brother, Saloth Sar, who attended the small French private school École Miche. In 1975, he would overturn Cambodian society and in the following year, he adopted the name "Pol Pot." But that was all a long way in the future.

SON NGOC THANH AND THE START
OF KHMER NATIONALISM

Because Cochinchina was a French colony, but Cambodia and the rest of Vietnam were French Protectorates, the people in Cochinchina had greater access
to schools and, for the brightest, a university education in France. Although
some wealthy Cambodians from Phnom Penh and elsewhere in Cambodia
were able to go to school in Vietnam, with many attending Lycée Chasselouop-
Laubat in Saigon, these were very much the exceptions. The Cambodian minority in Cochinchina, the Khmer Krom, however, who grew up in Vietnam
(some of whom spoke Vietnamese as their first language), could attend schools
in Cochinchina, and it was not long before they came to have an unusually
influential role in Cambodian politics. The first of the Khmer Krom to arrive
on the scene in Phnom Penh was Son Ngoc Thanh.

Thanh had been born in Cochinchina, and his father was a Khmer Krom
landowner, while his mother was from a Chinese-Vietnamese family. He had
gone to school in Saigon, and then accepted a French government scholarship
to study in France. He studied law for a year, and in 1933, he returned to French
Indochina, taking up a position at the National Library in Phnom Penh. He
then became friends with former students of Collège Sisowath, which, in 1934,
was transformed into a *lycée*, and joined the alumni association, even though
he had never attended the school. He also became closely associated with the
Buddhist Institute in Phnom Penh, which had been founded in 1930 by the
French Buddhist scholar Suzanne Karpelès. It was not long before Son Ngoc
Thanh began involving himself in politics.

In 1936, Thanh established the newspaper *Nagara Vatta* ("Angkor Wat"). This
weekly paper was the first Cambodian-language newspaper ever, and it had
a circulation of between 4,000 and 5,000. Others involved with the newspaper
included Pach Chhoeun, who had served in the Cambodian forces in Flanders
in World War I and then made a career working in banks, and Sim Var, an interpreter and secretary in the judicial courts. The paper appealed to shop keepers
and other small-time capitalists, and was remarkably popular in managing
to attract a stable of good writers and intellectuals.

The paper was still flourishing when, on September 3, 1939, France declared
war on Germany and World War II began. With the French declaration of war,
feelings amongst the French in Cambodia led to Phnom Penh being bedecked
by French tricolors, and King Sisowath Monivong quickly and publically declared his support for France. Most Cambodians expected the war to be similar to World War I—some rallies and patriotic speeches, Cambodians enlisting
to serve in the French army, and ultimate victory over Germany. An article in
Nagara Vatta had compared Hitler's aggression in Europe to that of the Vietnamese in 19th-century Cambodia, and it was quite clear that there was a new
elite who were happy to support the paper, which must have had some 20,000

or so readers in a city with, as of 1936, a population of barely 100,000. The paper discussed Cambodian nationalism, but few people had reckoned that the French Protectorate in Cambodia would not last for much longer.

The fall of France to Germany in June 1940 shocked the French and Cambodians in Cambodia, along with many people around the world (and, indeed, France itself). Prince Sisowath Monireth and Prince Sisowath Monipong had served on the famous Maginot Line, and they returned to Cambodia greatly chastened by the French defeat in Europe. The new Vichy government in France then replaced the acting governor Georges Catroux with Jean Decoux. The Siamese government recognized the weakness of the Vichy administration in Indochina, and decided that it was a good opportunity to try to expand their country. In June 1939, the ultra-nationalist government of Phibun Songgram had renamed the country Thailand, "the land of the Thai people," which, for the first time, associated the country with an ethnic group. In November 1940, fighting broke out on the Thai-Cambodian and Thai-Laotian borders, with the Thai army attacking the French in Indochina. In attacking on land and moving into Cambodia, the Thai army was led by Kriangsak, who would later become the Prime Minister of Thailand, and it drove back the French and colonial armies with relative ease. However, they were unable to follow this up with a naval assault when the French air force managed to bomb much of the Thai navy. To stop the fighting, the matter was referred to the Japanese, who mediated. They awarded the Thais some 25,000 square miles (65,000 square kilometers) of territory, including Battambang, most of the Siem Reap province, and a section of Southern Laos. The Cambodians managed to keep Angkor Wat, but they lost their second-biggest city, Battambang. The reason that the Cambodians accepted a French Protectorate had been that they wanted protection. King Monivong was so angered that the French had not managed to protect his country that he refused to speak French anymore or meet with any more French officials. He died on April 24, 1941.

4

The Road to Independence (1941–1953)

The impending death of King Sisowath Monivong left the French colonial administration with the problem of who should succeed him. The obvious choice was Monivong's older son, Prince Sisowath Monireth. He had trained as a French army officer and was bright, intelligent, and shrewd, but some people recognized that he was perhaps a little too shrewd. They could also choose Prince Monipong, Monireth's younger brother. Monipong had trained in the French Air Force, and was married to a French woman. He would be loyal to France, but his marriage might be a problem for court officials. Certainly, the choice of a client ruler was fraught with problems. In 1916, the French had chosen the 12-year-old Bao Dai as Emperor of Vietnam and sent him to school in France. When he returned to Vietnam at age 19, he had been intent on making major changes to the country, but quickly found his reform efforts stymied by the French. As a result, he ended up seeking solace in living the life of a playboy. In 1939, the Dutch in Java had chosen Hamengkubuwono IX as, they hoped, a quiet client Sultan of Yogyakarta. In the aftermath of World War II, he was to prove anything but subservient, emerging as a nationalist hero and the second Vice-President of Indonesia.

The French had decided on Prince Norodom Sihanouk, a cheerful and like-able music-loving teenager who was attending school at Lycée Chasseloup-Laubat in Saigon at the time. Born on October 31, 1922, in Phnom Penh, he had attended François Baudouin Primary School in Phnom Penh, and then Lycée Sisowath, before going to Saigon to complete his schooling. His mother, Princess Kossomak, was a daughter of King Monivong, and a careful business-woman herself. The descent from Monivong to Sihanouk through a female line echoed the debate in the French scholastic community during this period on whether royal succession in Angkor went through the male or female line. However, Sihanouk's father, Prince Norodom Suramarit, was a grandson of King Norodom I., Sihanouk was descended from both Norodom and Siso-wath, bringing together the two branches of the Royal Family. Genealogically, this ancestry meant that he had two grandfathers, and, effectively, two great-grandfathers and one great-great-grandfather, King Ang Duong.

Norodom Sihanouk was crowned on April 25, 1941, in Phnom Penh. For advice, he listened attentively to his mother and her brother, Prince Monireth. He was a little estranged from his father, who had used his money to help back the *Nagara Vatta* newspaper, and was certainly an ardent Cambodian nation-alist. Prince Monireth always gave sage advice, and Sihanouk began to intro-duce a program of modest reforms. This involved finally retiring Thiounn, who had, as Minister of the Palace, enriched himself at the government's ex-pense for 43 years. The King also opened a school, Collège Sihanouk, the sec-ond high school in the country after Lycée Sisowath, with Thailand having taken control of the other one in Battambang. However, the King had to be cautious, as by August 1941, the Japanese had deployed 8,000 soldiers to the country. The French colonial administration, through its links to the Vichy government in France and, through them, the German government, was un-able to do anything to prevent this deployment. When the Pacific War broke out on December 7 and 8, 1941, the Japanese were able to use their bases in Cambodia to send soldiers to Bangkok, and more importantly, to launch their attack on northern Malaya.

The *Nagara Vatta* started publishing articles that supported the Japanese and began opposing French colonial rule. When Singapore surrendered on Febru-ary 15, 1942, and the Japanese had taken the vast majority of the Netherlands East Indies by the end of that month, as well as most of Burma two months later, it was clear that the political situation in the region had changed forever. The French colonial establishment was technically still in power in Indochina, but it was apparent that they would remain there only until the Japanese de-cided to eject them. In 1941, Cambodians in Bangkok came to form the Khmer Issarak ("Independence") Committee under Thai auspices. It was to launch an armed struggle against the French. However, the first problem for the French was how to deal with peaceful protests.

THE UMBRELLA PROTEST AND
THE FRENCH REACTION

In July 1942, some nationalists in Phnom Penh decided to plan a march against the French. The ringleader was a monk called Hem Chhieu who taught monks at the Pali School in the Cambodian capital. He mentioned some of his ideas to Cambodian militiamen and on July 17, one of them arrested him. The seizure of a senior monk outraged many, and the people planning the protest decided to rally in support of Hem Chhieu. Son Ngoc Thanh believed that the Japanese had promised to help the rally, which took place on July 20, 1942.

The rally headed for the office of the acting French *Résident Supérieur*, Jean de Lens. There, the protestors, led by Pach Chhoeun, demanded Hem Chhieu's release. This event attracted some 1,000 to 2,000 ordinary people, as well as 500 monks, and captured the imagination of many. Pach Chhoeun's wife's youngest brother, Douc Rasy, described many years later how as a 16-year-old schoolboy, he watched with great pride as the demonstrators marched through Phnom Penh. Because the monks in the protest carried umbrellas, the event was often referred to as the "Umbrella Protest."

The French reacted harshly. They had agents following the protestors and photographing them. These photographs were used to identify who was in the demonstration, and Pach Chhoeun was dragged before a French court and sentenced to death, and then had the sentence commuted to life in prison. The harshness of that sentence—nobody had been killed in the demonstration—shocked and cowed many people. Pach Chhoeun was taken to the French penal settlement on the island of Poulo Condore, where Hem Chhieu was also held. Chhieu died within two years of arriving there, and when Pach Chhoeun was finally released less than three years after his arrest, he was, physically, a shadow of his former self. The event, however, was to join many others in the folklore of the Cambodian nationalists and in 1979, the government of the People's Republic of Kampuchea renamed the street along which the demonstration traveled after Hem Chhieu to commemorate the monk, who was one of the early martyrs of the nationalist struggle.

Son Ngoc Thanh had expected the Japanese to act to protect the demonstrators and when it became clear that this was not going to happen, he fled for safety to the house of a Japanese officer, and then went to live in Battambang, moving to Tokyo in 1943, where he tried to urge the Cambodian nationalists to resist the French.

The arrest of Hem Chhieu had led to simmering discontent in Buddhist circles, and this discontent became worse when, in 1943, the newly appointed French *Résident Supérieur*, Georges Armand Léon Gauthier, decided to replace the Cambodian alphabet of 47 letters with a romanized one. The aim was to adhere to the phonetics of the spoken language, but also to change it as the

French had done in Vietnam, the British had done in Malaya, and Kemal Ataturk had done in Turkey. The monks felt this would debase Cambodian culture, but the French pushed the change through.

CAMBODIAN "INDEPENDENCE" ACHIEVED

In June 1944, the Allies had landed on the coast of Normandy in the D-Day Operation, and from August 24 to 25, the liberation of Paris took place. With the Free French in control of the French capital, and the Germans and the Vichy French fleeing France, it became clear that French Indochina was also about to change. The French had enjoyed a relatively comfortable war up to that point. They had managed to broker a deal with the Japanese, and none of the French were interned like the British and Dutch soldiers and civilians in Malaya, Singapore, and the Netherlands East Indies. Now, with the Free French in control of France, the Japanese expected that the French in Indochina might quickly align with the Allied cause, as it appeared likely that they would win the war in Europe. This would seriously affect Japanese plans to try to hold as much of the Asian mainland as they could. The sign that war was going to sweep Cambodia came in February 1945, when an American Flying Fortress was sent to bomb the Japanese military headquarters in Phnom Penh. It missed and its bombs killed hundreds of Cambodians. One of the unexploded bombs was found nearly 50 years later.

On March 9, 1945, the Japanese seized control of Phnom Penh, and indeed the whole of French Indochina in what became known as the *coup de force*. Although scores of French died in Vietnam, the event was relatively benign in the Cambodian capital, where only a few guards and militiamen were killed. On March 13, 1945, at the express demand of the Japanese, King Sihanouk formally declared that Cambodia was now the independent Kingdom of Kampuchea. He nullified the Franco-Cambodian agreements and also ended the romanization of the Cambodian language. On March 18, Ung Hy became the first prime minister of Cambodia, taking the title *Akkamohasena*.

Because of the fighting in Vietnam, which had led to the deaths of some French, including a few senior officers, rumors had spread that the French in France were going to intern (and possibly kill) all of the Vietnamese in France. The Vietnamese in Phnom Penh, who largely lived in the north of the city, rioted and attacked the French, who lived mainly in the center of Phnom Penh. The Japanese quickly moved to protect the French and then decided to intern them all as they awaited further developments.

The Japanese released all political prisoners and Pach Chhoeun returned to Phnom Penh a physical wreck, although his spirit was not yet broken. In April, Son Ngoc Thanh flew in from Tokyo, and was given a government position. The Cambodian capital was by now seething with political ferment. On August 6, 1945, there was a demonstration against the French that was attended by as many as 30,000 people, a quarter of the capital's population. Finally, on August 12, a small group of radicals and, later, Prince Norodom Thon and some other members of the National Guard stormed the Royal Palace and demanded the resignation of Ung Hy and the appointment of Son Ngoc Thanh as the *Akkamohasena*. The King bowed to these demands and Thanh took the title of Prime Minister. Once in power, he held a brief poll about whether or not people supported his rule and independence from the French. He received two negative responses and published the results as 541,470 in favor and 2 opposed. This does appear to indicate that Thanh did include women in the voting, not that, of course, anybody actually voted.

On August 14, Japan surrendered following the bombing of Hiroshima and Nagasaki, and under an agreement between the Allies, Cambodia (and indeed the whole of Indochina) was to be returned to the French. Because there were no French in the region at the time, the task of securing southern Vietnam and Cambodia was assigned to the British who arrived in Saigon. Khim Tit, a veteran of World War I, and Thanh's Defense Minister, betrayed Thanh to the British who arrived in Phnom Penh on October 12. As David Chandler reported, on the morning of that day, Thanh reopened Lycée Sisowath, and had a late lunch in the Central Prison in Saigon. There, he was tried and sentenced to 20 years in jail, and was later commuted to house arrest in France, where he lived comfortably and completed the law degree he had started to pursue about 15 years earlier.

THE RETURN OF THE FRENCH

For most people, the return of the French to Phnom Penh was greeted apathetically. Few people felt that the French had actually won the war. Indeed, at the Japanese surrender ceremony in Phnom Penh, the Japanese commander had presented his sword not to the British commander, but to a Gurkha. He was keen to indicate that the war had not been won by Europeans, but by Asians.

Prince Sisowath Monireth, who had recognized that the French were going to restore their rule whether or not the Cambodians tried to resist, became the new Prime Minister, and his brother Prince Monipong was the new Minister of Foreign Affairs. The right to exercise independent foreign policy is enjoyed only by sovereign states, so in making that appointment, Monireth was clearly showing that Cambodia did retain some semblance of independence. The French were certainly not able to restore the same type of rule that they had enjoyed before World War II. In Vietnam, their attempts to take back northern Vietnam from the Vietnamese Communists were openly resisted. The French were keen to minimize their enemies and on January 7, 1946, they signed a modus vivendi agreement with the Cambodian government by which

Cambodia would be granted autonomy, while the negotiations over the exact relationship between the French Republic and Cambodia were still in progress.

Some of the most difficult problems were actually overcome with ease. The Thai government quickly returned the provinces of Battambang and Siem Reap, as well as the northern Malay States that they had taken from the British in 1943, in the expectation that they would not lose any of their original territory. The negotiations for the return of western Cambodia were, in part, undertaken by the then-Governor of Kratie, Lon Nol, who would become a major figure in Cambodian governments after full independence was achieved in 1953; he would go on to become the first (and, indeed, the only) president of Cambodia.

The other problem was a constitutional one. The decision was made that there would be elections held for a Constituent Assembly that would then decide on a Constitution, and after that, elections could be held for a National Assembly, which would have significant powers over events and developments in Cambodia. As this process started, Prince Norodom Norindeth, a pro-French member of the Royal Family, and a wealthy landowner in his own right, established the Liberal Party, the first Cambodian political party established in the country's history. It gained support from some French bureaucrats, including Louis Manipoud, a schoolteacher at Lycée Sisowath who was in charge of the local education system for the country. Politically, the party was pro-French and would obtain the support of, Norindeth hoped, the elite, the Cham Muslim minority, and the people who would be induced to support a strong anti-Communist government.

The next political party to be established was the Democrat Party. Its founders were three supporters of Son Ngoc Thanh: Sim Var, who had worked on *Nagara Vatta*, Ieu Koeus, and a schoolmaster called Chhean Vam. All three, who would all subsequently become prime ministers of the country, decided that they needed a really charismatic leader, and turned to Prince Sisowath Youtévong, a brilliant scientist who had spent the World War II years living in Nazi-occupied Paris, gaining a doctorate in mathematics. He had established important connections in the French Socialist Party, and had been flown briefly to the United States in a French diplomatic delegation just before the end of the war. He was also the great-great-grandson of Prince Ang Em, who had died in Vietnamese custody in 1844. The party was quickly organized with branches in all of the provinces and districts, where local school teachers and others helped rally up support. The third political party, the Democratic Progressive Party of Prince Norodom Montana, never achieved much success.

When the elections were held on September 1, 1946, the first ever in the history of the country to gain a large franchise—small elections had been held in the 1930s for advisory positions, with 100 or 200 people voting—there was widespread popular support for the process, and the Democrats won 50 of the 67 seats at stake, with the Liberals securing 14, and independents winning the other 3 (with 2 of those going to Democrat allies). Prince Youtévong became the Prime Minister in December 1946, with a mandate to change the country. The Constitution, which was agreed upon in May 1947, included a number of important checks and balances. It created two houses for the legislature: the National Assembly, directly elected by people in the constituencies, and the High Council of the Kingdom, which would be comprised of major interest groups, with civil servants, the Palace, provinces, and the like electing (or nominating, in the case of the Palace) members who were usually from their own ranks. However, on July 17, 1947, Prince Youtévong died—probably owing to overwork and strain. This left another member of the Royal Family, Prince Sisowath Watchayavong, as the Prime Minister, and a Cambodian Buddhist scholar from the Khmer Krom, Son Sann, as Deputy Prime Minister.

As Cambodia headed to the polls for elections under the new Constitution, two more political parties were formed: the Khmer Renewal Party of Lon Nol and Nhiek Tioulong, both of whom were hard-line right-wingers with strong Palace ties, and the National Union created by Khim Tit, which unapologetically represented the elite. On December 21, 1947, the Democrats won 55 of the 75 seats in the first National Assembly—the number of seats had been enlarged to allow for voting in Siem Reap and Battambang, which had not been included in voting for the Constituent Assembly in the previous year. The Liberals won the remaining 20 seats. The Khmer Renewal Party picked up 3.3 percent of the vote, with Lon Nol coming in last for the seat he contested. In January 1948, elections were held for the High Council of the Kingdom, and the National Union, which had won 0.4 percent of the vote in the National Assembly elections for seats with a very limited franchise, managed to win a third of the High Council seats. However, the Democrats were able to take advantage of a split in the smaller parties and gain control of the High Council, with the Democrat leader Chhean Vam becoming the new Prime Minister.

THE DEMOCRATIC PARTY

The Democrats had been formed to introduce socialism into Cambodia. They supported the construction of more schools, especially high schools, throughout the country. They believed in improved health service and a form of welfare state. They had also promised scholarships to universities in France for the best and brightest Cambodian students. How they were going to pay for all of these initiatives had not yet been determined. Most ardent nationalists supported Son Ngoc Thanh and desired his unconditional return to Cambodia. Many provided passive support to the few Cambodian Issarak rebels holding out against the French, and some gave them actual support. They also wanted a process that would lead to independence.

The massive majority that the Democrats enjoyed led, however, to factionalism. Penn Nouth, a Democrat who was to become one of Sihanouk' most loyal advisers, became Prime Minister, and was soon succeeded by an ambitious politician, Yèm Sambaur. In July 1949, Yèm Sambaur and another leading Democrat, Sam Nhean, along with their supporters—16 other deputies— resigned from the Democrat Party and decided to set up their own parties. Yèm Sambaur used a procedural motion to bring down the government and in February 1949, he became Prime Minister, filling the government positions with his supporters, and establishing a casino that quickly started raising enough money to pay for his projects. He managed one great success: the negotiation of the Franco-Cambodian Agreement of November 8, 1949, which saw the France devolve all power to the Cambodians, except over military matters and foreign affairs. However, it was clear that Yèm Sambaur's government did not enjoy the support of a majority in the National Assembly, and he refused to submit to a vote. He then persuaded Prince Sihanouk to dissolve the assembly and with a Democrat, Ieu Koeus, as interim Prime Minister, election plans were drawn up.

From 1949 to 1950, there was massive violence throughout the country, as the Vietnamese Communists and their supporters were keeping up their attacks on the French and had masterminded the establishment of a Cambodian Communist arm that was occasionally allied to Issarak groups. The fighting in the countryside led to widespread banditry and lawlessness. After eight days, as interim Prime Minister, the new Democrat leader Ieu Koeus was outmaneuvered and Yèm Sambaur returned as Prime Minister. Four months later, Ieu Koeus was murdered in his office when somebody rolled a hand grenade under his desk while he was working. A man who initially claimed he worked for Prince Norindeth of the Liberal Party was apprehended, and then denied responsibility. Norindeth fled the country and with the anti-Democrat Police Chief Lon Nol leading the investigation, nothing was ever proved. King Sihanouk briefly—from May 3 to May 31, 1950—served as Prime Minister, and he, in turn, was succeeded by his uncle, Prince Monipong, and then by a bureaucrat, Oum Chheang Sun.

Yèm Sambaur consolidated his supporters into the National Recovery Party, while Sam Nhean formed his People's Party. Yèm Sambaur had managed, with the help of Sihanouk, to mastermind a program that saw many Issarak rallying in support of the government and being granted military positions, with their soldiers then integrated into the Royal Army. One of the men who ended his rebellion and rallied was a pseudo-warlord in Siem Reap, Dap Chhuon. Dap Chhuon set up his own party, which took in some more disgruntled Democrats led by Mao Chay.

Although the political infighting dominated the attention of Cambodians during the election campaign, most of the press coverage outside the country centered on the career of an unfortunate pachyderm who was sent by Sihanouk as a gift to U.S. President Harry S. Truman. Sihanouk was keen to send the Americans a present, and although they had stated that they would like a tiger, the Saigon press started publishing details about a white elephant being dispatched. Some Cambodians pointed out that a white elephant could only be given to a supreme ruler, and the offer was soon downgraded to an ordinary elephant. Americans joked about a Democrat president receiving a Republican Party symbol. The elephant's mahout fell ill in Saigon, and the elephant had to leave without the replacement mahout, who was flown to Singapore, where the elephant and the new mahout (who only spoke Cambodian) then continued their journey. Sadly, on September 8, the day before the election, the elephant died on the ship off Cape Town, South Africa, and was buried at sea. Sihanouk then offered to send a statue from Angkor, which he felt would be more appropriate.

Finally, on September 9, 1951, elections were held for a new National Assembly. Yèm Sambaur expected an outright victory, while Mao Chay and Sam Nhean were less ambitious, and merely hoped that they might hold the balance of power. The problem was that the National Recovery Party and Dap Chhuon's Victorious Northeastern Khmer Party (VNKP), the Khmer Renewal Party, the Liberal Party, and the Democratic Progressive Party all had similar right-wing anti-Democrat policies. Not surprisingly, they split the right-wing vote five ways. Far from winning by a landslide, Yèm Sambaur's party did not gain a single seat, and he lost his own seat by 32 votes. The Democrats only lost one seat overall, the Liberals lost two, and the VNKP picked up four and the Khmer Renewal Party won two. Lon Nol once again failed to be elected, and did not contest another election until 1972, when he felt certain of victory.

THE END OF THE DEMOCRATS

The Democrats had won their third election in a row and Huy Kanthoul, one of the original supporters of Son Ngoc Thanh, became Prime Minister. Son Ngoc Thanh returned to Phnom Penh in triumph on October 29, 1951. Tens of thousands of his supporters lined his route as he went from the airport to Phnom Penh. On the same day, the French *Résident* of Cambodia, Jean de Raymond, was murdered by one of his servants. The two events were totally unrelated, but nevertheless contributed to a tense atmosphere. Thanh collected $40,000 in back pay for the six years salary he had not claimed, but found the parliamentary process difficult. While he had been in comfortable exile in France, Cambodia had transformed and gained political consciousness. Although Thanh was welcomed as a hero, many sought to use him for their own ends. He was unsure what to do, and was annoyed that the French were still technically in control of the country. On March 9, 1952, he and some colleagues drove out into the countryside and joined rebel Issarak, forming an armed resistance to the continued French rule. He had hoped that this would sweep him back to Phnom Penh within months, but it was 18 years before he was able to return to the city again.

Although he had clearly lost the 1951 elections, Yêm Sambaur held onto his government residence, car, and chauffeur, and still enjoyed the prerequisites that accompanied the position of minister, which he had not enjoyed since May 1950. The Huy Kanthoul government was worried that removing these privileges might cause more trouble than it was worth. But finally, the Democrats had enough. They sent in police to arrest Yêm Sambaur and Lon Nol. The latter was held in custody for four hours, something that outraged him for years, and a search of Yêm Sambaur's house uncovered hand grenades, which implicated him in the murder of Ieu Koeus. It was unclear how far this investigation could go, and on June 15, 1952, at the request of King Sihanouk, French colonial soldiers and French troops surrounded the National Assembly and the Prime Minister, Huy Kanthoul, was overthrown.

The reaction in Phnom Penh was relatively muted. Pach Chhoeun immediately retired from politics and took up a position at the National Library. Another leading Democrat and former Prime Minister, Chhean Vam, also left politics to run a jewelry business. Some Democrats raged, but most decided to wait out the crisis. However, the overthrow of Huy Kanthoul enraged the Cambodian students studying in France, many of whom were there on scholarships that had been sponsored by the Democrat government. Two students, Saloth Sar (later known as Pol Pot) and Ieng Sary, who had helped the Democrats in the 1947 election campaign, had been offered scholarships to France. The former left after two years, without completing his course of study, but the latter stayed and completed his degree. Both joined the French Communist Party, and on their return to Cambodia, they would become leading figures in the underground Cambodian Communist movement. That a democratically elected government could be overthrown seemed to have inured both of them against any plans for the Communists coming to power in an election, given that the results could be so easily overturned.

King Norodom Sihanouk had decided to act for a number of reasons. He was not just intervening to save his friend Yêm Sambaur. Sihanouk had always admired the 12th- and 13th-century ruler Jayavarman VII, and the Buddhist concept of a monarchy by which the King looked after his people. Sihanouk had been horrified by the reports of fighting in the countryside, and was genuinely worried that the Communists could come to power in Cambodia if the fighting against the French worsened. He had seen Emperor Bao Dai of Vietnam—who had traveled to Phnom Penh on an official visit on November 22, 1942—unceremoniously forced to resign in 1945, only to be brought back by the French and appointed to a powerless position. Although he did not like Bao Dai, monarchs tend to enjoy the respect that people around the world have for monarchies, and he believed that an attack on one monarch could be seen as an attack on the institution.

Appointing himself as Prime Minister, King Sihanouk decided to launch his Royal Crusade for Independence. Part of this, according to Sihanouk's own account, was influenced by the death of his favorite daughter, Princess Kanthi Bopha, from leukemia on December 14, 1952, at age four. It reminded him of his own mortality, and he sought to get the French to agree to concede independence as quickly as possible.

Sihanouk tried to attract international attention to the plight of Cambodia; he contacted many world leaders and went overseas, where he pressed his case. Most leaders, especially from newly independent countries, were supportive of Sihanouk, but one reaction from a world leader that is worth mentioning was that of the British Prime Minister, Winston Churchill. When he heard about Cambodia's problems on April 28, 1953, he exclaimed, "I have lived 78 years without hearing of bloody places like Cambodia."

Penn Nouth became Prime Minister, presiding over a government that was restructured to feature King Sihanouk as President of the Council, Penn Nouth in the official designation of Prime Minister, and four other members of the Royal Family serving in various capacities, including one of Prince Aruna Yukanthor's daughters, Princess Pengpas Yukanthor, overseeing the portfolios of public instruction and the fine arts. The other Royal appointees were the brothers Prince Sisowath Sirik Matak and Sisowath Essaro, and Sihanouk's uncle, Monipong. A fifth prince, Prince Norodom Viriya, was to join the ministerial line-up in July.

The French had hoped to cobble together a Federation of Indochina by which Cambodia, Laos, Cochinchina, Annam, and Tonkin would be brought together as equal parties, and with the first three supporting France, the other two could be outvoted. It was clearly a gerrymander to prevent the wishes of the majority in Vietnam from being expressed, as the five parts had unequal populations, and the plan was quickly shelved. By mid-1953, the French were clearly losing the military conflict in Vietnam, and decided to reach an agreement with Sihanouk; they would grant Cambodia independence and in return, he would guarantee the French property in the country. Sihanouk readily agreed. It was a very small price to pay for independence, and Sihanouk was a Francophile anyway. On November 8, 1953, France granted "full and satisfactory" independence to Cambodia.

5

The "Golden Years" under Sihanouk (1953–1970)

The proclamation of independence on November 9, 1953, led to euphoria throughout Cambodia. King Sihanouk rode in triumph through Phnom Penh, choosing the same route that Son Ngoc Thanh had used in his return to the Cambodian capital just over two years earlier. Sihanouk was cheered by a larger crowd as the man who had achieved independence without fighting. By November 1953, Sihanouk was the country's hero, and Son Ngoc Thanh was somewhere in the jungle, where he was to continue a spirited but hopeless struggle for most of the rest of his life. As the British Prime Minister Harold Wilson was to later remark, "A week is a long time in politics." Sihanouk had already realized this and would do everything he could to encourage the impetus gained from the Royal Crusade for Independence.

Cambodian independence, which had followed independence for Laos on October 23, 1953, meant that the French could concentrate their efforts on trying to maintain their control of Vietnam. However, by the time the Sihanouk had started his triumphal ride through the streets of Phnom Penh on November 9, both the French and the Vietnamese Communists had decided to stake everything on the battle of Dien Bien Phu. Sihanouk would later remark that the French had come to Indochina and left, the Japanese had also come and left, and the Americans had come, and would eventually go, but Vietnam was going to be Cambodia's neighbor forever and that was essentially the grim reality of Cambodia's geo-political position. Sihanouk knew that whatever was going to happen in Cambodia would be influenced by the outcome of the fighting at Dien Bien Phu.

Cambodian folklore still related stories of battles, with Cambodia trapped between Thailand and Vietnam, but few Cambodians feared invasion by Thailand. In fact, given its geographic boundaries, Thailand had more to fear from invasion by or through Cambodia, as demonstrated when Vietnamese soldiers captured most of Cambodia in January 1979. Furthermore, in Vietnam, the pressure on the population along the Cambodian-Vietnamese border was so intense that Cambodians expected, with good reason, that illegal immigrants from Vietnam would flood into Cambodia. In the 1950s and 1960s, the Cambodian government gazettes, the *Journal Officiel*, made regular announcements of lists of Vietnamese who had been deported.

If illegal Vietnamese immigrants were one problem, another, more serious issue was the possible annexation of part or, indeed, all of Cambodia by the Vietnamese government. While the French were in Vietnam, this was never a danger. But if the French left—and in November 1953, this was a real possibility—then a united Communist Vietnam could easily pose a risk to Sihanouk's newly independent country. Sihanouk had always liked publicity, but from the moment Cambodia achieved independence, Sihanouk decided that his country should have a high profile on the international stage as a "good international citizen," to quote a phrase from the 1990s. Tourists were welcomed to the country, and treated well. They visited the temples, spent their money, moved around in safety, and left, telling others about the great time they had at Angkor Wat, or riding an elephant through the nearby jungles.

Sihanouk also made a point of personally answering many of the letters he was sent from around the world. In fact, he continued to do so throughout his entire life, even during his periods of exile, ceasing this practice only when ill health forced him from the public eye in the mid-2000s. He corresponded with countless school children, stamp collectors, coin collectors, and the like. His secretary during the 1990s, Julio Jeldres, first befriended him when he wrote to Sihanouk while still a schoolboy in Chile. If an article appeared in a newspaper or magazine about Cambodia, Sihanouk's embassy staff had to write to congratulate the author, or send in corrections. They would then send Sihanouk details, and he would annotate it, often writing back to the authors himself to point something out or congratulate them. University lecturers and journalists were invited to visit the country, as well. Some people scoffed at the idea, but it worked, and a relatively small price (in monetary terms) was paid for 17 years of peace and prosperity that are still thought of by many Cambodians, even those who are not old enough to remember them, as the "Golden Years."

Chan Nak became Prime Minister of the country on November 23, 1953, followed by Sihanouk five months later and then, after ten days, Penn Nouth became Prime Minister, heading three consecutive governments until Leng Ngeth, a lawyer who was also Sihanouk's personal legal adviser, became Prime Minister from January 26, 1955, until September 30, 1955. In spite of these changes, the government administration remained in the hands of Royalists, and Sihanouk had also built up a large civil service, although his critics would claim it was too large.

By courting world attention, Sihanouk hoped to increase his international prestige, which he did, and this would help guarantee Cambodia's independence. On March 13, 1954, only four months after Cambodia became independent, the French were defeated at Dien Bien Phu. This coincided with the Geneva Conference held to discuss matters in Korea and Indochina. Independence provided international recognition for the Cambodian government, which seems to have led so many books and published articles to incorrectly cite 1954 as the date Cambodian independence was acquired.

At Geneva, the Cambodian communists were sidelined. Sihanouk was able to show that they had little support and that his government was the legitimate government of the country. Initially, Sihanouk was able to align with the West as an ally of the United States. However, some of his Court already had reservations about the role the United States wanted to play in the country. Prince Monireth found the U.S. diplomats with whom he dealt intrusive and naïve. Others were far more disparaging, feeling that they were interfering in the country. However, the most important decision Cambodia made at Geneva was that Vietnam would be partitioned, with plans—by the Communists at any rate—to hold elections in 1956. This left Vietnam divided for at least two years, and with the South Vietnamese government rejecting the holding of elections when they could not freely campaign in the northern half of the country, the division might well have lasted much longer. Cambodia was safe from attack by Vietnam, for the time being. The country had a long border with South Vietnam, which would be too involved in survival to think of attacking Cambodia; it had no border with North Vietnam.

On February 7, 1955, Sihanouk held a referendum on his achieving independence and on his role as the country's leader. He won, with 925,667 votes cast for him, and 1,834 cast against him—1,231 of those votes were made when a column of Communist guerillas crossed the frontier and voted at a single polling booth in Kampot, and then marched back to Vietnam. Sihanouk had the endorsement he wanted, and on March 2, he shocked everybody, including many members of his family, by announcing his abdication as King in favor of his father Norodom Suramarit. He argued that this would help him concentrate on politics, while his father could rule as King and remain above party politics. Sihanouk would then have the task of uniting his people as Cambodia went to the polls to elect a new National Assembly. In April 1955, Sihanouk was feted at the Bandung Conference in Indonesia, where he met Chinese Prime Minister Zhou Enlai, the Indonesian President Sukarno, the Yugoslav leader Josip Tito, and other world leaders, some of whom would later visit Cambodia.

Following on from Bandung, the leaders of the five contending right-wing political parties had finally decided to unite. The Khmer Renewal Party and the VNKP had banded together and declared themselves to be "rightist, monarchist, traditionalist, and in principle opposed to party politics." The power of Sihanouk's new-found zeal brought them together with the other political groupings of the right, and he formed Sangkum Reastr Niyum, the Popular Socialist Community. It was a political movement that hoped to end Cambodia's fractious nine-party democratic system. Sangkum was never a political party as such, and to join, you had to vow that you were not a member of any political party. Instead, Sangkum favored a system that removed the party machines from politics, allowing the most talented people of any political persuasion to help run a country that had a small trained elite. Rather than form a one-party system, as some other countries had attempted to do, Sangkum's aim was a no-party system, but for the 1955 elections, he had to take on the existing political parties head-on.

The Democrats suddenly realized that they would have to contend with the five right-wing parties, as well as the People's Party, with the Palace, the establishment, and the police all forming an alliance against them. The Democrat Party had also changed considerably. Keng Vannsak, a Khmer philologist, and a group of left-wing friends had taken control of the party's executive committee and the party was now very much to the left of the political center, and its policy was socialism and also—at its more extreme fringes—collaboration with Communism. A rump of the Liberal Party and the National Recovery Party had kept going, but they would not split the vote of their opponents. Some of the traditional Democrat base was also going to be eroded by the formation of the Pracheachon, or People's Party, a left-wing party with undisputed links to the Communists. However, the Democrats began the fight in good spirits. The election campaign was headed by Keng Vannsak, but three days before the voting would take place, his election rally was broken up by Sam Nhean's son, Sam Sary, who was accompanied by the police. They arrested the Democrat leader, and Keng Vannsak spent the day of the election, September 11, in jail.

The election was internationally supervised, but the published reports by the British contingent certainly did not reveal any very close scrutiny. The election results were that Sangkum won all 91 seats in the National Assembly, with 83 percent of the vote. However, what is believed to be the only surviving copy of the semi-official *Cambodge* newspaper for September 12, which had formerly been housed in the National Library of Cambodia, showed that a piece of paper had been stuck over a column on the table of results, revealing that non-Sangkum candidates—probably Democrats—had won 9 seats. The Pracheachon was declared to have won only three percent of the vote, and the Cambodian Communists returned to the jungle. They would not take part in a contested election again until 1993, when a pro-Vietnamese faction known as Pracheachon, the Cambodian People's Party, would lose an election and then force themselves on the victors. Khim Tit's loyalty was finally rewarded when he became Prime Minister from April until September 1956, with San Yun as Prime Minister from October 1956 until April 1957, and Sim Var as Prime Minister from July 1957 until January 1958, followed by Ek Yioun, then Penn Nouth again, then Sim Var again, and then Sihanouk as Prime Minister of the next three governments.

PRINCE NORODOM SIHANOUK AS LEADER

Sangkum was able to control political life in the country until 1970, and politicians from Sangkum for five years thereafter. With the 1955 elections, Prince Norodom Sihanouk was now the political master and he toured the world, becoming a close friend of the Chinese Communist leaders Mao Zedong and Zhou Enlai, and investing both of them with Royal Cambodian honors. Foreign countries—especially China—offered Cambodia financial aid, and Sihanouk accepted this offers with open arms, using the money to built a deep-water port at Kompong Som (which was renamed Sihanoukville), railways, hospitals, and schools. If Sihanouk became famous for traveling around the world, he was well known in Cambodia for his regular appearances at rallies and for meeting people. Disgruntled individuals could come and present themselves at his Palace and seek redress, and he would deal with many of their problems. He became approachable for many Cambodians, and the peasants loved him, as he shared bawdy jokes with them, made fun of pompous officials, and showed them films that he had directed and starred in.

On a personal front, Sihanouk's private life had also settled down. He had a reputation in his youth as a playboy, although he did later say that he had "never concurred any Vietnamese woman" during this time. He had fallen in love with Monique Izzi, and he left his previous wives—in fact, he had left some of them already—for her. Monique was the daughter of François Izzi, a Frenchman of Italian origin who had come to Cambodia, where he had married Mme. Pomme Peang, who had previously been married to a Cambodian Court official called Oum Phankeo. Oum and Pomme Peang already had three children; one, Oum Winavuth, served with distinction in the French forces and had been killed by the Vietnamese Communists, and another, Oum Mannorine, was a police officer in Phnom Penh. After Mr. Izzi left his wife and went back to Europe (he died in World War II), Monique and her sisters were brought up in the household of Prince Sisowath Sirik Matak, where one of them, Nanette, married Sirik Matak's brother, Prince Sisowath Methavi. Although Oum Mannorine and Prince Methavi never held very senior posts under Sihanouk— the former ended up as a junior cabinet minister, and the latter as Ambassador to East Germany—they wielded enormous influence with Prince Sihanouk. This was a time when Sihanouk was also moving away from relying on his uncle Prince Monireth for advice. Indeed, Monireth had effectively withdrawn from the political scene, but his brother, Prince Monipong, did take up the position of Ambassador to France, where he died in 1956.

Another man who also became a close confidante of Prince Sihanouk was Sam Sary, the easy going son of the politician Sam Nhean. Sam Sary had been a close personal friend of Sihanouk for many years, and Sihanouk had rewarded him by making him Ambassador to the Court of St. James in London. However, while there, Sam Sary was involved in a public scandal when one of his maids went to the police. Sam Sary was recalled, but still enjoyed Sihanouk's confidence as Cambodia went to the polls in 1958. On this occasion, Sangkum nominated one candidate for each seat, and only one seat was contested when Keo Meas, a diehard member of the Pracheachon who was still convinced that his party could win at the polls, contested, but was crushed, receiving 396 votes to Sangkum's 13,542 votes for the seat of Phnom Penh. The elections were, however, far more important in one other way; they marked the first time that women were able to vote—Sihanouk's Sangkum government had extended the franchise to include women—and a former school headmistress, Mme. Pung Peng Cheng, became the first woman elected to the National Assembly.

Right after the election, Sam Sary launched his own opposition party and then produced a free newspaper that carried no advertising and was obviously being bankrolled by somebody. Suspicion focused on the U.S. Embassy and on January 13, 1959, Sihanouk referred to a "Bangkok Plot" to overthrow him. Sam Sary disappeared, and his house was searched by police, who found incriminating material there. Rumors later emerged that Sihanouk had allowed Sam Sary to flee the country. This certainly seems possible, as Sihanouk always showed a level of loyalty to longtime friends, rather than dumping them when there was a scandal, which many politicians have seen as the expedient course of action. Sam Sary was hunted down by assassins hired by Police Chief Lon Nol, escaped an attempt on his life in Vientiane, and was murdered soon afterwards, probably in Saigon. Sam Sary's son, Sam Rainsy, was 10 when his father fled the country, but his grandfather was still alive and he helped look after Sam Sary's children. In 1965, when he turned 16, Sam Rainsy went to France, where he became a prominent banker before he returned to Cambodia in the 1990s, and is now the leader of the main opposition party in the country, which is named after him.

Sihanouk had always liked Sam Sary, but he had never really had anything in common with Dap Chhuon, the warlord who lived in Siem Reap, which he ran like his personal fiefdom. Dap Chhuon was a passionate anti-Communist and this had come to the attention of the South Vietnamese government and also the Americans, who were becoming involved in Vietnam. Boum Oum, the leading anti-Communist, controlled the southern part of Southern Laos, being that he was from the Royal House of Champassac, the hereditary rulers of that region dating back to late medieval times. This led some people to feel that Boum Oum and Dap Chhuon could secede from Laos and Cambodia, respectively, and form their own country, which could be a bastion against Communism and gain U.S. backing. It would have no coastline, and its industry would be based on tourism to Angkor Wat, and opium, but it would also obviously be able to rely on generous U.S. funds. Dap Chhuon, however, became nervous and told the head of police, Lon Nol. The two were very interested in mysticism and had been friends of a sort. In fact, Sihanouk later claimed that Lon Nol was part of the conspiracy all along and that explained why the Police Chief rushed up to Siem Reap and why Dap Chhuon was killed before he was able to make any confession. Victor Matsui, a U.S. diplomat who was there, as well, fled the country under suspicious circumstances. Some of the plotters were executed.

Matters grew considerably worse when, on August 31, 1959, two suitcases containing presents exploded in the Royal Palace in Phnom Penh, killing the Chief of Protocol, Prince Norodom Vakrivan, as he opened the one addressed to him. It appeared that the bomb in the other suitcase, which had been addressed to Prince Sihanouk, had detonated prematurely. On February 2, 1960, a 15-year-old boy turned up at the U.S. Embassy asking for help to assassinate Prince Sihanouk. The Embassy staff suspected entrapment and called the Cambodian police, who threw the boy in prison, where he languished for the next 10 years.

GROWING PROBLEMS WITH VIETNAM

On April 3, 1960, King Norodom Suramarit died. He had been a popular king who had done a great deal to enhance the prestige of the throne. An active nationalist in the 1940s, as King, Suramarit had remained above politics and was widely revered and respected; even some of the cynical elite had found him to be a good King. His death introduced the problem of succession. After splitting from Princess Kossomak, Sihanouk's mother, Suramarit had taken a second wife and they had two children, the 13-year-old Princess Norodom Vichara and the 8-year-old Prince Norodom Sirivudh. There was also Sihanouk's eldest son, Prince Norodom Yuvaneath, who was 17. As Sihanouk had foresworn the throne, there was a constitutional crisis, which was resolved by Queen Kossomak being made the head of state, retaining the prestige and symbolic power of the throne, although the real power would remain in the hands of her son, Sihanouk.

To approve this major constitutional change, Sihanouk appointed a little-known bureaucrat, Chuop Hell, as the interim Head of State and a referendum was held in which voters could choose between him, Son Ngoc Thanh (sentenced to death in absentia), the Communists, or "No Opinion." Sihanouk received 2,020,349 of the vote. Some 133 voted for Thanh, and the same number voted for the Communists, while 93 professed "No Opinion." People questioned these results, but the sentiment was clear: Sihanouk was popular and most people in the country wanted him to continue running Cambodia. If any year could be described as the peak of Sihanouk's career, this was it.

However, the fighting in Vietnam had led to serious disquiet in Cambodia, which shared a long border with South Vietnam. Much of the border was unmarked, and there were—indeed, there still are—disputes over it. Cambodian scholar Sarin Chhak spent his student days writing a thesis about the borders of Cambodia, and his work is still treated with reverence by Cambodians in their regular disputes with Vietnam. The major border dispute with Thailand, over the temple at Preah Vihear, had been solved amicably by international arbitration, during which Cambodia's claim to the temple was upheld—although this conflict flared up again in 2008. But once again, Cambodia's problems with Vietnam were far more serious.

The Vietnamese Communists had hoped that after the Geneva Agreement, there might be elections, which they expected to win. However, the anti-Communist Ngo Dinh Diem government in South Vietnam had never agreed to hold these elections, especially as they would not be able to organize in the other half of the country. Diem's police network was also able to locate and neutralize so many of the Communists operating in South Vietnam that in December 1960, the southern Communists formed the National Front for the Liberation of South Vietnam (NFL) and formed an armed wing, which soon gained the pejorative nickname "Vietcong." They called for support from North Vietnam, and the Vietnam War formally began.

Soon after the fighting started in 1961, it became clear that the North Vietnamese would have to obtain large amounts of military and other supplies for their southern "allies," as they called them, or "puppets," as others referred to them. The logical route ran along jungle paths from North Vietnam through Laos and northeastern Cambodia into the central highlands of South Vietnam. If the Communists went through east-central Cambodia, it would be possible to launch an attack on Saigon itself. This route was to become known as the Ho Chi Minh Trail.

Sihanouk had declared Cambodia neutral in the Vietnam War, but he weighed the consequences of the war very shrewdly. The U.S. objective was to save South Vietnam. For them, victory would be achieved through an end to the fighting and the maintenance of a pro-U.S. government in South Vietnam. Not even the most optimistic of U.S. generals or politicians could conceive of taking North Vietnam. Although Sihanouk disliked Diem, and there could be trouble, especially with the Mekong River, he believed that South Vietnam would be so worried about attack that it would not dare mount an unprovoked assault on Cambodia with the aim of annexing part or all of it. If the status quo was maintained, Cambodia was safe. However, the Communist objective was to take over the south, and then reunite Vietnam. A united Vietnam would pose a very serious risk to the future of Cambodia. As a result, Sihanouk reached a secret understanding with the Vietnamese Communists; they would be allowed to use the Ho Chi Minh Trail, provided that they did so surreptitiously. The Royal Cambodian Army would not notice and would not actively help—at least that was the theory. In return, when the Communists won the war, which Sihanouk saw as inevitable, the new Communist government of a united Vietnam would respect Cambodian sovereignty and borders. Obviously, the agreement could not be made public at the time, but Sihanouk has subsequently confirmed that this was what transpired in the 1960s. It was a delicate line that Sihanouk was treading, and although some have blamed him for so many things eventually turning sour, that he managed to balance on the "tightrope" for as long as he did was evidence of his political skill. Sihanouk himself said, "I'll keep maneuvering as long as I have cards in my hand. First a little to the left, then a little to the right. And when I have no more cards to play, I'll stop."

THE SANGKUM REGIME

The first government that was sworn in under the new regime—with Queen Kossomak as head of state, but Sihanouk actually running the country—included Pho Proeung as the new Prime Minister. A bureaucrat, he was also the head of Cambodia's internal intelligence services, and his family was regarded as the second in seniority in the country, after the Royal Family. The Deputy Prime Minister in the former government, Nhiek Tioulong, a long-time friend of Sihanouk, remained in office. During the 1960s, Tioulong had become one of the most powerful figures in the country. He had been the co-founder of the Khmer Renewal Party with Lon Nol, and the two—Tioulong as a military man, and Lon Nol as a police chief—became stalwarts in Sangkum. Although Sihanouk never really trusted the latter, he enjoyed Tioulong's company. Tioulong had reorganized the Cambodian army just after independence when a Vietnamese Communist attack occurred as expected, and since then, he had held a number of portfolios, including a brief tenure as Cambodia's Ambassador to France, and later, the Soviet Union. Tioulong and his family appeared in a number of Sihanouk's films, and one of his daughters was to marry Sihanouk's third son, Prince Chakrapong, while another was to marry another member of the Royal Family.

When the Pho Proeung government collapsed after allegations of corruption were made against some of its members, Penn Nouth returned as Prime Minister. He was followed as Prime Minister by Penn Nouth again, then Sihanouk again, and from February until August 1962, Nhiek Tioulong was Prime Minister. Amid these many changes in prime ministers, many of the ministers held the same portfolios, one of whom was Lon Nol, who remained Minister of National Defense. He was building up a following among army officers who wanted closer links with the United States and the West. Sihanouk, however, had other ideas.

On June 10, 1962, Cambodia went to the polls. With Sangkum candidates standing unopposed in each constituency, the turnout figures and the voting record were, to one extent, academic. However, they did get people used to the mechanics of voting, which would be of significant value in 1966. Throughout the changes in governments and ministers, Sihanouk remained firmly in charge. He would hold court at his Palace and at the public meetings held every six months, anybody, including many poor peasants who trekked in from the countryside, could bring up grievances with him personally. The ministers would then be told to fix whatever the problem was. Sometimes, they would be berated. On one of these occasions, the Secretary of State for Trade, Khieu Samphan, was criticized and felt humiliated.

Khieu Samphan had been a student in France, where he had completed a thesis on problems with the Cambodian economy. He saw the crisis as stemming from the gradual erosion of landownership by the peasants and the intrusive nature of Chinese money-lenders, and he wanted greater state support for, and protection of, agriculture and industry within the country to prevent Cambodia from being flooded with cheaper imports. His arguments had won over many people in the Cambodian government, and had some influence on Sihanouk—Khieu Samphan's strong Communist leanings were not seen as suspicious at the time. Khieu Samphan had been a school teacher before being elected to the National Assembly in 1958, and he traveled to Parliament by bicycle, rejecting the offer of a free Mercedes Benz car in exchange for pushing an important business deal through. In 1960, Khieu Samphan had fallen afoul of Kou Roun, the head of the security police, and on July 13, police agents had grabbed Khieu Samphan in the street and stripped him of his clothes, leaving him to scuttle home naked. It was a humiliation that was to come back to haunt the Royal Government many years later. But in the meantime, Khieu Samphan bided his time. He was forced to resign from the government in July 1963, and Sihanouk then asked the gathered politicians if anybody wanted his position. When one man called Nim Nirom said something, he was immediately given the Trade portfolio. He did not remain minister for very long, though.

THE CAMBODIAN COMMUNISTS

Soon after Sihanouk changed the political system based on his 1960 refer-endum, on September 30, 1960, the Cambodian Communists held a secret Con-gress in a room at the railway station in Phnom Penh. They were unsure of what their role could be in Cambodia—they were a handful of activists who had been rocked by a number of incidents. After Ho Chi Minh had established the Indochina Communist Party, some Cambodian Communists had felt that the Vietnamese planned to use the Communist movement to dominate the region. This seemed to be confirmed in the Indochina War when many Cambodian Communists fought alongside the Viet Minh, and focused much of their fight-ing on the French in southern Vietnam. In 1954, a significant number of Cam-bodian communists were evacuated from the country on a Polish ship, the *Jan Kilinski*, and were in Hanoi, leaving the rump of the Cambodian Communist movement in Phnom Penh. There, they operated an underground existence, having been routed in the 1955 elections and intimidated in the 1958 elections. A number, such as Saloth Sar and his wife, Khieu Ponnary, were school teach-ers. Some worked in the state system, but a small important group was asso-ciated with the Chamroeun Vichea ("Progressive Knowledge"), a private school in Phnom Penh where students were taught new ideas. With many Commu-nists on its teaching staff, it soon became a place where Communists could meet and also befriend like-minded students.

The Communist movement in Cambodia—Sihanouk called the members the Khmer Rouge ("Red Cambodians")—was held together with the belief that they would be able to take over the country. In 1960, this might have seemed impossible, but 15 years later, they would be in charge of Cambodia, introduc-ing one of the most savage revolutions of the 1960s. They were relying to some extent on the Socialist views of Sihanouk, and some Communists had tried to show their support for Sihanouk's neutralist foreign policy and his alliance with Communist China. But the Cambodian Communists were not certain whether they could rely on support from the Chinese. Mao Zedong's *Little Red Book* was never translated into Khmer, and the Chinese were keen supporters of Sihanouk and would do nothing to weaken his regime.

In 1962, the Communist movement was shaken when its General Secre-tary, Tou Samouth, was arrested by the government. He was taken to Lon Nol's house by the police and tortured for a week before he was killed and his body disposed of in Stung Meanchey in Phnom Penh. During that time, Tou Samouth had refused to divulge the members of the Khmer People's Revolutionary Party, as the Cambodian Communist Party was known, but the members were not sure about this. They went into hiding and waited for what they expected would be the inevitable police raids. When these did not come, the Communists reformed and on July 20, 1962, appointed Saloth Sar as the acting Secretary General of the party, which was renamed the Workers' Party of Kampuchea.

Although Tou Samouth had not divulged the names of the Communists, some were well known and a list of 34 was published in the newspapers in March 1963, and those on the list were invited to meet Sihanouk. Saloth Sar, who had been confirmed as the Secretary of the Workers' Party of Kampuchea during the previous month, was on the list, but chose not to attend. Those who did were verbally berated by Sihanouk and then physically assaulted by his police force right after he left the meeting. Sihanouk was not present at the actual attacks, but they felt that he would have known about them, and, indeed, arranged them beforehand. The event certainly shook the Communists and in May 1963, Saloth Sar and other leading Communists decided to leave the capital for the jungles.

Saloth Sar had been educated at École Miche, a small private school in Phnom Penh, and then at Collège Preah Sihanouk in Kompong Cham, before working for the Democrats and then spent two years in France, where he studied, joined the French Communist Party, and became interested in Communist activism. He was intelligent, quiet, polite, and deferential in his appearance, but this masked a deep resentment for what he saw as the major problems with Cambodian society. He detested the Court and Palace structure he had grown up within, and he resented the international attention foisted on Prince Sihanouk, as well as the Prince's mannerisms and flamboyant style. He hated the cronyism that existed, and the rich Chinese families that dominated business life in the country. Determined to change it all, he set his sights on revolution with a fervor that was to be magnified by the Red Guards in China in 1966.

PROBLEMS AHEAD

For many reasons, 1963 was a turning point in Sihanouk's Cambodia and signaled a major change in his policies. Prince Norodom Kantol was the Prime minister. Some, such as Bernard Hamel, a French adviser to Sihanouk, have seen this year as the turning point. Intellectuals saw it as the end of the Golden Years, but for the peasants, *their* prince was still *their* savior, ready to help them and show them courtesies that many of the Western-educated elite in Phnom Penh would not. On May 1, 1963, the Chinese President, Liu Shaoqi, visited Cambodia. Some Chinese Nationalists connected with Taiwan had planned an assassination attempt, but they were arrested. For Sihanouk, Liu Shaoqi's visit was a sign of support, as the Vietnam War was about to impinge on Cambodia more than ever before. The crisis arose on November 1, 1963, when there was a coup d'état in neighboring South Vietnam. Ngo Dinh Diem, the President of South Vietnam, and his brother and chief adviser, Ngo Dinh Nhu, were captured and killed by pro-American generals in a coup that the U.S. clearly had foreknowledge of and supported. Sihanouk was shocked. He was no friend of Diem—in fact, the two despised each other—but the Prince could not believe that the U.S. government would stand by and let one of its most loyal allies be overthrown and murdered. Sihanouk was not a U.S. ally and he certainly feared that there might be a renewed assassination attempt on himself. In Laos, Quinim Pholsena, the neutralist foreign minister, had been murdered on April 1.

On November 12, 1963, Sihanouk took the unusual step of naming Prince Norodom Naradipo, his fourth son, as his successor. Immediately afterwards, the National Congress of the Sangkum Movement stated that Cambodia should and would reject U.S. aid. Sihanouk made some bitter comments about the death of John F. Kennedy, and when, on December 8, the prime minister and dictator of Thailand, Sarit Thanarat, also died—albeit of natural causes— Sihanouk hailed the removal of his enemies in the West and the East, as well as the man who had controlled both of them. It was an ill-judged comment, but showed the level of anger that Sihanouk felt over U.S. foreign policy.

The rejection of U.S. aid signaled a major change in economic policy that would be adopted by the Cambodian government. Up to this point, the government had been moderately Socialist, building up the education system, upon which Sihanouk lavished funds, making teachers some of the best-paid government employees in the country. The expansion of the education system since Cambodia achieved independence in 1953 had led to a great demand for university graduates, and helped to create a large supply of them. While many students continued to study in France, as well as in other countries, the Khmer Royal University had been opened in Phnom Penh in 1960, and this was to be followed by the establishment of other universities. Sihanouk had created a society where peasant children hungry for knowledge had been able to excel in the education system, and could not only aspire to, but also obtain, white-collar jobs in a massively expanded civil service.

However, in 1963, the civil service was unable to recruit the large number of graduates who had completed their degrees that year. Many were unable to find work. The degrees and qualifications they had earned often meant they did not want to return to the farms in the countryside, from which many of them had hailed. These people were not destitute—they often remained at home, living with their parents or other relatives—but they became a vitriolic target of criticism. Some believed that Communism might solve this problem, but others thought that a freeing-up of the country's economy might provide free-enterprise jobs that would help reduce the high levels of urban unemployment.

Sihanouk did not want to create a free-market economy. Instead, he wanted to go the other way. He was worried about the control of the economy by a relatively small number of extremely wealthy Chinese and Sino-Khmer businessmen. He felt that nationalizing the major companies and then creating large government enterprises and corporations would solve the problem, and in January 1963, he organized the nationalization of Cambodia's private banks. However, this, and many of his other moves, led to scandals that were not of his making. A banker named Kitchpanish Songsakd fled Phnom Penh for Saigon and then for Bangkok with some $4 million in assets from the Bank of Phnom Penh. It was a financial scandal, but Kitchpanish, in exile, also started helping Son Ngoc Thanh's small Khmer Serei ("Free Khmer") movement and this angered Sihanouk.

The fury of Sihanouk fell on a young student, Preap In. Hailing from a farming family, Preap In had studied at the Collège Technique ("Technical College") at the same time as Saloth Sar. However, rather than joining the Communists, he had thrown in his lot with the Khmer Serei. At age 26, he believed that he would be offered amnesty to return to Cambodia and did so. However, he was seized by Cambodian police and subjected to a public trial, where he was publically berated by Prince Sihanouk. Preap In refused to apologize for his actions and did not crave the mercy of the Prince. He was sentenced to death and publicly executed. Sihanouk ordered the film of his execution to be shown in cinemas around the country. Many people were disgusted by this and saw Preap In as a misguided young man who was made a scapegoat for the inability of Sihanouk's police to find Son Ngoc Thanh.

THE BREAK WITH THE UNITED STATES

On October 27, 1964, the Cambodian government threatened to break diplomatic relations with the United States, citing violations of Cambodian sovereignty by U.S. troops and aircraft along the border with South Vietnam. This was exacerbated by an article in *Newsweek* magazine that claimed that Queen Kossomak was living off immoral earnings, and that she was the owner of some properties that were being used as brothels. Although this was the case, the Queen had actually leased out the places to others, who had, in turn, leased them out to the brothel owners. The Queen was not a large-scale property owner, but given her commitments at the Palace, she scarcely bothered with the details of all her land holdings. Sihanouk saw the article for what it was: a deliberate slight against his mother to get to him. When, on May 1, the U.S. forces from South Vietnam bombed the "parrot's beak," the part of eastern Cambodia that protruded into South Vietnam, it was the final straw. Cambodia broke diplomatic relations with the United States, closed down their embassy, and ordered their staff from the country.

The break with the United States was hailed by many Cambodians. A left-wing member of the National Assembly, Hou Youn, championed Prince Sihanouk's neutralist stance, as did many other politicians. The opinions of people in the Royal Court were divided. Some were worried about this affront to the

United States, but others hated Americans and were quite happy to see them ejected from the country. Lon Nol, the Police Chief, and a hard-line anti-Communist, was concerned that the lack of U.S. aid would damage Cambodia's ability to secure its frontiers. However, true to form, he kept his own council. The Australian Embassy in Phnom Penh looked after U.S. interests—and it should be added that the Australian Embassy in Saigon had been looking after Cambodian interests in South Vietnam since the break in diplomatic relations following the Buddhist Crisis in Saigon in mid-1963.

Some foreign celebrities lauded Prince Sihanouk. The doctor-turned-writer Han Suyin, author of *A Many Splendoured Thing* (1952), extolled Sihanouk's decision. She was closely identified with the left wing, and had already traveled to Cambodia, a trip she used as the basis for her book *The Four Faces* (1963). In it, she eulogized Sihanouk, with Sim Var later commenting that the praise she heaped on Sihanouk helped buoy the Prince in the international arena. The French President, Charles de Gaulle, by this time breaking his country's support for the United States and pursuing his own foreign policy objectives, visited Phnom Penh in August and early September of 1966. Other leaders who traveled to Cambodia included President Sukarno of Indonesia, Emperor Haile Selassie of Ethiopia, and President Josip Tito of Yugoslavia in January 1968. With a publicly stated policy of neutrality, they embraced Sihanouk as one of their allies in the Non-Aligned Movement. Princess Margaret from Britain visited Phnom Penh in September 1969, and U Nu of Burma and President Diori of Niger visited in November 1969.

THE 1966 ELECTIONS

With the country seemingly united behind Sihanouk, National Assembly elections were held on September 11, 1966. By this time, the Cambodian economy had stagnated. The government-run corporations established by Sihanouk had floundered badly. Most were headed by members of his circle, and some started showing losses owing to inexperience or inefficiency, while others were clearly having their money siphoned off. It was in this period of economic malaise that the elections were held, and Sihanouk, exhausted by matters of state, decided to allow any member of Sangkum to nominate. The election saw 425 candidates contest the 82 seats in the National Assembly, with only 43 of the outgoing deputies being renominated. Sihanouk only personally intervened in four elections. He was critical of Douc Rasy of the right wing, and Hou Youn, Hu Nim, and Khieu Samphan of the left. All four were easily reelected, with newspaper editor Soth Polin later commenting that the added publicity of Sihanouk's attacks had actually made all four better known in their constituencies than would otherwise have been the case. Of the 82 elected, 5 could be seen as representing the left wing. The socialists, who had received some Royal patronage in 1962, found themselves to be a spent force, electorally. Six leading right-wing Cambodians, Douc Rasy, Sim Var, Yêm Sambaur, Op Kim Ang, Trinh Hoanh, and Long Boret, all won seats. Douc Rasy, the brother-in-law of early Nationalist Pach Chhoeun, was one of the few politicians who was not afraid to criticize Sihanouk personally, and he would indeed become a bitter critic of the Prince. Sim Var and Yêm Sambaur were both former Prime Ministers, Trinh Hoanh and Long Boret were writers, Trinh Hoanh was a journalist, and Long Boret authored romance stories, many of which were serialized in newspapers.

The election results were certainly a victory for somebody who was not even running in the elections. The man who gained the most from the polls, and who was then sworn in as Prime Minister, was 53-year-old Lon Nol, the longtime Defense Minister and a fervent Buddhist and mystic. He always allowed visiting monks to stay in his compound in Phnom Penh, and portrayed himself as a man keen on recognizing piety in others. However, he was also a schemer and had used his long involvement in politics, the police, and government to build up dossiers on his political opponents. Often reserved in giving his own opinion, he was very much the opposite of Sihanouk. Lon Nol wanted to reverse some of Sihanouk's measures, which had led to the economy being placed under state control. Lon Nol's government included three women cabinet ministers, and he was determined to push through his agenda. Sihanouk responded by setting up the "Counter-Administration"—a loyal opposition in the British or French Parliamentary sense. This, he hoped, would keep Lon Nol in check, and it was certainly a delicate moment in Asia. In September of the previous year, 1965, the Indonesian Communist Party had been destroyed in the wake of events that occurred in Jakarta, the Indonesian capital—events that are still a little hazy. Some Communists may have planned a coup d'état, and they may have had the support of President Sukarno. If this was the case, and this does seem likely, the plan failed, and Sukarno was reduced to a figurehead, and would soon be removed even from that position. In December 1965, Ferdinand Marcos had been elected in the Philippines, signifying the establishment of a new government dedicated to ending corruption and changing Filipino society for the better—although some years later, this government came to embody some of the greatest excesses of government corruption and graft. In May 1966, Mao Zedong in China had launched what was to become known as the Great Proletarian Cultural Revolution, a significant turn to the left.

In Cambodia, the reaction to the new Lon Nol government was mixed. Many of the elite welcomed it, as did, presumably, many of the peasants who voted for the politicians who would form the Lon Nol ministry. However, some peasant farmers in the province of Battambang were angry. In the district of Samlaut, there were disturbances, although their significance is a matter of dispute in academic circles. Australian-American academic Ben Kiernan wrote his original Honors thesis on the "Samlaut Rebellion," as he termed it, and went on to write about this subject many times in his future works. He viewed the events in Samlaut as the turning point in Cambodian history, arguing that they signified the start of the armed struggle that would lead, in 1975, to a Communist victory. Sihanouk has publicly rejected this view, claiming that there was never any such rebellion, although he later moderated his approach, arguing that there was peasant discontent, but that it was directed against Lon Nol, not him, and this does seem possible. The crackdown launched by Lon Nol led Khieu Samphan and Hou Youn to flee Phnom Penh to join the Communist resistance in the jungle on April 25, 1966. Wild stories quickly circulated that they had been murdered by Lon Nol, but he denied it. At the time, Sihanouk was certainly unhappy with Lon Nol, and on April 30, 1966, he summoned Lon Nol to see him. Lon Nol tendered his resignation, citing ill health.

THE ROAD TO MARCH 1970

The resignation of Lon Nol led to the appointment of longtime politician Son Sann as the new Prime Minister. Son Sann was from a Khmer Krom family whose ancestors had been involved in fighting the Vietnamese. His father had moved to Phnom Penh, where he had been born in 1911, and Son Sann had been educated in France and Britain, and then served in the government administration from 1935 onward, holding many ministerial positions, and serving as Director of the National Bank of Cambodia from 1964 until 1968. He was a revered Buddhist intellectual, a man of grace and charm, for whom, a journalist later wrote, Paris would be a second home, although Beijing never could be one.

Son Sann tried to restore some balance to the government by including a mixture of rightist and centrist politicians. Not long afterwards, the Cambodian government allowed the National Front for the Liberation of South Vietnam—which the Americans dubbed the "Vietcong"—to set up an office in Phnom Penh. By now, serious questions were being asked about the disappearance of the two left-wing politicians. On August 7, Sihanouk claimed that Khieu Samphan and Hou Youn were still alive, but not many people believed him; they were still convinced that Sihanouk had them murdered. On October 7, a third deputy, Hu Nim, fled to the jungle to join the Communists, and elections had to be held for the three seats vacated in the National Assembly. Mention should also be made of a student, Hun Sen, who also fled to the jungle to join the Communists at this time. He would later adjust the date of his move to the jungle to 1970, a more politically acceptable date. But that was all in the future. On January 31, 1968, Penn Nouth became Prime Minister, but the political crisis was already mounting.

It was abundantly clear to most observers that the Vietnamese Communists were openly flouting Cambodia's neutrality and using not only the Ho Chi

Minh Trail, but also the port of Sihanoukville (formerly Kompong Som), to bring supplies overland to their jungle bases along the border with South Vietnam. It was subsequently claimed that Nhiek Tioulong made a large fortune by helping the arms and materiel shipments and lorry convoys. On March 18, 1969, the United States, its patience at an end, started secretly bombing Cambodia to try to destroy the Vietnamese Communist bases there. They might have expected howls of protest from Cambodia. However, on the contrary, on June 11, Cambodia restored diplomatic relations with the United States, and the U.S. National Security Adviser Henry Kissinger claimed this justified the continued bombing. He said that he felt Sihanouk was turning a blind eye to the bombing. Kissinger might have been correct in his sentiments, or Sihanouk might have realized that there was nothing else he could do.

On August 14, 1969, Lon Nol became Prime Minister again, and when, on September 3, Sihanouk went to Hanoi for the funeral of Ho Chi Minh, plots began to be formulated for his overthrow. Around the same time, Nhiek Tioulong saw the proverbial writing on the wall, and left Cambodia for a comfortable exile in Paris. Lon Nol was soon able to act, and with the support of Prince Sirik Matak, a friend from childhood days who was now Deputy Prime Minister, plans were advanced for removing Sihanouk from power, or possibly even changing the status of Cambodia to that of a Republic, based on the French model. However, by the end of 1969, Lon Nol was in Europe seeking medical treatment, and Sihanouk was worn out.

Angkor Wat. [Courtesy of the author]

The entrance to Angkor Thom.
[Courtesy of the author]

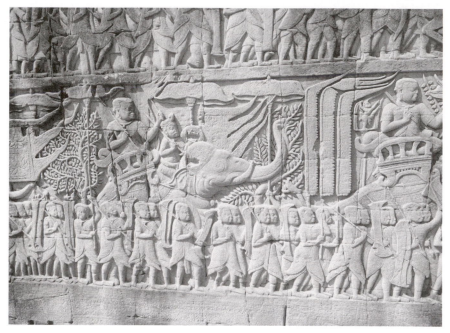

Wall carving at Angkor Thom showing Khmer war elephants in battle against the Cham. [Courtesy of the author]

King Sisowath Monivong is carried in a golden palanquin from the Royal Palace through the streets of Phnom Penh, September 10, 1928, following his coronation. [AP Photo]

King Norodom Suramarit, Queen Kossomak, Prince Norodom Sihanouk, Prince Sisowath Monireth, Prince Sisowath Monipong.

Prince Norodom Sihanouk sits on stage during the dedication of an infirmary in a village in Cambodia. [Courtesy of the Library of Congress]

Cambodian Prime Minister, Lon Nol, after the flag of the Khmer Republic was raised, following its proclamation on October 9, 1970, in Phnom Penh. [AP Photo/Ludwig]

Photographs of some of the 11,000 people killed at Tuol Sleng during Democratic Kampuchea. [Courtesy of the author]

Prime Minister Hun Sen. during his first visit to Australia. [Courtesy of the author]

Prince Norodom Ranariddh, First Prime Mister of Cambodia, addressing a United Nations news conference in 1997. [AP Photo/Richard Drew]

Sam Rainsy, Cambodia's opposition leader. [Courtesy of the author]

6

The Khmer Republic
(1970–1975)

On January 4, 1970, an official from Sihanouk's office telephoned Air France and reserved the first-class section on the flight that was leaving Phnom Penh on the following day. The first-class section of that flight, as well as the January 6 flight, was also booked. With packing starting at the Palace, it was clear that Prince Sihanouk, who was in the hospital at that time, was going to leave the country. By the time he turned up at Pochentong Airport, there was a small crowd of politicians and other well-wishers. The official reason given for the trip was that Sihanouk was going to France to seek medical treatment from his doctor in Grasse in the south of France, but that was clearly not the actual reason. A doctor could have quite easily traveled to Phnom Penh—money being no object. The real reason seems to be that the Prince was worn out. He was exhausted by the state affairs that had dominated his life for the last 15 years, and he wanted to rest and relax. At the airport, he was overheard remarking that he would be back to plough the first furrow of the agricultural year, which was in April. This event was one of the important royal festivals that Sihanouk had resurrected and, unlike some of the other ceremonies, it had previously existed.

As Sihanouk was heading to France for medical reasons, Lon Nol, the Prime Minister, was returning from his own medical treatment in France. The two men's paths crossed at Rome Airport in Italy, and the two spoke during what was obviously a prearranged meeting. What they discussed has been hotly debated. Thach Reng, an army officer accompanying Lon Nol and who would later become the head of the Special Forces, said that Sihanouk had told Lon Nol that he would be returning to Phnom Penh in the middle of March, and that on his way back, he would stop in Moscow and then Beijing. He wanted the two major Communist powers to put pressure on the Vietnamese Communists to withdraw their soldiers from his country—or, at the very least, to lessen their presence in the country. In order to strengthen his bargaining position, Sihanouk was reported to have asked Lon Nol to organize demonstrations against the Vietnamese in Phnom Penh.

It has been suggested that Lon Nol had been musing over whether or not to stage a coup d'état and overthrow Sihanouk during the 1960s. This seems unlikely. Lon Nol was a relatively unimaginative police officer who had ended up as the Defense Minister for long periods of time, and although openly pro-American, he had never really deviated from his course of service to Sihanouk and the elected government. However, his political ally, Prince Sisowath Sirik Matak, was quite different. Sirik Matak was an important member of the Royal Family. Intelligent, polished, and wealthy with a hint of arrogance, he disliked the way Sihanouk had been running the country. In late 1969, he had returned to the country after serving as Ambassador to China and then to Japan. In Japan, he had come to realize the power of the market economy, and disliked the socialist economic model that Sihanouk had introduced in the mid-1960s. Many of his friends in the elite had children who could not find work in the overstrained bureaucracy, and Sirik Matak felt that freeing up the economy would offer more opportunities for everyone. Despite the claim in many published works that he felt slighted because Sihanouk had become King in 1941 instead of himself, there seems to be no truth to this whatsoever. With Sihanouk overseas, Prince Sirik Matak now saw that he had the opportunity to act, and to try to do so constitutionally. He was aided by one of his brothers, Prince Sisowath Essaro, who lived in Paris, where he looked after the welfare of Cambodian students in the French capital.

Sihanouk was relatively confident of his popularity. He never doubted that the peasants would stand by him, and on December 28, 1969, he called for a vote of confidence on him by all the members of the National Assembly. Only Douc Rasy voted against him. He was, however, concerned about Prince Sirik Matak. To watch over him, Sihanouk had left the militia ("surface defense") in the hands of his trusted brother-in-law, Oum Mannorine, a man whose loyalty to Sihanouk and to the Throne was beyond any doubt. Oum Mannorine had the network and the ability to monitor any plans for a coup d'état, and he was prepared to do whatever it took to defend the Throne.

There was, however, a legal issue that Sihanouk had not foreseen. A king was, in effect, "anointed by God," with some supernatural element to his rule, but Sihanouk was no longer King. He had abdicated in 1955, and now held an uncertain constitutional position in the country. Sihanouk was undoubtedly the leader of Cambodia, his mother was technically the head of state, and Lon Nol was legally the head of government. Sihanouk owed his position as leader to the referendum of 1960, which had confirmed his power. If, as opposition deputy Douc Rasy, a trained lawyer, argued at the time, and later in his book on the subject, Sihanouk was appointed by a vote of the people and confirmed by the National Assembly and the High Council of the Kingdom, surely he could also be ousted by the vote of the National Assembly and the High Council of the Kingdom. This was an idea that Prince Sirik Matak favored. Lon Nol was uncertain, so Prince Sirik Matak and his supporters had to force the issue.

Their main problem was that if the matter went before a vote in the National Assembly and the High Council of the Kingdom, and Sihanouk's supporters won the day, or even managed a good showing, then there would be major trouble, possibly a civil war. In that instance, Sihanouk would return to Phnom Penh, and quickly take control. However, if the vote to overthrow Sihanouk was overwhelming, chances were that he (Sihanouk) might be persuaded to quietly go into exile in France or somewhere else. It was a risk that Prince Sirik Matak felt that he could and should take for the sake of the country.

On March 11, 1970, large numbers of monks and students, together with police in plain clothes, marched through Phnom Penh to protest the presence of Vietnamese Communists in the country. The demonstration headed to the Embassy of the Provisional Revolutionary Government (the political arm of the Vietcong) and there, it turned into a riot, with people first pillaging that building and then the North Vietnamese Embassy and the Office of the North Vietnamese commercial attaché. Some students, exuberant over what they had done, then charged over to the Chinese Embassy, but soldiers ringed that building with orders to shoot if provoked. The protests were to be limited to the offices of Vietnamese Communists. In Paris, when Sihanouk heard what had happened, he was outraged and publicly denounced the actions in an interview granted outside the residence of the Cambodian Ambassador to Paris. The pillages were far more serious than he had planned or expected. Inside the residence, he railed against Lon Nol and Prince Sirik Matak, threatening to execute most of the government when he returned. Sirik Matak's brother, Essaro, secretly taped the outburst. The tape was then flown back to Phnom Penh and played to a meeting convened by Sirik Matak and Lon Nol. Many of those who had wavered in their support of the overthrow of Sihanouk were horrified.

Sihanouk, obviously realizing that something was afoot, flew to Moscow, where he hoped to enlist Soviet support to urge the Vietnamese Communists to leave the country. He had just arrived when, on March 16, a large student demonstration outside the National Assembly led to speculation concerning

whether or not Sihanouk could be legally deposed. To test the deputies, corruption charges were brought against Oum Mannorine. This move against
somebody so close to Sihanouk was unprecedented, and the case against Oum
Mannorine was, at best, unproven. Some silk, valued at $60,000, had arrived
in the country with his name on the bags, and there had been an attempt to
avoid paying import duties. Oum Mannorine denied having anything to do
with this, and it seems that a local businessman might have mentioned the
Minister's name as a way of circumventing the customs service. A very beautiful young lady was said to have been involved in the smuggling, and the
local press in Cambodia had a field day. The debate in the National Assembly
revealed that if members of Sihanouk's inner circle could be attacked, then so
could the Prince. The plan to overthrow Sihanouk began to be enacted. On the
nights of March 16 and 17, Oum Mannorine finally acted and moved loyalist
troops to arrest Lon Nol and Sirik Matak. However, the two were forewarned
of this arrest, and it was Oum Mannorine and his circle who found themselves
arrested and held without trial for the next three years.

Early in the morning of March 18, 1970, a heated argument took place at
Lon Nol's house. Lon Nol had finally agreed to support the overthrow, but
now Prince Sirik Matak wanted Lon Nol to pledge to end the Cambodian monarchy and declare a republic. It was too much for Lon Nol, but he finally re-
lented. The two set off for the National Assembly building which, by this time,
was ringed with soldiers. There, in a joint closed session, the members of the
National Assembly and the High Council of the Kingdom met and voted on
the dismissal of Sihanouk as leader of Cambodia. Three deputies argued
Sihanouk's case, with one storming out of the Assembly rather than take part
in the vote, and the other two, one of whom was Mme. Pung Peng Cheng, the
first woman to be elected to the National Assembly, were distraught, but eventually persuaded by the other members to vote. The final tally was a surprise
to even Prince Sirik Matak—it was unanimous. Sihanouk was overthrown.
Although few realized it at the time, this was a crucial decision that would
change Cambodia forever.

The possibility of foreign involvement in the overthrow of Sihanouk has
been a source of debate for years. The evidence points to the U.S. Embassy in
Phnom Penh not being involved. It would have been closely watched, and if
the C.I.A. had been involved, this organization probably would have worked
through the embassies of friendly nations, such as that of Australia. There was
a very high level South Vietnamese involvement, and the South Vietnamese
vice-president, Nguyen Cao Ky, made at least two secret visits to Phnom Penh
in the days leading up to March 18. But for many of the Cambodians involved
in the overthrow, the matter of whether of not the Americans were involved
was irrelevant. Given the openly pro-Western sympathies of Prince Sirik Matak
and Lon Nol, it would have been surprising if the United States had not ap-

proached them at some time, and as Sirik Matak and Lon Nol pointed out, their overthrow was entirely legal. Thus, the United States did not need to engineer a coup d'état. Instead, the United States and South Vietnam supported elements within the country that moved to have Sihanouk deposed constitutionally for their own internal reasons.

THE REACTION TO SIHANOUK'S OVERTHROW

The ease of the Parliamentary vote to depose Sihanouk surprised many of the conspirators. Some of the senior plotters held cabinet positions, but did not have seats in the National Assembly, so they had been nervous about how the vote would go. When she was given the news of her son's deposing, Queen Kossomak said, "Serves him right."

Because the entire procedure followed the law, Cheng Heng, the President of the National Assembly, became the head of state. He was a wealthy businessman with his own private menagerie in the back of his house. After losing his seat in the 1966 elections, he won another one in a by-election, and was somebody who was never likely to challenge Lon Nol or Sirik Matak. For the conspirators, he was the ideal choice. In Phnom Penh, the news of the overthrow of Sihanouk dampened the atmosphere, with some people unable to believe the news they heard on the radio. There were many who were overjoyed by the news, while others sat around wondering what was going to happen next.

Sihanouk was leaving Moscow for Beijing when he was informed by the Soviet Prime Minister Aleksei Kosygin that he had been overthrown. President Podgorny had offered Soviet help to fly Sihanouk home ahead of the overthrow. It was now too late for Sihanouk to return to Phnom Penh. Uncertain about what to do, and what the reception would be like in Beijing, Sihanouk and his staff were nervous as they flew to China. When they arrived at Beijing, the Chinese welcomed Sihanouk as a head of state. He was greeted by the French Ambassador Étienne Manac'h, who offered him asylum in France, and then he met with the Chinese leadership. They had tried to seek assurances from Lon Nol that the Vietnamese Communists could continue to use their bases along the Cambodian-Vietnamese border, and they were rebuffed; that was against everything that Lon Nol and Sirik Matak stood for. The Chinese then offered Sihanouk the support of the Communists—Vietnamese and Cambodian—if he would declare the Lon Nol government illegal and launch an armed struggle to take back the country. It was after this that Nay Valentin, the Cambodian Ambassador to Beijing, gave Sihanouk the official news of his deposition. Sihanouk tore up the notification, and the scene was set for war.

On March 20, Colonel Seng Sunthay, an officer who was very close to Prince Sirik Matak, was found shot dead in a hotel in Phnom Penh. It was rumored that he had offered to shoot Sihanouk dead if the Prince returned. It seemed that the Sihanouk loyalists were starting to take their revenge as the Lon Nol government went through the process to declare their country a Republic. To show that the new government supported the freedom of the press, all political prisoners were released. Many of those prisoners were Communists, some of whom rallied to Lon Nol, but most of whom drifted away and would form a vitriolic opposition. Then, ritual denunciations on the radio and in the newspapers started against Sihanouk. These attacks were launched on his policies, his person, his mother, his wife, her mother, and his children. For the conservative Sirik Matak, the situation was getting out of hand. Some felt that he wanted his own son-in-law, Prince Duongchivin, to become the new king, and reinvigorate the country with a coronation resplendent in pomp and ceremony. This soon became impossible.

Large mobs of Sihanouk loyalists demonstrated in the countryside, and when two deputies went to talk to them—one, incidentally, being the only deputy who had not voted to overthrow Sihanouk—they were literally torn to pieces by the mob, as was one of Lon Nol's brothers. The mobs then marched from provincial capitals on Phnom Penh. Lon Nol sent out the troops to block the main roads and this succeeded in preventing chaos in the capital. However, the worst was yet to come. The North Vietnamese and the Vietcong suddenly decided to throw their lot in with Sihanouk, undoubtedly on orders from Hanoi, which was taking instructions from Beijing. They quickly consolidated their positions as Lon Nol was warned by his supporters that full-scale war was about to break out.

Lon Nol immediately called up volunteers to fight the North Vietnamese and the Vietcong. His appeal for 10,000 was answered by 70,000, mainly students who wanted to drive the Vietnamese Communists, and indeed all Vietnamese, from their land. Pent-up hatred going back centuries was unleashed as Cambodian youths, often badly armed, engaged the Vietnamese Communists in the countryside. They were no match for the seasoned veterans of the Vietnam War, and were driven back with huge losses. However, they then rampaged through Vietnamese districts in Phnom Penh, taking out their fury on innocent Vietnamese civilians. It was now a holy war by which the Buddhist Cambodians sought to expunge the Vietnamese from their country—most of the Vietnamese civilians were Roman Catholic, and the Communists were atheists. Prince Sirik Matak intervened whenever he could to prevent the massacres of Vietnamese civilians, but was unable to prevent the escalating carnage. The Lon Nol-Sirik Matak government, which had promised liberal Western-style democracy, was soon denounced around the world as perpetrating racist atrocities.

With war breaking out in Cambodia, mercenaries and journalists arrived in the country. The Cambodian government lacked the money to hire the former and most left, while some of the latter started going out into the countryside to cover the fighting. Overall, 31 journalists, including Sean Flynn, the son of the actor Errol Flynn, disappeared in the next few months as they were captured by the Communists and murdered. Of all the Western journalists killed in the 15 years of the Vietnam War, a third were killed within a few months in Cambodia.

With the Vietnamese Communists quickly gaining the upper hand in the countryside—in Prey Veng, they brought in a statue of Sihanouk to show their support for the deposed Prince—the Americans and South Vietnamese realized that they were approaching the abyss. If Vietnamese Communists were surreptitiously using the Cambodian jungles to launch attacks on South Vietnamese and U.S. positions in South Vietnam, the situation would become disastrous were to take over the whole country of Cambodia. U.S. President Richard Nixon was withdrawing U.S. soldiers from Vietnam, but events in Cambodia would clearly hinder his plan to reduce U.S. casualties ahead of the November 1972 elections. On May 1, a large U.S. and South Vietnamese military force invaded Cambodia. They sought permission from Lon Nol soon afterwards; they were undoubtedly worried that if they gave advance notice, word of the invasion would be leaked by Cambodians. As a military operation, it achieved its objectives and swept the Vietnamese Communists from the region bordering South Vietnam. For Cambodia, the invasion was a disaster. The Communists were driven deeper into Cambodia, and Lon Nol's lack of foreknowledge made him appear to be a U.S. puppet. There was a demonstration against the U.S. involvement at Kent State University in Ohio, where four students were shot dead. Sihanouk was particularly touched and wrote of his great sadness, given the way they had turned out to see him when he visited the campus in 1960.

Some felt that even at this late stage, Sihanouk might have been able to return to the country and avert a crisis. However, this ceased to be a possibility in July 1970, when Sihanouk was put on trial in Phnom Penh. In August, he was found guilty of various crimes against the country and sentenced to death in absentia. The trial did not demonstrate any semblance of fairness, but it did ensure that Sihanouk would fear execution if he decided to return. Moderate Sihanoukists were then purged from government positions, as, on October 9, 1970, some nearly 1,800 years of monarchical tradition in Cambodia ended. The descent from the Funan Royal Family to that of Angkor and Sihanouk was broken. Cambodia became the Khmer Republic, "One and Invisible," and the song officially known as "Khmers Stand Up!" but more correctly translated as "Khmers Arise!" or "Khmers Rise Up!" became the new national anthem.

THE KHMER REPUBLIC

The choice of the name "Khmer Republic," rather than the "Republic of Cambodia," was telling. The term "Khmer" was used by nationalists to specifically exclude those groups which were not deemed "proper" Cambodians, specifically the Vietnamese and the Chinese. This was a bold statement that the country was now for the Khmers, and those who wanted to make it ethnically pure had the ear of the government. Organizations such as the Mon-Khmer Institute were established to study the historical differences between the Khmers and others, as well similarities with the Mon people of Burma. Lon Nol wrote a pamphlet called *Neo-Khmerism* describing his philosophy, if one could be imaginative enough to suggest that there was any coherent thread in it. Lon Nol had wanted to preside over the country as somebody like King Suramarit had done from 1955 to 1960, and to be the man who embodied the spiritual nature of the nation. Despite his military rank, he did not want to be a military leader, but instead had that forced upon him.

The military situation started to settle down as a battle began around the world with both the Khmer Republic and Sihanouk's government-in-exile, the Royal Government of National Union of Kampuchea (GRUNK), vying for recognition from world bodies and foreign governments. Militarily, the Khmer Republic had to hold Phnom Penh, as whoever held the capital effectively controlled the country. The capital was where Lon Nol had the most support, and where he deployed his best soldiers. Since its establishment in the 15th century, the city had been protected by the Mekong River. In the wet season, the river swelled in size and this protected it from attack by the east bank. In the wet season, the defenders also had the advantage in most other parts of the country, as bad roads slowed down any attack. But in the dry season, which extended from late December to late April, the Mekong would become narrower and it was then possible to fire rockets from the east bank into the city. That was when the Lon Nol government would be most tested, and as a result, it was then that they launched many of their military offensives.

In late 1970, and again in December 1971, Lon Nol's troops had taken part in two major military attacks on their opponents, a combination of poorly armed Sihanoukists, Cambodian Communists (now referred to by many as the Khmer Rouge), and heavily armed Vietnamese Communists. These attacks were known as Operation Chenla I and Operation Chenla II. Both were imbued with spiritual significance by Lon Nol, who saw the deities supporting him in his battle against the atheist Communists. Both Chenla I and Chenla II reflected cavalier planning, and resulted in Lon Nol losing much military hardware. However, the Communists were not strong enough to make good on their attack.

Lon Nol also had serious health problems. On February 8, 1971, he had a stroke while taking a shower, and was rushed to Hawaii for emergency treatment. Sirik Matak took over as a growing rift between his supporters and those of Lon Nol appeared. Lon Nol's younger brother, Lon Non, launched Operation Akineth Moha Padevuth, managing to drive the Communists back from some villages they had held for nearly a year. Its aim was not military, but political, and Lon Non was soon ready to launch his Socio-Republican Party.

After the proclamation of the Khmer Republic, the deputies from the National Assembly had had their terms extended to decide on a new constitution. They had failed to reach any agreement, so a Constitutional Drafting Committee was convened, with preparations made for elections to be held in 1972. The pressure for these elections was international, as well as national. The U.S. government was negotiating with the Vietnamese Communists at Paris, and the South Vietnamese president, Nguyen Van Thieu, had held elections (of a sort) in November 1971 to show his continued popularity and mandate, and it was expected that Lon Nol would do the same.

THE 1972 ELECTIONS

By January 1972, the war was dragging on, and corruption was starting to sap the morale of Lon Nol's army. Not only were some officers selling army supplies to the public, others were even selling military materiel to the enemy. Many had invented fictitious soldiers, whose names existed only in pay slips. This left some army units seriously depleted and unable to militarily achieve some of the results that were expected of them. The delays in drawing up a Constitution were also annoying many people, not least of them Lon Nol.

On February 25, 1972, Lon Nol delivered a savage attack on Sihanouk and Keo Ann at a press conference in the presence of Cheng Heng and the Buddhist Patriarchs. The ferocity of this attack, and the unlikely person who gave it, led to the reaction that ensued. Keo Ann was an eccentric law professor who very much owed his position in society to the education system of the French and, most of all, to Sihanouk. His family had been peasant farmers in Svay Rieng in the east of the country, and he had managed to obtain a scholarship first to Lycée Sisowath in Phnom Penh, and finished his secondary schooling just before Cambodia gained independence. He then went to France, where he gained his doctorate from the Sorbonne in Paris, with his thesis topic being the Cambodian Customs Service, and he had held a minor ministerial post in the late 1960s. A popular lecturer, he denounced Lon Nol for not clamping down on open corruption and flagrant abuses of power by the military and politicians. He also criticized Sirik Matak, who he felt still wanted to restore a monarchy. The speech was damning, but Lon Nol overplayed his hand by also attacking Keo Ann. The student movement, which had been supportive of Lon Nol, then turned against him to defend their lecturer, with one student, Koy Pech, denouncing Lon Nol in such colorful (and indecent) language that soldiers were sent to arrest him for insulting behavior. It was not long before two deputies—Ung Mung and Hoeur Lay Inn—physically fought each other in the National Assembly, and soon afterwards, another deputy, Prince Sisowath Sovannareth, who had been critical of Ung Mung, lost both his hands and his legs when a hand grenade was dropped into his car while he was driving in Phnom Penh.

Keen to take the political initiative, Lon Nol appointed Son Ngoc Thanh as Prime Minister—he had last held that position in 1945—and then made himself President of the Khmer Republic, with an Executive Cabinet of Advisers to later run into the hundreds (all of whom were paid salaries equivalent to those of cabinet ministers). As this occurred, rumors began circulating that Lon Nol was negotiating a peace agreement through his brother, Lon Non, who had worked through his contacts in the radical movement to try to get the Soviet Union to back a ceasefire. The French were also working on this negotiation, with Étienne Mannac'h, their Ambassador to China, being the lynchpin of many of their plans. However, the Chinese Premier, Zhou Enlai, denounced the planned peace agreement in a banquet held to honor Sihanouk, and any hope of a quick ceasefire ended.

This left Lon Nol with the need to get his Constitution approved by the people. On April 30, 1972, a referendum was held on the new Constitution, and it was approved with the support of 97.2 percent of the voters. Even if the results were inflated, the move was popular. This left the Presidential Elections to be held on June 4. Longtime nationalist Sim Var, the Ambassador to Tokyo, was nominated, and had the support of some of the popular press (which he and his son-in-law owned). Speculation then started that an obscure right-wing reactionary called Huy Mong was going to stand. This would split the vote of the military, upon which Lon Nol was relying. In Tam, one of the main plotters in the 1970 overthrow of Sihanouk, was then nominated, but when Keo Ann went to lodge his candidacy, his election deposit was embezzled, so Queen Kossomak came up with the money for the second lodgement of his nomination. As the nominations were about to close, Lon Nol and Huy Mong both nominated as candidates. The first few days were tough, and Sim Var was disqualified because his wife was Japanese. Huy Mong then dropped out, and the election became a direct choice between In Tam, Keo Ann, and Lon Nol.

Everybody knew what Lon Nol stood for, and he had remained surprisingly popular, managing to separate himself a little untouched from the corruption that surrounded him. In Tam's underlying politics were similar to those of Lon Nol, although he was more of a democrat (without Lon Nol's reputation for mysticism), and wanted the Khmer Republic to be a truly liberal democracy. He believed that he could fight against corruption, and lead a more efficient and Khmer Republic to victory against its foes. In contrast, Keo Ann proclaimed that he would end the war through a ceasefire, and allow Sihanouk to return to the country as a private citizen. By the end of his campaign, his message was certainly that a vote for him was a vote for Sihanouk, although it is doubtful that he ever specifically stated this.

The two-week election campaign showed that all three candidates were popular, and all held large, well-attended rallies. These were to be the last openly contested elections in the country until 1993. The voting went smoothly and the provisional results for Phnom Penh showed that 51 percent supported In Tam, 42 percent voted for Lon Nol, and 7 percent supported Keo Ann. Then, the results started changing, especially in provincial areas. Lon Non bought off a newspaper editor, Buoy Sreng, and all of the copies of his newspaper when it began printing some of the early results. Soon, the results showed that Lon Nol had won with 54.9 percent of the vote, preventing a second-round runoff (which occurs when the winner receives less than 50 percent of the vote). In Tam (who was given 24.4 percent of the vote) and Keo Ann (with 20.6 percent) cried foul. Later analysis showed that In Tam almost certainly achieved more votes in the polls than Lon Nol, who may have achieved less than 20 percent. However, given that many peasants in the countryside, who would have tended to favor a pro-Sihanoukist candidate, were not able to vote because they lived in the war zone, and that a quarter of the overall population lived in areas occupied by Sihanouk's GRUNK, Keo Ann might well have had the advantage in a second round held throughout the entire country.

THE CAMBODIAN COMMUNISTS

While the Khmer Republic was going through the election process, Prince Sihanouk's Royal Government of the National Union of Kampuchea (GRUNK) was being transformed, both openly and secretly. When Sihanouk made his call for patriotic Cambodians to support him in 1970, he knew the peasants would rally to him if they could. He had hoped to win support from Cambodian intellectuals. Some of these overseas intellectuals, such as Nhiek Tioulong, had given him their support, while others remained on the sidelines. The Cambodian Communist movement, however, rallied to Sihanouk; whether they did so based on instructions from Beijing, or because they saw this as being in their own best interests is largely academic. The foremost Cambodian Communists were Khieu Samphan, Hu Nim, and Hou Youn, the three deputies who had fled to the jungles in 1967. At the time, Sihanouk had been accused of having them killed. However, they now aligned with him, and blamed the excesses of 1967 on Lon Nol who was, after all, Prime Minister at the time. Sihanouk accepted their apologies and welcomed their support.

But in the shadows were the three men who were actually running the Communist Party: Saloth Sar and Ieng Sary, who were married to sisters, and Son Sen, who was a distant relative of Ieng Sary. These men had been in the jungles since 1963, and had realized that while their movement had little chance of defeating the Royal Army in the 1960s, if they allied with the Vietnamese Communists, and with the international support and prestige of Sihanouk, they might come to power. They secretly infiltrated Sihanouk's movement and by 1972, they started easing out Royalists and replacing them with hardline Communists. They had no qualms about using Sihanouk. In 1973, the Prince quipped to the Italian journalist Oriana Fallaci that they would spit him out "like a cherry stone" when they came to power.

However, they also had a far more secret agenda: Ieng Sary and Son Sen were Khmer Krom, Cambodians from Vietnam. Ieng Sary had even had a Vietnamese name when he was young, which he had shed in his student days. The two of them, as well as Saloth Sar, hated the Vietnamese and the pro-Vietnamese Communists, dubbed the Khmer Viet Minh. The three believed in an ethnically pure Cambodia, in the same way that Lon Nol did, but they harked back to the Khmer *Loeu*, the highland Khmers, rather than the Hindu-Buddhist civilization of Angkor that Sihanouk and Lon Nol preferred. Thus, as they remade Sihanouk's movement, those who favored a long-term alliance with Vietnam were also eased out, and some of them indeed disappeared. As for using the Vietnamese Communists to help them in the war, it is doubtful that Saloth Sar and his colleagues lost a moment's sleep over that.

THE FAILURE OF DEMOCRACY IN THE KHMER REPUBLIC

Lon Nol's victory in the presidential elections of June 1972 led, finally, to the formation of his Socio-Republican Party. In Tam had established his Democratic Party with support from, amongst others, Douc Rasy, while Prince Sirik Matak's friends in the Sino-Khmer elite had helped him to form the Republican Party. There was even a Women's Party campaigning for more rights for women. Thus, it could be expected that a democratic structure for the elections to the new Legislature and Senate of the Khmer Republic would be established, as in 1946. Alas, this was not to be the case.

Lon Nol's Socio-Republican Party was essentially an alliance of two factions that became known as Dangkor and Dangrek. The former were comprised of the circle that circulated around Lon Non, who had been a radical in his youth and still harbored the notion of using the Soviet Union and France to achieve a peace settlement, cutting out China, although Non was now seen as far more conservative. The Dangrek faction was for the old-time radicals who centered on Son Ngoc Thanh and Hang Thun Hak, later to become Prime Minister. A large myriad of other politicians came to be associated with the Socio-Republican Party as Lon Nol extended the size of his team of presidential advisers, enabling him to provide significant government salaries to the most senior political figures in the country in exchange for their advice, which he sought once a month or more infrequently. This helped to corrupt an entire political class.

With the economy of the country being kept going only by the U.S. money that was still pouring in, the elections for the Legislature were held on September 3, 1972. The Legislature was to reflect the will of the entire country, and all provinces were represented, even when the entire area was in GRUNK hands and the only voters were a handful of refugees. The Democratic Party and the Republican Party refused to have anything to do with the elections, and Lon Non was worried that if all of his friends were elected unopposed, outside observers might question how genuine the democracy actually was. He had prepared for that eventuality; some of his radical associates established the Pracheachon Party, or People's Party. One of these associates was Saloth Chhay, the editor of a newspaper owned by Lon Non; Saloth Chhay was also the older brother of Saloth Sar (Pol Pot). Another member of this Pracheachon Party was Khieu Seng Kim, the younger brother of Khieu Samphan. The election results were not disputed: the Socio-Republican Party won every seat, easily defeating the Pracheachon Party candidates, who offered no more than token resistance, and received no more than a token vote. The Senate was elected, and then another ten military members of the Senate were nominated by the Army High Command.

As Hang Thun Hak from the Dangrek faction of the Socio-Republican Party was sworn in as Prime Minister on October 17, 1972, the military situation remained largely unchanged. During the dry season, the GRUNK and the Cambodian Communists—the Vietnamese Communists were having less and less to do with the war—would gain territory, but would be driven back, and during the wet season, there would be a military stalemate. Because the Cooper-Church Amendment had been passed by the U.S. Congress, the U.S. government was not allowed to send ground troops or advisors to Cambodia; that loophole had been closed. However, the United States Air Force was used to bomb the Communist bases. The carpet bombing of large parts of the countryside led to the deaths of countless civilians, and many more fled to the towns, provincial capitals, or Phnom Penh, where their presence inflated the number of people technically under the control of the Khmer Republic. In terms of the international competition for recognition, by early 1973, GRUNK controlled more of the country, but the Khmer Republic controlled the capital and some 75 percent of the population.

In the villages close to the areas that were bombed, the Cambodian peasants were, not unnaturally, terrified and the Cambodian Communists used this to embitter them not just against the Khmer Republic's government, but also against the city people, who were largely untouched by this devastation. The city-country divide, which was already great in 1970, was made far worse by the war, and helps explain the anger the peasants from the countryside felt when they did eventually, in the form of the Khmer Rouge army, storm the capital in 1975.

On March 18, 1973, a pilot in the Cambodian Air Force, So Photra, who was the husband of Princess Bopha Devi, the eldest daughter of Sihanouk, flew his aircraft over Lon Nol's Presidential Palace and bombed it. Some 47 people were killed in a compound where the families of the Palace Guards lived. This attack coincided with a teacher's strike and the reemergence of Keo Ann on the political stage. Lon Nol immediately declared a State of Siege and suspended many of the safeguards in the new Constitution. He banned newspapers, arrested dissidents, and threw some 55 members of the Royal Family in prison, including Sihanouk's fourth son, Prince Norodom Chakrapong, who led the police on a spectacular car chase through Phnom Penh.

By this time, the political violence in Phnom Penh had worsened. One of Prince Sirik Matak's close aides, Tep Khunnah, the Head of the Independent Republican Association, was driving his jeep near the Korean Embassy on March 25, when a motorcycle passed him and the pillion passenger deposited a hand grenade in his car. He was able to grab it and throw it into the street before it exploded. This was certainly a sign that political assassinations, which had been largely unheard of up to that point, were going to become more common.

Later that month, Prince Sihanouk stole the limelight as film footage was released of him dressed in black wearing a checkered scarf, the costume that was to become symbolic of the Khmer Rouge. The footage showed him near Angkor Wat, washing from a wash-tub, chatting to the Communists, and even embracing some of them. One of those he embraced was Saloth Sar, who was emerging as the secret power in GRUNK, and would become better-known to the world as Pol Pot. It also showed that Hu Nim, Hou Youn, and Khieu Samphan were all well.

THE REPUBLICANS REGROUP

To try to paper over the cracks in the Khmer Republic, and under intense pressure from the United States and its other foreign backers, the Republican government transformed itself. Lon Non resigned and prepared to head overseas. When he arrived in France, customs officials discovered some $170,000 stuffed inside a toy dog carried through the airport by one of his children. In Paris, Tep Khunnah met Lon Non in a night club and punched him so badly that the latter lost some of his teeth. He had been stripped of his former power. Lon Nol's 93 advisers were reduced to 10, and the "Four Men of March 18, 1970" came together to form the High Political Council. This consisted of Lon Nol, (Prince) Sirik Matak, Cheng Heng, and In Tam.

Finally, on May 15, 1973, In Tam became Prime Minister and tried to preside over a change in the government by attempting to draw in many politicians, but this quickly led to a bloated cabinet. This was followed by Lon Nol trying to regain control. He wanted to try to reach an agreement with Sihanouk and the Communists, and released all the members of the Royal Family who had been held under house arrest or in jail. Former prime minister Son Sann, now in Paris, offered to serve as an intermediary. The need to do something was desperate as, on August 15, 1973, owing to the implementation of a U.S. Congressional ban, the U.S. air force was no longer able to bomb the Communists in Cambodia. For some observers, this signaled that the Khmer Republic would collapse, but it continued for another 20 months. On August 7, only a week before the bombing ban, U.S. aircraft had accidentally bombed the Republican naval base at Neak Luong, destroying much of the town and killing hundreds of loyal Republicans.

In Tam reshuffled his government on October 22, 1973, but on December 26, he was forced to hand the reins over to Long Boret, who became the last Prime Minister of the Khmer Republic. Long Boret was affable and popular, and able to present the Khmer Republic positively in international relations, having managed to lead the campaign to retain the Republic's seat at the United Nations and other world bodies. He tried to prevent luxury cars from being imported into Phnom Penh, which was still under siege. After only a week in office, he faced his first major military action when the Cambodian Communists launched a dry season offensive and, with the Mekong River shrinking in size, the Communists were able to fire rockets into the capital where, during one raid on February 11, 1974, some 139 civilians were killed, with the fire leaving another 10,000 homeless. The carnage that resulted from the rocket attacks started sapping the capital's strength, but the Republican soldiers held out. Evidence of what was going to happen when the country finally fell to the Communists, was seen on March 28, when the former royal capital of Udong was captured by the Cambodian Communists, who emptied the city of all of its inhabitants, and then proceeded to murder soldiers, civil servants, and teachers. The ominous potent of what was going to happen to Phnom Penh was lost on the world media, many of whom ridiculed the Khmer Republic and complained about its eccentricities and problems.

The new U.S. Ambassador to Cambodia, John Gunther Dean, arrived in Phnom Penh on March 31, and four days later, he presented his credentials to Lon Nol. A few weeks later, as the annual rains began, the Republican soldiers were able to rest as the Mekong River swelled in size, making it much harder for the Communists to shell the capital. The rains elsewhere in the country also served to prevent any major Communist attack. While the wet season did stop the Communists from capturing Phnom Penh, it did not prevent infighting in the city, where student protestors seized former minister, Thach Chia, and the Minister of Health, Dr. Keo Sangkim, who were then both shot dead by a gunman. The students who were involved in the protest were horrified and unable to find the assassin, who had fled. There have been many debates about who organized this dual assassination. The newspaper *Nokor Thom* accused Prince Sirik Matak of being behind the killing, and the editor, Soth Polin, fled the country as his paper hit the news-stands. Other theories were even wilder. It was not until the 1990s that the gunman—or, at any rate, somebody who claimed to be the gunman—emerged in Phnom Penh as a member of Hun Sen's Cambodian People's Party, and claimed he was sent in by the Communists to discredit the student demonstrators.

If the gunman was a Communist determined to destabilize the government, he certainly succeeded. Members of Prince Sirik Matak's Republican Party resigned from their ministerial positions, and a Socio-Republican government was formed on June 16, 1974. Two months later, the Khmer Republic celebrated, having survived a year since the end of the U.S. bombing, with Lon Nol and Prince Sirik Matak presiding over a parade through central Phnom Penh. In the following month, Lon Non returned to the country, with many politicians hopeful that he might have been able to use his connections in the Soviet Union to obtain a ceasefire.

THE 1975 COMMUNIST OFFENSIVE

On January 1, 1975, the Cambodian Communists launched their Dry Season Offensive, and once again, they were hoping to capture Phnom Penh in four months. By this time, the Sihanoukists no longer played any role in the military events in the country. Some of Sihanouk's overseas supporters held back as the Khmer Rouge launched a terrifying rocket bombardment of Phnom Penh. It was not long before there was heavy fighting in South Vietnam, and it was quite clear that South Vietnam might also collapse, or be reduced to a rump area around Saigon. The fighting in Cambodia was particularly fierce along the Mekong River, with the Communists eager to be able to set up their artillery and shell Phnom Penh, which was now flooded with refugees. The city had barely been able to cope with 500,000 refugees before the war started, and already had a population of up to four times that number; it was sustained by a U.S. humanitarian airlift of rice and other food to keep people from starving.

Lon Nol was in a severe depression as the Communists attacked the strategic river port township of Neak Luong—reinforced after the 1973 bombing—which they did not capture until April 1. The Republican soldiers valiantly held out, protecting a civilian population of about 50,000. Its fall meant that river convoys could now no longer reach Phnom Penh, and it allowed the Communists to wage the bulk of their forces against the capital, which they were desperate to capture before the rainy season began.

With a disastrous military position, Lon Non decided to move against his political opponents and at the Socio-Republican Party Congress in Phnom Penh, he pushed for greater representation of his faction, winning key positions for leading anti-Communists. However, many people realized that it was only a matter of time before the Communists won the war. There was a larger than normal exodus of foreign ambassadors and representatives, including Michael Tung, who had represented the Republic of China (Taiwan) since the overthrow of Sihanouk. The newly accredited British Ambassador to the Khmer Republic was ordered to remain in Saigon, and Lloyds of London, the insurance market for the world, announced that it had cancelled all war-risk insurance on any future aircraft traveling to Phnom Penh. By mid-February, the U.S., French, and Japanese embassies warned all of their citizens to leave.

Some intellectuals, including an engineer Pin Yathay, were involved in trying to establish a group that could try to undermine Lon Nol and, if at all possible, reach some form of accommodation with the Khmer Rouge. However, they felt that they were being undermined by the United States, as the senior political figures of the Khmer Republic left the country. Yèm Sambaur had been the Honorary Consul for Haiti in the Khmer Republic since 1973, and he left in his official capacity, as did one senator who was observed requiring the help of three airline staff to get his small briefcase onto the plane. Then, General Sosthène Fernandez, the Minister of Defense, left. Replacing Fernandez was a slightly younger man, Sak Suthsakhan. At the end of World War II, he had served in the anti-French Greenshirt militia, and then had a long and respected role in the army as an honest soldier who was tried to salvage victory or, at any rate, a reprieve from disaster.

On March 21, 1975, Prime Minister Long Boret announced a cabinet reshuffle that strengthened the Dangrek faction, with Hang Thun Hak as his deputy. The Communists then announced that they had sentenced seven "super-traitors" to death: Lon Nol, Prince Sirik Matak, Cheng Heng, Long Boret, Son Ngoc Thanh, In Tam, and Sothène Fernandez. These men would be executed as soon as the Communists captured Phnom Penh, but the other government officials would all be spared, according to the related radio announcement. Soon afterwards, Cheng Heng left after reading a short statement in which he said that he hoped his departure would make it easier for a peace settlement to be reached. He moved to the United States and settled in Texas. Pressure then mounted for Lon Nol to leave.

Always proud, Lon Nol did not want to leave his country, which he had led into a disastrous war. A face-saving solution was reached whereby President Suharto of Indonesia invited him to go to Bali. In tears, Nol emerged from the Presidential Palace on April 1, 1975. Neak Luong was just about to fall as he bowed to the flag of the Khmer Republic and then, with his wife, children, and Mme. Lon Non, he boarded a helicopter bound for the airport. When Lon Nol reached the top of the aircraft's steps, he turned and looked over the country that was now in ruins before him. It was the land he had loved, and that had been devastated by a war he knew that he had caused. He quietly entered the aircraft and then a Communist rocket hissed into the airport compound, landing nearby. His aides, who were still climbing the steps to the airplane, charged into the plane, pushing each other and pushing Lon Nol himself over as they closed the door and the plane taxied away. Better composed, Lon Nol did manage to meet Suharto, who was returning to Indonesia after receiving medical treatment in Bali. At the same time, two of Lon Nol's sons were withdrawn from school in Singapore, and with goods being shipped to Hawaii, the final destination of Lon Nol's exile was finally known.

The fall of Neak Luong on April 1 allowed the Communists to focus their energies on trying to take Phnom Penh's Pochentong Airport, located to the west of the city. However, it was heavily protected and flights were still possible. Indeed, Long Boret was able to leave for Bangkok, where he met with Prince Norodom Yuvaneath, the eldest son of Sihanouk. Sihanouk said that if Long Boret immediately resigned and invited the exiled prince to return to Phnom Penh, then Sihanouk would fly back and try to take charge. He had long since realized that the Communists had taken over his movement, using his name to gain support, and a victory for them would spell disaster for him and the Throne.

For the politicians in Phnom Penh, accepting Sihanouk's offer might have prevented the horrendous carnage that was to take place when the Communists did come to power. However, in spite of the warnings provided by what had happened after the fall of Udong and Neak Luong, few expected the bloodbath that occurred. The Republicans felt that if they held out for three or four more weeks, the rainy season would start and they would be able to hold their positions until the end of the year. By that time, the diplomats and world powers might be able to negotiate a passable solution to the conflict. That was certainly their hope.

However, the military reality was quite different. In South Vietnam, the Communists were driving toward Saigon, and the South Vietnamese government was crumbling. With Lon Nol no longer in the country, and because there was no vice president, the head of state was Saukham Khoy, the President of the Senate, a respected army officer who had served Sihanouk until 1970, and then Lon Nol. He was overwhelmed by the task facing his government. He immediately attempted to improve his military position by trying to shore up morale in Battambang. If Phnom Penh fell, the Republicans might try to hold out there. His first major task was to decide on the plan that Long Boret brought back from Bangkok. The cabinet rejected it as impractical, and as news leaked to the *Bangkok Post* newspaper, Sihanouk backtracked and denounced the plan as an attempt to split him from the Chinese—which it certainly was. Saukham Khoy suggested that a coalition government with a Sihanoukist leftist called Chau Sau might be possible, but the Communists were not in the mood for compromise. By April 10, they had pushed forward to within three kilometers of Pochentong Airport. The Republican government responded by cancelling exit visas for all men of military age, and recalling all those abroad. The executive order was easy, but to return was not that easy, and to enforce this order was impossible.

OPERATION EAGLE PULL

Realizing that Phnom Penh was about to fall, a British journalist, Jon Swain, prepared to fly from Bangkok to Phnom Penh. On the morning of April 12, at Pochentong Airport, a civil engineer called Hok Peng Hieng, a descendant of King Norodom, who had also attended school with Pol Pot, and his family prepared to leave the country. Both flights were delayed as the U.S. Air Force took control of the air space over Phnom Penh. The night before, the U.S. Ambassador John Gunther Dean had visited various senior politicians in Phnom Penh to tell them that the United States was going to evacuate all of its embassy personnel on the following morning. The scene was set for Operation Eagle Pull. Prince Sirik Matak responded furiously:

Dear Excellency and Friend,

I thank you very sincerely for your letter and your offer to transport me towards freedom. I cannot, alas, leave in such a cowardly fashion.

As for you and in particular for your great country, I never believed for a moment that you would have this sentiment of abandoning a people which has chosen liberty. You have refused us your protection and we can do nothing about it. You leave and it is my wish that you and your country will find happiness under the sky.

But mark it well that, if I shall die here on the spot and in my country that I love, it is too bad because we all are born and must die one day. I have only committed this mistake of believing in you, the Americans. Please accept, Excellency, my dear friend, my faithful and friendly sentiments.

—Sirik Matak

U.S. marines arrived in Phnom Penh to secure the U.S. Embassy and a nearby field, which was used for the evacuation itself, conducted via helicopter. Some 276 people were evacuated, but there was the capacity available to take many more. Saukham Khoy accepted this offer, and through a misunderstanding, so did Long Botta, the Minister of Culture. Long Boret presided over a cabinet meeting at the time of the evacuation and all of the other senior politicians in the country chose to remain at their posts. A few American reporters, notably Sydney Schanberg, Richard Boyle, and Al Rockoff, remained. On the following day, they were joined by Jon Swain, who flew in on a largely empty plane. The scene was set for the demise of the Khmer Republic.

With Saukham Khoy's departure, General Sak Suthsakhan, the commander-in-chief of the Republican Army, took control and appointed himself chairman of a Supreme Committee. His aim was to try to hold out for two or, at the most, three weeks until the rainy season started. It was a hopeless task. On April 15, Pochentong Airport fell. Although there were no incoming flights for three days, it was a useful drop-off point for supplies arriving by parachute, and the Communists captured the fuel, ammunition, and food stored there. On the following morning, Long Boret started to draft a deed of surrender, but the generals were unwilling to agree to this. Sak Suthsakhan offered to declare Phnom Penh an open city and sent the request to Sihanouk in Beijing.

THE FALL OF PHNOM PENH

On the morning of April 17, 1975, Cambodian Communists broke through Republican lines all around Phnom Penh and made for the center of the city. Very early in the morning, the cabinet members were called to the Bottum Vaddey Pagoda to board helicopters to leave, but the helicopters never turned up. They returned home. Three hours later, at 7 A.M., the Republican Army Radio Station broadcast a surrender that was to take effect in two hours. Sak Suthsakhan and Long Boret then made for the Olympic Stadium, where three helicopters were placed on standby by Brigadier-General Thach Reng of the Special Forces. Sak Suthsakhan and the others boarded the first helicopter, which took off immediately. From the air, they saw Long Boret and his family rush from one helicopter to the last one. Neither took off, and it is probable that they stalled or the engines were flooded and unable to be started. Long Boret then returned to his desk and sat there waiting for a formal handover of power. Apparently when the Communists entered the room, Long Boret stood up to greet them. When it was quite clear that they might kill him, he fled through a side door.

In central Phnom Penh, Lon Non and his brother-in-law, Brigadier General Chhim Chhoun, worked on their next plan. While the cabinet was planning for the evacuation, some of their supporters were donning Communist uniforms and planning to steal victory. They headed to Monivong Boulevard, where they were greeted by cheering from the populace, who thought the war was over and that peace would return to the country. This was certainly not going to be the case. The leader of Lon Non's men, Hem Keth Dara, made a speech outside the Information Ministry in which he stated that he had taken control of central Phnom Penh. However, soon after his speech ended, the real Communists arrived on the scene. Their demeanor was very different.

7

Democratic Kampuchea
(1975–1979)

As the Republican General Mey Sichan was announcing the surrender and transfer of power, a Cambodian Communist cadre seized the radio microphone and announced that he had not arrived to negotiate and that the city had fallen. A chill ran down the spines of many people listening to their radios when they heard this. Lon Non, Chhim Chhoun, and their bodyguards at the Ministry of Information were detained, along with Long Boret and Hem Keth Dara. All were to be killed soon afterwards. By this time, the Cambodian Communists had ordered the evacuation of the entire population from Phnom Penh. That same morning, the Communists also took control of Battambang and the other cities and towns still held by the Republicans.

The evacuation of Phnom Penh and, indeed, all other urban centers in Cambodia on April 17, 1975, immediately characterized the Cambodian Communist Revolution as one that would be far more savage and far-reaching than most other revolutions in the 20th century. Some saw it as stemming from the Cambodian Communist hatred of cities. The cities, particularly Phnom Penh, had been the focus of power since the period of the French, and it had been the center of the Royal Court, which the Communists detested. But the evacuation of Phnom Penh, Battambang, and other places was executed for more than mere revenge. It has been suggested that the forced evacuation of Phnom

Penh, as well as the way that the countryside population was then reduced to virtual slavery, was similar to what had happened to cities in this region during medieval and early-modern times. This had occurred at Angkor in 1432, when it was overthrown by the Siamese, and at Ayuthia in 1767, when the Burmese destroyed that city. Certainly, there are close parallels, but the Cambodian Communists also had other reasons that were far more mundane.

Ieng Sary, who would become the Cambodian Communist Foreign Minister, argued that without the U.S. airlift of supplies, which had ended with Operation Eagle Pull, the population was going to starve, as there was only a small window of time before the rice had to be planted ahead of the wet season. This was certainly a factor, and many of the people were able to plant rice, alleviating a famine in 1976. However, the real reason might have been that this move would help the Communists control the population more easily. The country had been at war for five years and it was likely that some Republican soldiers might have established strongpoints in the city, which they could use to launch attacks on the Communists and prevent them from ruling effectively. Not only was it likely that this did happen, but some of the foreigners seeking refuge in the French Embassy heard gunfire around the city for days after the surrender, implying that this indeed was the case.

Although most of the population joined the forced evacuation from Phnom Penh, including the injured and sick from hospitals, many of whom believed the Communists who told them over the loud speakers that the United States was about to bomb the city, others fled for safety to places thought to offer any form of protection. Many surged into the Red Cross Headquarters, but it soon became clear that the Communists were going to chase them out of that compound. The bulk of them then fled to the French Embassy, overwhelming the diplomats and officials at the entrance, who were trying to stop this from happening. By the evening of April 17, the vast majority of the population was either streaming out of the capital or waiting their turn on congested roads. Hundreds of Cambodians and foreigners, however, were in the French Embassy and it quickly became clear that the Communists were not going to tolerate this.

On April 19, when the streets of Phnom Penh were finally clear of the last stragglers of the evacuation, a Communist official turned up at the French Embassy and demanded that senior Cambodian politicians there be handed over to them. To this day, nobody knows who told the Communists about the presence of these officials, but there remain suspicions. The French had hidden Prince Sirik Matak in a cupboard, but somebody had betrayed him. He cleaned his glasses, put on a new shirt, and bravely went out to hand himself over. Luong Nal, the former Republican Minister of Health, also went out to meet his fate, as did Ung Boun Hor, the President of the National Assembly. They were all killed. Later on April 19, other Republican officials and many civilians left the French Embassy, being taken to the nearby Lambert stadium, where they were processed, while officials were taken away to be killed. The others were forced out into the countryside. The foreigners in the embassy were then allowed to leave for Thailand. On April 30, the government of South Vietnam collapsed, and the Communists had also won the Vietnam War.

YEAR ZERO

The new Communist government of Cambodia sought to secure the country, implementing their hardline policies. By this time, they were already known internationally as the Khmer Rouge, and had isolated Prince Norodom Sihanouk, who was not allowed to return to Cambodia until September 9. In the intervening five months, the Communists had evacuated all of the cities and established an almost entirely rural population. In the cities, they destroyed icons of the old regime—the Roman Catholic Cathedral where the French and the Vietnamese worshipped for so many years, and the World War I War memorial showing a French soldier and a Cambodian soldier holding hands were some of the first sites destroyed. Foreign cemeteries, banks, car showrooms, and the like were trashed. But some places, such as the National Museum and the National Library, survived. So did many of the Embassies.

There was a central plan underlining Khmer Rouge policies, but its implementation was left to local officials, who were haphazard in their zeal. When the Western journalists Sydney Schanberg, Al Rockoff, and Jon Swain were captured by Khmer Rouge on April 17, 1975, a scene vividly recalled in the film *The Killing Fields,* their initial captors were peasants who were unable to read. When they tried to pass off Dith Pran's faked passport at the embassy several days later, it turned out that the Khmer Rouge official who was dealing with the French had a degree from the Sorbonne. Many of those who survived the initial screening by the Khmer Rouge did so by chance, including Sydney Scanberg's assistant, Dith Pran. When all of the other Cambodians were ejected from the French Embassy, he tried to remain, placing hope in his false passport. Those who were taken out were checked by Khmer Rouge, and many were taken off and killed. When Dith Pran was forced to leave the embassy, the reception committee had left, and he was able to wander off and end up in a village as though he had no contact with the West.

The former city residents forced into villages became known as the "New People." They were discriminated against in favor of the original villagers, who greeted the new arrivals with disdain. During the five years of the war, the peasants in the countryside had endured massive hardship, and some had experienced their farmland or that of relatives and friends being bombed by the Americans and the Republicans. Even before then, under Sihanouk, they had felt like second-class citizens in the country, although Sihanouk had done far more for the peasants than any previous leader of the country. Sihanouk had opened primary schools in or near many villages, but the peasants' children had to go to towns for secondary education, which was conducted in the French language. Lon Nol had changed the medium of secondary education to Khmer, but he was certainly in no position to make the lives of peasants any better. The Cambodian Communists had, however, worked with the peasants through the five years of war, and many of the peasants enjoyed seeing the city people having to work in the fields.

In enforcing their rule over the population, the edicts of the Cambodian Communists took its toll on the city people. Many were not used to working in the fields, and some quickly succumbed to overwork, malnutrition, illness—the Communists did not have any system of imported medicines—or simply from a broken heart after having seen so many of their family members killed or living in such impoverished circumstances and being regarded with suspicion and, indeed, hatred by the peasants. Buddhist monks were defrocked and had to join others in the fields.

The Communists also sought out their enemies—members of the Republican government, or class enemies. Denunciations in villages would lead to immediate arrest and almost certain execution. Many of the people who had evacuated from Phnom Penh headed back to areas where they had family roots. These evacuees were, all too often, identified by other people there and many were then murdered by local Communist leaders, who ruled their villages like feudal lords with absolute power over the life or death of so many of their villagers. There were certainly Communists who treated their villagers well, but they were definitely the exception. However, some politicians did escape the purges. Chhean Vam, the much-respected Democrat who had been Prime Minister in 1948, would certainly have been recognized by somebody, but he survived. So, too, did Kol Touch, one of Sihanouk's ministers of industry, a humble man who had done a great deal to help people during his brief tenure as a cabinet minister. Evacuated to Svay Rieng, he also survived. Most, however, were not so lucky. Norodom Chantaraingsey, a Republican General (he had renounced his title of "Prince"), had decided not to surrender to the Communists. He remained in the jungle with his men, but his wife was captured by the Communists and he was killed in a desperate effort to save her.

Although the Communists killed most of their enemies, either when they found them or in regional torture centers, those suspected of being major figures in the former regime were sent to Phnom Penh, where the Communist government operated a skeleton civil service. They had destroyed the National Bank soon after coming to power, and had established an economy with no money, where food was produced and then consumed on a village level. The airport was cleared to allow Chinese flights to come and go, but apart from that, the country was sealed to the rest of the world. By accident, a U.S. cargo ship, the *Mayaguez*, sailed into Cambodian waters, where it was seized by the Communist; the crew was only freed when U.S. marines were sent in. There were no letters into or out of the country, nor were there any telephone connections. The telex line was, however, maintained, and the government does seem to have later established a communications network from their government offices to China.

The new government was headed by a number of people, the most important being Saloth Sar, who had transformed himself with his new name, "Pol Pot." Whereas Saloth Sar had been a well-educated member of the middle class who had Palace connections and had studied in France—albeit without any success—Pol Pot was from a poor peasant family. Khieu Samphan, the former member of Parliament, also had a leadership position, as did Ieng Sary, Pol Pot's brother-in-law, and Son Sen, a distant relative. They had managed to purge the new government of Royalists, and the Khmer Viet Minh, Communists who supported an alliance with Vietnam.

Sihanouk finally returned to Phnom Penh on September 9, and was taken to a wing of the Royal Palace, where he was confined under house arrest, except for brief, organized visits to the countryside, until January 1979. For him, it was an unhappy existence and he certainly feared for his life. The Chinese leader Mao Zedong had told the Cambodian Communists to look after Prince Sihanouk, Monique, and *their* children—and the Communists certainly did so, ensuring that they neither Prince Sihamoni, nor Prince Norindrapong were harmed, as the latter had supported the Communists. However, Sihanouk's children from his other wives, and his other relatives fared less well. They, as well as many of Sihanouk's supporters, returned to the country, only to disappear soon after their arrival.

A few anti-Communist resistance groups remained in the jungles for a short period of time. Some of these were associated with In Tam and operated along the Thai-Cambodian border, especially in the province of Battambang. There were also other groups that held out, of which the most well-known was *Khleang Moeung*, named after the 15th-century general in the armies of Angkor who committed suicide so that in heaven, he could call on the spirits to attack the invading Siamese forces. Other groups included the *Sereikka Odder Tus* ("Northern Group"), *Cobra*, and the Khmer Liberation Movement. For the most part, these groups were only able to survive, and to occasionally extricate somebody to Thailand in exchange for money from a wealthy Cambodian exile. However, they did manage some successes. Cobra bombed Siem Reap in March 1976, inflicting casualties on the Communists there, and bombed the Kompong Som refinery in late 1977. These actions made the Communist leadership even more paranoid than it had been before. They saw these and smaller attacks as the work of saboteurs within their own ranks. This led the Communists to conduct regular purges of their own members.

There has been much publicity given to Tuol Sleng, or S-21, as it is sometimes known, although the latter was the name of the security team that ran the detention center. Located in Phnom Penh in the Lycée Ponhea Yat, Tuol Sleng was a center where high-level enemies of the state were sent for interrogation and eventual execution. Most opponents of the Khmer Rouge were executed in the villages where they lived, with their bodies being buried in pits or left in clearings in the jungle which became known as the "Killing Fields." Some were sent to provincial detention centers, and those suspected of working to undermine the state, including many Communists, were sent to Tuol Sleng, as the Communist government wanted to ensure that not only that they were executed, but that all their associates had been identified, captured, interrogated—with detailed confessions recorded—and then eliminated. Thus, if one was taken to Tuol Sleng, he would either die there or be executed afterwards, most often at Choeung Ek, the site of a former Chinese burial ground.

The confessions from Tuol Sleng that survived have provided scholars with detailed knowledge not only of the detention center process, but also an insight into the Cambodian Communist Movement, given the number of Communists who were interrogated and then killed. The people killed at Tuol Sleng or Choeung Ek include one of the early Communist leaders, Keo Meas, and other senior Communists, such as Hu Nim and Phouk Chhay, with the latter two surviving until their execution in July 1977. By that time, some of the interrogators at Tuol Sleng were also deemed to have been "contaminated" and were also executed by newly recruited guards. The commandant, Comrade Deuch (Kang Kech Ieu), a former school teacher, presided over this torture and execution center all of this time.

For most of the outside world, little was known about what was happening inside Cambodia. Many Cambodians overseas had celebrated the end of the war in April 1975, and some had tried to return. Of those who did, nothing was heard from them. Laurence Picq, the French wife of a Cambodian Communist, went back and subsequently wrote her memoirs. She described being taken to Long Boret's former house, where the returnees spent their first night. Many were from middle-class backgrounds and were so keen to prove that they had changed that they rushed in and cleaned the lavatories, which were soon sparkling. Some ended up in the small Communist civil service, others were sent to the countryside, and the rest were murdered.

The first major news that reached the outside world about the Communist regime was the April 1976 announcement that the promulgation of the new Constitution of Democratic Kampuchea had taken place in January, and had been followed by elections for an Assembly of People's Representatives. There was no evidence of any voting taking place in that part of the country and although a list of those elected was read on the radio, the names meant nothing to most of the listeners who heard them. Certainly, very few recognized the name Pol Pot as the man now in charge of the country. It was then announced that Prince Sihanouk had resigned as head of state and that Khieu Samphan was the new head of the State Praesidium, with Pol Pot being the prime minister of the new government. On September 27, Pol Pot was replaced by Nuon Chea, and in October, Pol Pot was back as Prime Minister.

By this time, it was clear that Pol Pot was in charge of the government, but he was presiding over a paranoid leadership circle, which lived in the otherwise uninhabited city of Phnom Penh. They feared assassination attempts, and Pol Pot always surrounded himself with his loyal bodyguards, many of whom were drawn from the Khmer *Loeu* highland peoples. He is believed to have slept in a different place each night, and kept his movements secret. Clearly, this was not because he feared any attack from the Americans, or even the Republicans or Thais; he was afraid that another member of the Cambodian Communist leadership might try to kill him. The conundrum was that Pol Pot himself was always affable and deferential in public. Sporting a Chinese fan, he engaged in discussions with ordinary people, such as workers at the bicycle factory in Phnom Penh, and made them feel at ease. Yet, behind this friendly façade was clearly a heart of steel. While he seemed genial in person, he sent many people to their deaths, and was responsible for the murder of so many more.

Historians, politicians, statisticians, and demographers have long debated how many people were killed by the Communists between April 1975 and the time of their ouster in January 1979. Some 15,000 people were executed at Tuol Sleng or Choeung Ek, so there is no doubt that the number killed must greatly exceed that figure. Refugees fleeing Cambodia for Thailand in the late 1970s spoke of terrible massacres, and coming across fields of dead bodies—the Killing Fields. Their reports were published by the French priest François Ponchaud, and also in the *Reader's Digest Magazine*, but were initially and widely rejected by people who felt that the refugees had exaggerated the hardships and the danger they were in order to get other countries to take them in. Only later were many of these stories determined to be true.

It seems likely that more than a million people—out of a population of 7.3 million—died during the rule of Pol Pot between April 1975 and January 1979. It is possible that at least 100,000 were executed or, more precisely, murdered since very few had anything amounting to even the most rudimentary of trials. Of the remainder, these were the ones—both former city dwellers and also villagers—who died through malnutrition, starvation, or untreated disease, or because they simply lacked the will to live. Pol Pot and his circle certainly bear the responsibility for all of these deaths because it was through their leadership and incompetence that they were allowed to die. For many, however, he did not specifically seek them out to kill them, an important distinction, but he nonetheless quite rightly shares the blame for their deaths.

Pol Pot, Nuon Chea, and other Cambodian Communists have long been accused of having been involved in war crimes and genocide. The problem was that the people were not killed in war, and that the Communist leadership was made up of ethnic Khmers and the people they were killing were also, by and large, ethnic Khmers. However, Australian scholar Ben Kiernan and others have sought to collect evidence that they deliberately targeted the Chams—Cambodian Muslims. They comprised a separate ethnic group, and the death rate they suffered was certainly higher than that of the ordinary population.

But Pol Pot was not alone in this carnage. Other Communists later claimed that they were forced to remain loyal to Pol Pot for fear of their lives. In his book, published in 2007, Khieu Samphan was to famously comment that he was not involved in the killings and bore no responsibility for them. Some 16 years earlier, in his paper *Pol Pot and Khieu Samphan*, previously titled *Moloch's Poodle*, Stephen Heder argued that Khieu Samphan was so clearly implicated in the killings that this defense was unfeasible. Pol Pot's brother-in-law Ieng Sary, the foreign minister, also sought to avoid responsibility. He traveled overseas to promote the government, and he for one could easily have defected if he had wanted to do so. There were other important Communists, as well: Nuon Chea, Ta Mok, and Vorn Veth (purged and killed in 1978).

What would bring down Pol Pot was not the manner in which he terrorized his own people, but his views on, and actions against, Vietnam. Only two weeks after the Cambodian Communists had taken power, the Vietnamese Communists had taken control of South Vietnam, arresting Son Ngoc Thanh, who was to die in a Vietnamese prison camp two years later. These two crucial weeks in late April 1975 provided a great sense of pride for the Cambodian Communists, who were able to argue that they had won their war ahead of their Vietnamese counterparts. But this period also underlined a deep hatred that was developing between the two groups. Pol Pot hated the Vietnamese, as did much of the leadership of his Democratic Kampuchea (DK) regime. Soon after he came to power, he introduced moves to expel the entire Vietnamese population. He also armed his soldiers against any incursions from Vietnam.

In January 1977, DK troops launched a number of cross-border raids into Vietnam. This quickly gained the enmity of the government of the new united Vietnam, which initially tried to avoid conflict with the Cambodians, having so recently finished their 30-year civil war. However, these attacks continued through 1977, and the Vietnamese then seem to have decided that their best response was a military one. They launched a major assault on Cambodia in late 1977, sending Vietnamese troops a long way into their neighbor's territory. On December 31, the DK government announced that they had broken diplomatic relations with Vietnam, and it was not long before both sides were arming for war.

With Vietnam united, Cambodia was, historically, at its most vulnerable since the 1850s, but the isolated and paranoid DK leadership did not see this. They had long feared that the Vietnamese planned to annex Cambodia, and they might have been correct. During the late 1990s, vast quantities of Khmer-Vietnamese dictionaries came up for sale in Vietnamese markets, all of which were all printed in 1977. Some might ask why these dictionaries needed to be published at this time—unless the Vietnamese expected that a large number of them would have to speak Khmer. The relatively small diplomatic links in 1977 certainly did not justify printing these books in these quantities.

There were also growing splits in the DK regime. Some Cambodian Communists had always seen Vietnam as a friend and mentor, and they started to leave Cambodia, seeking refuge in Vietnam. One of these was undoubtedly Pen Sovan, a longtime Communist who had lived for many years in Hanoi and fallen out with Pol Pot. Another was a Communist regimental commander in the Eastern Zone of Democratic Kampuchea called Hun Sen, who fled overnight, leaving some of his family behind. A third refugee was Heng Samrin, a Communist from a border family with connections in Vietnam. However, he did not defect to Vietnam until May 25, 1978. All of these men were Communists who had served in the movement from the 1960s, and Pol Pot was probably right to assume that there were many more Communists with Vietnamese sympathies.

But if Vietnam was planning to invade Cambodia in 1977, there is the question of why they did not do so. They had the military potential to easily achieve this goal, especially after the collapse of the coalition government in Laos on December 2, 1975, given that its replacement was a pro-Vietnamese government led by Prince Souphanouvong. The answer was clearly that the Vietnamese government was worried that any attack on Cambodia might be followed by China attacking northern Vietnam. The Cambodian government enjoyed warm relations in Beijing, in spite of Pol Pot's close links to Mme. Mao and the other three members of the Gang of Four, who had been overthrown and arrested in 1976—when he was told of the arrest of the Gang of Four, Ieng Sary, who was in Yugoslavia, exclaimed "They are good people." But the new Chinese government under Hua Guofeng was not about to end a long alliance with Cambodia, in spite of its obvious dislike of the Gang of Four. Thus, as the Vietnamese worried about whether they should invade Cambodia, China invaded them, and the Vietnamese immediately sought a closer alliance with the Soviet Union. This was achieved through a Soviet-Vietnamese treaty signed on November 3, 1978, by which time the scene had been set for war. From February 1978 forward, Radio Hanoi had urged in Khmer for an uprising in Cambodia against Pol Pot, and over the succeeding months, the border clashes became worse. Pol Pot then sought to purge pro-Vietnamese in the Eastern Zone of Democratic Kampuchea, and both sides armed for the inevitable battle.

It is curious that at this time, Pol Pot sought to make overtures to outside countries. A Yugoslav camera crew was allowed into the country, and their film included an exclusive interview with Pol Pot. Then, the DK government invited three foreigners to visit the country and observe that they were about to be attacked by Vietnam. American journalists Richard Dudman and Elizabeth Becker and Scottish academic Malcolm Caldwell went to Phnom Penh, where they were shown around the countryside by DK officials. By this time, war was imminent. On December 2, 1978, the United Front for the National Salvation of Kampuchea (UFNSK) was proclaimed a rival government to that of Democratic Kampuchea. They broadcast on radio transmitters in Vietnam and it was quite clear that an invasion was expected at any moment. On December 23, a gunman broke into the hostel, which was where Dudman, Becker, and Caldwell were staying. Caldwell was shot dead and the gunman escaped, although the body of a guard was found nearby. There were claims that this man had shot Caldwell and then committed suicide, but nobody really believed this story. Whether or not Caldwell was the intended victim was uncertain, but the shooting was a great embarrassment for Pol Pot. Rumors began to circulate that Pol Pot had had the academic killed because he had asked too many intrusive questions. This was unlikely, but with the Vietnamese Communists, who clearly had the capability to murder, beginning to use their propaganda machine, there was sufficient confusion.

Two days after Caldwell's death on December 25, with so much of the world celebrating Christmas, Vietnam finally invaded Cambodia, sending its soldiers straight for Phnom Penh. The speed of the Vietnamese army seems to have been based on an earlier time, possibly November, when the DK launched a preemptive strike against the Vietnamese, who allowed their army into southern Vietnam and cut it to pieces. This then left the Vietnamese able to turn their attention to a badly defended Cambodia.

As the rest of the world was reacting to the Vietnamese move, the Vietnamese army headed for Phnom Penh. Pol Pot fled the city on January 6 by helicopter, with Prince Sihanouk and his small circle also being whisked out by helicopter. The Vietnamese—who had hoped to capture Sihanouk and use him as part of their propaganda machine—arrived in Phnom Penh on January 7 to find that he had escaped their grasp. He was flown to Beijing, and lived there and in Pyongyang—off and on—for the next few years, and was always grateful for the hospitality shown to him by his hosts in both countries. This left the victorious Vietnamese, who had captured a largely deserted Phnom Penh where, on January 10, the People's Republic of Kampuchea was proclaimed.

8

The Second Civil War
(1979–1991)

The Vietnamese soldiers who invaded Cambodia on December 25, 1978, had seized control of some 90 percent of Cambodia by January 10, 1979, with their soldiers facing Thai soldiers at some border-crossing points. It was on that day that the People's Republic of Kampuchea (PRK) had been proclaimed. Installed by the Vietnamese, the new government was immediately recognized by Vietnam, the Soviet Union, and the pro-Soviet countries of Eastern Europe. With the DK soldiers having fled to the borders with Thailand, and the DK regime in tatters, the people who had lived in conditions of such privation since April 1975, and some since 1970, left their villages, which had become their prison camps. They headed out in search of their relatives, or to seek safety in Thailand.

China was infuriated by the Vietnamese actions and on February 17, the Chinese People's Liberation Army launched an attack on northern Vietnam. The Vietnamese had prepared for this attack, but they still had to withdraw many of their crack soldiers from Cambodia in order to defend their homeland. The Chinese had expected their attack to be easy and to punish Vietnam, but they quickly ran into a military deadlock, and the Vietnamese Communists invited Western journalists to their battle lines, something that would have been unthinkable only four years earlier. During the late 1970s, the United States had been wooing China, and the war in Vietnam seemed to put them in a difficult position. They soon had to justify support for the DK regime in Cambodia, as increasing evidence was emerging about the nature of that government. China was forced to withdraw from Vietnam on March 5, 1979.

Tens of thousands of Cambodian refugees fled to Thailand and large refugee camps started to appear on the Thai-Cambodian border. Initially, the Thai soldiers drove back the refugees, but it soon became clear that they had terrible stories to reveal about life under Pol Pot. To further complicate matters, some of the refugees were actually also supporters of Pol Pot, and these supporters sought a place where they could rearm and prepare to fight the Vietnamese and the PRK soldiers. The Thai government then went into a panic, worrying that the Vietnamese could press their military advantage and send their tanks toward Bangkok. It would have been hard for the Thais to stop this, and this scenario led the Thai government to decide to arm the DK soldiers and use them as a buffer against the Vietnamese. It was a tactical decision that would open them, and many Western diplomats, up to a great deal of criticism.

On March 5, 1979, the Khmer People's National Liberation Armed Forces (KPNLAF) was proclaimed on Cambodian territory near the Thai border. This group owed its origins to exiles who had met in Paris in late 1975, forming the Association des Cambodiens à l'Étranger (Association of Overseas Cambodians: ACE). The group included Nguon Pythoureth, who was elected secretary-general. He had been the military attaché at the Cambodian Embassy in Paris, but in September 1970, he transferred his allegiance from Lon Nol to Sihanouk, provoking fights among Cambodian students in the French capital. Later appointed as Sihanouk's Ambassador to Mauritania, he had chosen not to return to Phnom Penh after April 1975, and was regarded as a good organizer. Others who came to support the ACE were Mme Suon Kaset, the editor of *Kampuja* under Sihanouk, and then secretary to Prince Sisowath Sirik Matak, and Truong Mealy, a former school teacher. The members essentially represented the tradition of Son Ngoc Thanh, and they approached the respected Buddhist scholar, former central banker, and politician, Son Sann, who initially declined to become involved, although they did later obtain the support of Yèm Sambaur and Sim Var, both former prime ministers, who were in Paris. Son Monir, a son of Son Sann, and Dr. Chhay Hancheng, a son-in-law of Son Sann, also joined, and it was not long before Son Sann himself was a member. Gradually, the group branched out from cultural activities and decided that they would have to fight the Cambodian Communists. Son Sann was unsure about a military approach, but the group had managed to recruit some former Republican commanders, most notably Sak Suthsakhan and Dien Del, to come up with plans to establish a military movement that would operate from refugee camps on the Thai-Cambodian border. This was what was to become the KPNLAF. Their enemy was expected to be Pol Pot's Democratic Kampuchea. However, by the time they had established their movement, Pol Pot had been ousted, and a pro-Vietnamese Communist government was installed in Phnom Penh. With Thailand now helping the DK soldiers, and also the KPNLAF, it was not long before the DK and the KPNLAF would have a tactical alliance.

In Phnom Penh, the new PRK government was placed under the leadership of Heng Samrin, who had grown up on the Vietnamese-Cambodia border, where some of his ancestors had been smugglers for several generations. He had fought in the Communist forces against the Republicans in the early 1970s, and fearing that he would be purged, he had fled to Vietnam in 1978, where, as the most senior defector, he had been named Chairman of the People's Revolutionary Council, running the country as head of state until 1991. For the previous 150 years in Phnom Penh, governments had sought an alliance with the British, and then achieved alliances with the French, and even, tentatively, the Japanese, the Chinese, the Americans, and the Chinese again. These alliances were all aimed to achieve one goal: to protect the country from aggression from Vietnam. Now, for the first time since the early 19th century, a Cambodian government had turned the entire foreign policy of the country on its head, and formed a close alliance with Vietnam. This would lead to another civil war.

THE EMERGENCE OF HUN SEN

Under Heng Samrin, Hun Sen was placed in charge of foreign relations, with the position being formalized when he became foreign minister in 1981. Born in 1952, he had left to join the Communists in the jungle in 1968. Later, he altered the date of his joining the Communists to 1970, a more acceptable date, internationally speaking. In 1968, the Communists were a small movement hoping to overthrow Prince Norodom Sihanouk and the elected government in the country. The date of 1970 was when Prince Sihanouk established his Royal Government of National Union of Kampuchea and hence, Hun Sen leaving Phnom Penh on that date would make him a possible supporter of Sihanouk, not somebody who actually sought to overthrow him. The evidence pointing to Hun Sen's 1968 departure was apparent in an interview he gave the Australian academic Ben Kiernan in 1983, which was published in Kiernan's doctoral thesis, when the dates were not that important, as Hun Sen was still an opponent of Sihanouk, rather than trying to entice him into an alliance. But evidence can also be found in the pages of the government gazette, *Journal Officiel du Cambodge*, which records a visit by Prince Sihanouk to Lycée Indra Devi in 1968, and Hun Sen's name is nowhere to be found on the very long list of students there who were presented to Sihanouk.

Even at this early stage, Hun Sen was emerging as a possible leader. After meeting Ben Kiernan, he acquired Kiernan's thesis, *How Pol Pot Came to Power*, and had it translated into Cambodian so that he and other Communists could read about the early history of their party, which they did not know much about. At this stage, Hun Sen already differed from the Cambodian Communist ideologues with whom he mixed. He was a young man eager to learn, and anxious to discover as much as he could about the country, which had been devastated in the civil war from 1970 to 1975, and the rule of the Khmer Rouge, in which he had participated, and he was clearly a man of considerable initiative and iron resolve.

The third man in the PRK government was Pen Sovan, who was born in 1936. In 1951, at the age of 15, he joined the Khmer Issarak and in 1954, he was evacuated to Hanoi, where he remained until 1970. He then became the first secretary of the pro-Vietnamese People's Revolutionary Party of Kampuchea, but would soon turn against the Vietnamese and end up interned by them. To legitimize their new regime, a court was convened in Phnom Penh on August 15, whereby Pol Pot and Ieng Sary were put on trial in absentia and five days later, both were found guilty of taking part in massacres and population displacements, establishing repressive systems, abolishing social relationships, and five other counts, and sentenced to death. The PRK pointed to the Killing Fields and Tuol Sleng as evidence of the bestiality of the DK. The Vietnamese used this to justify their invasion, although many foreign observers were able to point out that the Vietnamese did not actually know about these atrocities until their invasion, and had actually sent Cambodian refugees back to certain death at the hands of the DK in 1976.

By this time, the PRK was in turmoil. When the population was allowed to leave the villages they had been kept in by the DK, they clogged the roads, with many seeking refuge in Thailand, and others going in search of family members or heading back to Phnom Penh or other cities and towns. Some were able to find their old homes, and reoccupied them. Others found other people's homes and occupied them. Most found that the city had been systematically looted by the Vietnamese soldiers in late January and February 1979. Many were still searching so desperately for family members that this did not concern them. Whatever was on their mind, the planting of the harvest was not, and by the middle of 1979, the country was running out of food and people started starving.

The plight of Cambodia was revealed to a horrified world by the Australian journalist John Pilger, who by this time lived in London. He had been a journalist in Vietnam during the last days of South Vietnam, and during the early 1970s, he had visited Cambodia. Pilger returned in 1979 to find a devastated country, with piles of bones at sites in the countryside where people had been murdered by the DK. He was able to write extensive accounts about Tuol Sleng, aided by Chantou Boua, the Cambodian wife of Ben Kiernan, and the picture emerged of a paranoid DK regime that was involved in murdering so many of its opponents and possible allies.

But John Pilger's attention was also engaged by the horrendous humanitarian problem facing the country, with hundreds of thousands of people short of food. He was able to document how the Western countries boycotted Cambodia, yet supplied the refugees along the Thai-Cambodian border, encouraging exodus to these camps and enlarging the humanitarian problem. However, he was most critical of the aid being given to the Khmer Rouge camps, and his documentaries, *Year Zero: the Silent Death of Cambodia,* followed by *Cambodia: The Betrayal,* and then *Cambodia: Return to Year Zero,* alerted many in the outside world to conditions in Cambodia.

THE FORMATION OF RESISTANCE GROUPS

With the KPNLAF and the DK forces arming refugees to fight the Vietnamese and the PRK militia, other would-be leaders arrived in refugee camps on the Thai-Cambodian border and offered to lead guerilla groups. On August 31, 1979, the Movement for the Liberation of Kampuchea (Molinaka) was established. It was the first of the new groups to swear fealty to Prince Norodom Sihanouk and it was soon clear that Sihanouk was about to make a political comeback. On October 9, the KPNLAF established its political wing, the Khmer People's National Liberation Front, and on November 14, the United Nations General Assembly voted on the first of its many resolutions demanding the immediate and unconditional withdrawal of all foreign forces from Cambodia. The DK retained its United Nations seat with support from China and the United States, and as evidence of DK actions in Cambodia continued to emerge, the DK leadership organized a reshuffle, with Khieu Samphan replacing Pol Pot as its prime minister. The scene was then set for the second civil war.

Many would-be leaders emerged in this unstable political situation, sometimes in a blaze of publicity. One of these leaders was André Oukthol, a former radical who had moved to support Lon Nol in 1973. He turned up on the border proclaiming that he was Prince Norodom Soriavong, and established his own "provisional government." Quickly nicknamed the "Mad Prince" by the Western press, he was killed in January 1980, in an interfactional dispute. Within months, the border war had begun in earnest and it increased in ferocity, with large numbers of mines planted by either side. The fighting continued with the formation of Sihanouk's new political vehicle, the National United Front for an Independent, Neutral, Peaceful, and Cooperative Cambodia (FUNCINPEC), which was enacted in February 1981. Thailand and the West were eager for the various factions on the border to form an alliance and on June 22, the Coalition Government of Democratic Kampuchea (CGDK) was formally established through an alliance between FUNCINPEC, the Party of Democratic Kampuchea (PDK), and the KPNLF. In a power-sharing deal, the Cambodian seat at the United Nations was passed to the CGDK.

The CGDK was a curious coalition. In the government-in-exile, Prince Sihanouk was the head of state, Son Sann of the KPNLF was the prime minister, and Khieu Samphan was the foreign minister. On a political front, Sihanouk lent the CGDK international credibility and widespread diplomatic recognition followed. However, the PDK dominated the military conflict, as their soldiers did most of the fighting. The coalition was a clear compromise, as it gave the PDK a smaller overt role than they would otherwise have achieved, and China had recognized that the PDK was politically unpopular in the West. With Sihanouk in charge, the Association of Southeast Asian Nations (ASEAN) was able to back Thailand's support of the CGDK—and, indeed, recognize the CGDK—as a bulwark against Vietnamese expansionism and hegemony in the region.

PROBLEMS IN CAMBODIA

The PRK was facing many of its own problems, most of which were not of its own making. Having taken over a country with a wrecked economy, the PRK had to establish a government from almost nothing. On March 20, 1980, they reintroduced money by decree—a coin for 5 sen, made from aluminum, had already been minted in the previous year. However, the new currency from March 1980 introduced the issuing of a series of banknotes ranging in value from 0.1 riel to 10 riels. The riel was officially valued as the equivalent of a kilogram of rice. The Communist symbol of the PRK appeared on all notes, decorated by various agrarian scenes, the Independence Monument, a school, and the Bayon. On April 10, 1980, the first PRK postage stamps were reintroduced, showing their soldiers and the Independence Monument. The money and stamps were clear attempts to get the country back together again.

On May 1, 1981, the PRK rulers felt sufficiently in control of much of the country to hold elections to their National Assembly. Although the only candidates were members of the government People's Revolutionary Party of Kampuchea (PRPK), it was the first elections of any kind since 1972, and it did begin to reestablish the system of elections that would enable democracy to return to Cambodia 12 years later. However, problems soon emerged with Pen Sovan, the general-secretary of the PRPK. He made a private speech to party members that acknowledged the role Vietnam had played in overthrowing the DK regime and forcing Pol Pot to flee. He then added that it was now time for the Vietnamese to leave the country, and urged that they do so; otherwise, they would appear to be aiming to take over Cambodia. The speech was very badly received by the Vietnamese, and on December 5, 1981, Pen Sovan was removed as general-secretary and replaced by Heng Samrin, who was more loyal to the Vietnamese. For critics of the Vietnamese occupation, the arrest of Pen Sovan had justified their arguments. When Pen Sovan was asked for a reason for his arrest, he said he was told by his jailers that he knew what it was for. A loyal Communist, but one who refused to be subservient to Hanoi, he was to be held by the Vietnamese for nearly ten years. He was replaced by Chan Si, a loyal Khmer Viet Minh who was in poor health. He died in Moscow of a heart attack in December 1984.

Throughout 1984, the Vietnamese launched major attacks on the refugee camps on the Thai-Cambodian border. This was also the year that Cambodia came to dominate public attention with the release of the film *The Killing Fields*. Directed by Roland Joffé and produced by David Puttnam, the story related the career of *New York Times* war correspondent Sydney Schanberg in the Khmer Republic and his relationship with his interpreter and assistant, Dith Pran, a role played by fellow Cambodian Haing Ngor. The film showed the devastation of the first civil war in the country, and also helped provide an image of a vicious and mindless DK regime. Son Sann, the Prime Minister of the CGDK, watched the premiere of the French-language version in Paris and left remarking that the film really needed a sequel and historically, he was correct. In the film, Dith Pran managed, through guile and with some help from a good Khmer Rouge official (played by Prince Sisowath Chivan Monirak), to escape from Democratic Kampuchea to Thailand during the Vietnamese invasion. What Son Sann was alluding to was that Dith Pran had actually remained in the country after the Vietnamese invasion of December 1978 to January 1979, and had escaped with help from supporters of Son Sann when he suspected that the PRK forces might arrest him. It was an important political issue—equating the PRK with the DK—but it was missed by most people. However, it did propel Haing Ngor, the actor, who spoke at the World Anti-Communist League in Taipei, and other right-wing occasions, into the limelight. While Dith Pran, the man he had played in the film, had managed to get his wife and four sons out of Cambodia in Operation Eagle Pull, Haing Ngor had lost his wife, and had only narrowly managed to save one photograph of her, which he wore in a locket around his neck. In 1996, while being mugged in Los Angeles, he refused to hand that locket to his attackers and they murdered him.

The Royalists in FUNCINPEC now formed their armed wing, the National Sihanoukist Army or Armée Nationale Sihanoukienne (ANS), which was led by Prince Norodom Ranariddh, the second son of Prince Sihanouk. Ranariddh had been a law lecturer in France and he was a firm anti-Communist. He resented cooperating with the PDK, and the ANS and the KPNLAF soon formed what became known as the Non-Communist Resistance, with aid from Thailand, China, the United States, and members of ASEAN. Ranariddh was certainly emerging as a leading political operator, and eclipsing his younger brother, Prince Norodom Chakrapong, who was also heavily involved in the ANS. Ranariddh looked like his father and also sounded like his father in his speeches. He was quickly able to gain prestige and important name recognition value around the Western world.

PEACE TALKS START

On January 14, 1985, in an effort to remake itself, Hun Sen became Prime Minister of the new PRK government. The civil war continued, and on September 1, Pol Pot announced that he had officially retired to write a history of the Party. With many people wearying of the war, peace plans began to be mooted. The CGDK raised an eight-point proposal to end the war in 1986, but this was rejected by Vietnam. Finally, from December 2 to 4, 1987, Hun Sen met with Prince Norodom Sihanouk at Fère-en-Tardennois in France. There, Hun Sen played on Sihanouk's ego—he spoke to Sihanouk deferentially, and publicly altered the date of his flight from Phnom Penh from 1968 to 1970, portraying himself as a lifelong Sihanoukist. From January 20 to 21, 1988, there were further talks between Hun Sen and Sihanouk. Prince Sihanouk was ill and he really wanted to return to his country. Hun Sen offered him a position if he returned straight away. Preparations were made in Phnom Penh to receive Sihanouk, but he did not turn up. Hun Sen's gambit had failed. However, a number of other former leading Cambodian officials were persuaded to return to Phnom Penh. Cheng Heng and In Tam had already returned to Phnom Penh before the Paris Peace Agreement, and others had followed.

On July 25, 1988, the First Jakarta Informal Meeting was held and was attended by the Cambodian factions. It was the first time that the CGDK and the PRK met, and it was a frosty meeting. The Second Jakarta Informal Meeting was held on February 19, 1989, as Gareth Evans, the Australian Foreign Minister, pushed forward with his Cambodian Peace Plan. It recognized the need for a ceasefire, a peacekeeping force, and the establishment of a nationally united government that would maintain the sovereignty of the country until elections were held. In some ways, the proposal was similar to the one that followed the Lancaster House peace talks in 1979, which led to elections being held in Rhodesia-Zimbabwe in 1980. Many years earlier, the suggestion had been made in *The Economist* that the Japanese could fund such an operation. They had enjoyed a good reputation during their occupation of Cambodia—about the only Asian country that did—and with Japan eager to send soldiers overseas again, unarmed (or lightly armed) Japanese peacekeepers could be deployed to Cambodia. For Japan, this would create a precedent of sending Japanese soldiers overseas for the first time since 1945. However, the overall cost of the peacekeeping operation was likely to be high.

As plans for a peace agreement began, Hun Sen showed his political guile. From April 29 to 30, 1989, he convened the PRK's National Assembly in Phnom Penh. It adopted a new constitution, renaming the country the State of Cambodia, a name carefully chosen to move away from a People's Republic and reflect ambiguity about its sovereignty. The red flag with a five-towered Angkor Wat was replaced with a blue and red flag with a three-towered Angkor Wat, and there was also a new national anthem. Buddhism was now declared the state religion, and the right to hold private property was reestablished and guaranteed by law. For Hun Sen, this was a bold move followed by the declaration that all Vietnamese soldiers would withdraw from Cambodia, an event dated to September 1989, although this withdrawal lacked international supervision. Foreign diplomats in Bangkok joked that the PRK government would last as long as it took a tank to roll from the Thai border to Phnom Penh. Hun Sen's army was, however, a match for the CGDK forces for a while longer.

Hun Sen had seen that the world was changing, and with the fall of the Berlin Wall on November 9, 1989, and the end of Communism in Eastern Europe, Hun Sen recognized that his government could no longer rely on largesse from other Communist countries. Although he was to retain his Communist mindset, he remade himself in the mold of a democrat. He found this task tricky at times, but he managed it with consummate political skill.

Peace talks continued with the First Paris Peace Conference on Cambodia, held in the French capital and adjourned on August 30, after one month of talks. On February 26, 1990, the Third Jakarta Informal Meeting was held, and the Supreme National Council (SNC) was established to safeguard Cambodian sovereignty. This new body, the SNC, was to have 12 members. FUNCINPEC, the KPNLF, and the PDK argued that they should have three seats each, and that the PRPK should also have three seats. It was the opening gambit, and Hun Sen refused. It was then agreed that the three factions in the CGDK would have two seats each, and the PRPK would have six. The six PRPK seats were allocated to Hun Sen and five others. The choice of the seats of the CGDK parties was much more interesting. The KPNLF nominated Son Sann, its president, and Ieng Mouly, its secretary-general. The PDK chose Khieu Samphan and Son Sen, its former security chief. The name "Pol Pot" was so badly tarnished that he agreed to take a backseat. The choice of FUNCINPEC was a surprise to everybody; the party chose Prince Norodom Ranariddh, Sihanouk's son and the man who had been leading the ANS, and they then nominated Chau Sen Cocsal, a highly respected politician from the Sihanoukist period who had briefly been Prime Minister for two months in 1962, but was not well-known internationally. Although Chau Sen Cocsal had been prominent in nationalist circles since the 1940s, and was an establishment figure in the 1960s, little had been heard of him since 1970, when he had withdrawn from politics, spending some of the mid-1970s helping people in refugee camps. The reason for his choice was soon obvious. Born in 1905, he was 86 and was—by a large margin—the oldest member of the SNC. This enabled him to chair the initial meetings, with the CGDK insisting that the chairmanship should be his on account of his age. Furthermore, the CGDK decreed that the published list of SNC members should be ranked in seniority according to age, which would put Hun Sen at the bottom of the list. However, there was another twist; FUNCINPEC had not nominated Sihanouk, who then demanded to be appointed as the 13th member of the SNC as the overall chair, with the casting vote. Hun Sen reluctantly agreed. Sihanouk had outmaneuvered Hun Sen.

Given these moves toward elections in Cambodia in 1990, some politicians decided to preempt the process. In May 1990, Ung Phan and a group of supporters tried to launch the Liberal Democratic Socialist Party. They were promptly arrested and thrown into jail without trial. On September 17, Hun Sen replaced his longtime colleague Kong Korm as Foreign Minister and appointed Hor Nam Hong. Kong Korm was quickly marginalized and would later turn against Hun Sen. Hor Nam Hong would become one of the strongmen of the regime.

In 1991, the SNC was accorded the Cambodian seat in the United Nations General Assembly, and at a special congress held in Phnom Penh, Hun Sen made a dramatic move. The PRPK renamed itself the Cambodian People's Party (CPP)—the Pracheachon—taking the name of the party that had fought the 1955 elections. They abandoned Marxism-Leninism and sought to portray themselves as a democratic political party. With this accomplished, the scene was set for the peace agreement. There was, however, one problem: Prince Sihanouk had claimed that Hor Nam Hong had worked in a "Khmer Rouge concentration camp," and it was at this camp that many people, specifically Prince Sisowath Methavi, a close friend and relative of Sihanouk, and his family had been murdered—Methavi's wife was the sister of Princess Monique. Hor Nam Hong denied this allegation. He was certainly at the camp, but he claimed that he was an inmate and had been given tasks to do by the guards in a similar manner to the *kapos* in the German concentration camps during World War II. This led Hor Nam Hong to launch a libel suit against Sihanouk in France. Hor Nam Hong won the first battle in the courts, and Sihanouk's lawyers appealed. For Sihanouk to turn up at the Peace Conference, this lawsuit would need to be dropped, however, and it was. On October 23, 1991, in the French capital, the Cambodian leaders met and signed the Paris Agreements, which initiated the U.N. peacekeeping mission in Cambodia, paving the way for elections.

9

The Road to Democracy
(1991–1997)

The Paris Peace Agreements signed on October 23, 1991, ended the fighting from the two civil wars, which had begun in 1970, and provided a peace settlement for the country, with United Nations Peacekeepers taking control of Phnom Penh and then fanning out throughout the country. The aim was to secure all of Cambodia in preparation for elections to be conducted under UN auspices. By this time, five main political parties were expected to compete. Hun Sen controlled his Cambodian People's Party, which was clearly one of the front-runners, as was the Royalist FUNCINPEC Party led by Prince Norodom Ranariddh. There were also three other political parties with deep roots. The Party of Democratic Kampuchea (PDK) led by Khieu Samphan remained a major force and was likely to gain the support of some of the peasants who had actually been treated relatively well during the Democratic Kampuchea period. The KPNLF, with its weaker political structure, split. This split could have been foreseen in December 1985, when Abdul Gaffar Peang Meath and others tried to break away, and formed the Provisional Central Committee for the Salvation of the KPNLF. In 1991, a breakaway faction led by Sak Suthsakhan announced the formation of the Liberal Democratic Party. They wrote to their members and informed them that they had the support of the United States, and were heading into the elections on their own—they were essentially the Dangkor faction of Lon Nol's Socio-Republican Party, following the policies and program of the government of the Khmer Republic in its early days. This left the loyalist members of the KPNLF with Son Sann and Ieng Mouly, in the Thanhist mould, as the inheritors of the Dangrek traditions of the Socio-Republican Party. Even though the electoral procedure had not yet been agreed upon, it was quite clear that the split would fatally divide the group. With early commentators believing that the PDK would gain as much as 15 percent of the vote, it was clear from the start that the election would be decided in a run-off between the CPP and FUNCINPEC.

To organize their respective political machines, many politicians started returning to Cambodia—for some, it was their first visit back to Phnom Penh since the 1970s. The first major arrival in the Cambodian capital was Prince Norodom Sihanouk. The country was, however, to remain the State of Cambodia for nearly two more years. Sihanouk and his wife, Monique, returned on November 14, and a large crowd came out to meet him. He wandered through the crowd of well-wishers, greeting many of them personally. He then recognized one of the men who, as a boy, had been with him at school. Warmly greeting Hoeur Lay Inn, who had served as an adviser to Lon Nol in the Khmer Republic, Sihanouk showed all of the people present that Cambodia was entering a new era. Sihanouk was then taken to the Royal Palace, which had been prepared for his return; the last time he had been there was just before his forced evacuation 12 years earlier, ahead of the Vietnamese soldiers capturing the capital. Of the other returnees, Sak Suthsakhan had also fled Phnom Penh by helicopter, four years before Sihanouk. Son Sann had last been in Phnom Penh in the early 1970s, when he had tried to work out a peace agreement during the first civil war. Nhiek Tioulong had departed in 1969.

On November 27, 1991, Khieu Samphan returned to Phnom Penh. His PDK had taken over a small building that was to be used as their campaign headquarters, and he had expected that his arrival would be uncontroversial, as Son Sen was already in the country, having laid the framework for the PDK's reintegration into mainstream politics. Khieu Samphan clearly planned to establish a political party capable of campaigning in the forthcoming elections, and he was accompanied by Chan Youran, a former career diplomat who had sided with the Communists during the first civil war and remained loyal to them since then. Youran clutched a bag containing a large quantity of U.S. dollars to help bankroll the new party. In Cambodia in 1991, few businesses would extend any credit or accept bank checks, least of all from the PDK, whose hatred of banks was legendary.

However, a large crowd met Khieu Samphan at the Phnom Penh airport. They shouted insults and abuses at him, and chased his car as he was driven into the city. Along the route from the airport to his office, Khieu Samphan and the PDK officials who were with him observed people lining the route and throwing things at his car. Although he did manage to get into his office, there were even larger crowds baying for his blood and shouting death threats around it; the situation was rapidly getting out of hand. Clearly, Khieu Samphan had not expected this kind of reception—he would not have returned if he had. In 1966, he had been cheered by the people after being elected to the National Assembly, in spite of Prince Sihanouk speaking out against him personally. Since then, he had lived an odd existence wherein peasants were forced to support him in Democratic Kampuchea and border refugee camps, and China, too, provided him with large crowds of cheering Chinese. Now, in 1991, the mob outside Khieu Samphan's house started kicking down the front door as the PDK leader desperately telephoned the Chinese government—one of the main guarantors of the election process—and also appealed to the nearby journalists to save him. It was not long before the lynch mob broke through into the house, chasing Khieu Samphan into an upstairs room, where people tried to hang him from a ceiling fan. It appeared that the sheer number of people trying to kill him at the same time saved his life, with China demanding that action be taken and Cambodian soldiers sent in to rescue him. He was able to escape the building on a ladder, his face bandaged, and he rushed back to the airport, where he immediately flew out of the country. Chan Youran, who seems to have been at the foot of the stairs when the lynch mob arrived, was held by the crowd and released—after having been relieved of the money he had on him. The involvement of the PDK in the election process was now doubtful.

There have been accusations that Hun Sen orchestrated the attack on Khieu Samphan. Some sources report that agents sent by Hun Sen masterminded the whole event and made sure that Samphan was not killed. They kept in regular telephone contact with the police in order to call them just before the Khmer Rouge leader was actually lynched. It certainly served Hun Sen's short-term interest because he detested Khieu Samphan and the feeling was clearly mutual. Some of the demonstrators and the lynch mob were supporters of Hun Sen, but there were enough people who hated Khieu Samphan to take part in the attack, regardless of government involvement or encouragement. To restrain a lynch mob in a fervor like the one attacking Khieu Samphan would have been difficult, even if Hun Sen had wanted to do so. The action basically forced the PDK out of the mainstream electoral process, but they were able to get revenge on Hun Sen in a number of ways when the official campaign began.

THE ESTABLISHMENT OF THE UNTAC

At the beginning of 1992, Yasushi Akashi arrived in Phnom Penh to head the United Nations Transitional Authority in Cambodia (UNTAC). He was—until then—a relatively obscure Japanese official who had been undersecretary-general for disarmament affairs. He immediately alienated many Cambodians with his plan to live in Bangkok, which he felt was much safer than Phnom Penh (even though he would have a large security detail), and commute into the Cambodian capital each day. That this plan was even considered demonstrated the amount of money the UNTAC had the ability to spend there. Many Cambodian civil servants and teachers earned only several dollars a month as an official salary. Their pay had increased, but the minor U.N. officials who had just arrived were being paid more per day than many Cambodian civil servants earned in a year, and the U.N. salaries were tax-free. The money was going to be saved up in foreign banks, rather than being used to help build up the country. Given their staggeringly high rates of pay and superior living conditions, it was a pity that the U.N. staff did not do more for the country. For some of them, the assignment functioned as, sadly, a feeding trough before they went to the next operation, and they were paid a fortune to do very little to help poor people. Living on massive foreign salaries, U.N. officials had a difficult time obtaining cooperation from civil servants, who were being paid a pittance. There were also many disagreements between various members of the UNTAC, with the French and Australians both anxious to dominate Cambodia after the United Nations left. The head of the UNTAC's military component was an Australian Lieutenant-General, John Sanderson, while the French were trying to control the civilian component.

One of the U.N.'s major projects, and the one that was completed with a minimum of controversy and the greatest success, was the resettlement of the 750,000 refugees living in camps along the Thai-Cambodian border. They were resettled in new villages in Cambodia, and provided with huts to live in, tools to work with, some food to tide them over the first few months, and seeds for the following season. They were all taught the rudiments of agriculture, and they returned to the depopulated Cambodian countryside and successfully settled in.

By mid-1992, as the UNTAC started increasing the number of staffers in Cambodia, reports began to be published in national and international newspapers regarding the actions of a number of U.N. staff members. The reports showed that HIV/AIDS had spread quickly throughout the country, and the evidence signaled that it had been spread by some of the U.N. units posted in remote areas. There were also many reports of U.N. officials driving callously through the country. Some had come from countries where people drove on the right hand side of the road, while others were from those where people drove on the left. Some of the young ones—national servicemen from formerly Communist Eastern Europe—may never have driven before. They were given 4WD SUVs and there were certainly incidents of U.N. staffers driving through market places and killing, injuring, and maiming people. When later asked about these reports, Ken Berry, a legal adviser with the UNTAC, commented on the horrendous toll inflicted on innocent people by, at best, bad driving by U.N. staff, and deplored the deaths. When asked, as a follow-up question, whether any U.N. officials had been fined, jailed, fired, or faced some other serious sanction over their actions, he replied that he had not heard about any cases where aberrant officials were punished for what are regarded, in many other countries, as serious criminal or civil offenses.

The United Nations arrived in Cambodia with so much goodwill, but it only took a small minority to wreck the reputation of the entire group when it became clear that the wrong doers were never going to be punished for actions that are crimes throughout the rest of the world. Uch Kim An, a PRK/CPP official, later commented that of the U.N. staff members who worked in Cambodia, the Australians, Malaysians, Singaporeans, and French quickly earned the respect of the people. They were taught about Cambodia before they arrived, and treated the local people with respect. For many of the others, it was better that they had not come.

Corruption was rife. U.N. equipment was stolen, and the Western media devoted a great deal of attention to the loss of U.N. cars, many of which were stolen while parked with the keys in the ignition and the doors unlocked. One of the men who owned a Mekong ferry boat was later accused of having stolen hundreds of cars from the United Nations, and some U.N. officials were held at gunpoint when they entered a compound owned by Chheam Vun, a CPP official who was later made Ambassador to Australia, in order to recover some of their cars, which they claimed were being housed there.

But there were also amazing stories that highlighted the humanity of some individual groups within the UNTAC. On one occasion, a group of Japanese peacekeepers were wandering through a village and speaking to one another in Japanese. A village lady sitting nearby suddenly had a flashback and was able to understand what they were saying. She had been a Japanese civilian in Cambodia during World War II and had been isolated and ended up marrying a Cambodian and living in a village, having—until then—totally forgotten about her Japanese roots. The Japanese peacekeepers immediately offered their help.

In June 1992, the forces of Democratic Kampuchea refused to disarm and by November, the PDK announced that they had formed the National Union Party of Kampuchea and were not going to register this party for the elections, which were set for May 1993. Pol Pot had money from China, weapons he had stockpiled during the last civil war, and friends in the Thai military. In his biography of Pol Pot, Philip Short stated that he felt that the Khmer Rouge were about to prepare for another war. They were back in the same position they had been in during the 1960s: the attainment of power was possible, but only after another struggle.

THE PREPARATIONS FOR THE ELECTIONS

A number of other political parties had been registered, many by exiles. These included the Khmer Neutral Party, the Partie Democrate, the Cambodia Free Independent Democracy Party, the Free Republican Party, the Liberal Reconciliation Party, the Cambodge Renaissance Party, and the Republican Coalition Party. There was also Molinaka, which decided to separate from FUNCINPEC, but its leader Prum Neakaareach did get into trouble with the UNTAC officials for anti-Vietnamese comments, which resulted in him banned from the elections. Indeed, anti-Vietnamese sentiments started running high in early 1993, as the election campaign began in earnest. Some Cambodians were worried that the Vietnamese settlers who had arrived in the country during the reign of the pro-Vietnamese PRK might manage to vote in elections. They would obviously support the CPP and given that there were hundreds of thousands of them in the country, many Cambodian nationalists cried foul. Allowing illegal immigrants to remain in the country was one matter, but having them decide a close election race was quite another. The Khmer Rouge took matters into their own hands, and a number of brutal massacres took place in Vietnamese village communities. The number of Vietnamese killed was not large, but the nature of their deaths was clearly horrific. These murders quickly achieved the desired result, as hundreds of thousands of Vietnamese fled, with some returning to Vietnam, while Vietnamese fishermen clogged the Mekong River trying to escape. They would not be voting in the election—the UNTAC was certain of that. Deprived of their electoral clout, the CPP was quick to disown these settlers, many of whom saw their livelihoods destroyed in a matter of days. The Khmer Rouge followed up these attacks by denouncing people who had "Khmer bodies but Vietnamese minds," showing that the attacks might be launched on any politician who supported an alliance with Vietnam.

As the election approached, the CPP began to enforce its rule in the countryside. Although the party had officially stood down as the administrator of the country, in favor of the UNTAC, in many places, especially the countryside, they were still powerful and had strong patronage ties. Local CPP leaders had acquired small or large fortunes involving themselves in illegal logging, or the seizing of property right before the reintroduction of private land ownership. They had the police on their side and intimidation was rife. Some BLDP campaign workers disappeared while handing out leaflets or campaigning in the countryside, and it soon became clear that they had been murdered by local CPP strongmen, who were exerting themselves in a kind of warlord status over the people living nearby. Whatever the CPP officials may have thought about Communism in theory, the intimidation worked in many areas, as the peasants were not keen on seeing their lot made any harsher.

FUNCINPEC was well organized for the election campaign, but many of their new printing presses were held up by CPP-controlled customs officials.

However, FUNCINPEC managed to operate its own radio transmission equipment to bring its message to the people. Prince Norodom Ranariddh toured the cities, towns, and countryside, where he was greeted by so many people who saw him as a reminder of his father. Although Sihanouk was not actually standing, the election was fought as though he was, and Ranariddh had a large public following. One of the men who masterminded the campaign was Ung Huot, a Cambodian who had lived in exile in Australia for many years. He had been a student activist and taken part in the March 1970 demonstrations against the Vietnamese communists, and in 1971, he won a scholarship to Australia, remaining there until 1991. During his 20 years in Australia, he had gained citizenship, worked for Telecom Australia, the telecommunications conglomerate, and was an active member of the local FUNCINPEC organization, serving on the staff of Prince Norodom Ranariddh. In 1991, he sold his house in Australia, returning to Phnom Penh, and worked ass FUNCINPEC's head of Public Relations, and then director of the party's election campaign. Suave, self-assured, and fluent in English (and French and Khmer), he managed FUNCINPEC's electoral strategy with great skill. Although he had the United Nations' support to take part in campaigning, the climate created by local CPP officials was distinctly hostile to FUNCINPEC workers and those from other parties.

THE 1993 ELECTIONS

The elections were finally held from May 23 to 28, 1993. The reason for extending them over five days was to allow the maximum number of people to participate. The country had enjoyed a good tradition of elections from 1946 until 1972, but many of the people voting in 1993 had not taken part in any serious election campaigns in their lives. They were now courted by 20 political parties, and a wide range of political traditions. The election system allowed voting by province, with each party providing a list of candidates in order, and seats allocated according to the number of votes achieved by each party in each province. Overseas Cambodians all had to register in Cambodia, but they were allowed to vote at a number of polling stations around the world: Bangkok (Thailand), Canberra (Australia), Jakarta (Indonesia), Paris (France), and Washington, D.C. Many people were angry that there were no polling stations on the west coast of the United States, where so many of the Cambodian exiles lived. However, thousands still made the trip to these foreign cities to cast their votes.

Exit polls were conducted by all of the major political parties in Cambodia, and after the first day of voting, it became quite clear that the election was effectively a head-to-head contest between the CPP and FUNCINPEC. Both parties then pushed themselves forward in a final burst of activity and campaigning to get as many people to vote as possible. The Khmer Rouge leadership, which had decided not to participate in the election, then held a series of high-level meetings. They despised FUNCINPEC, with its Royalist traditions, but they also hated Hun Sen and his CPP. Several days into the elections, when it was clear that the voting was going unhindered by Khmer Rouge, and that any election boycott would be meaningless to the outside world, the Khmer Rouge decided to throw their weight behind any candidates who stood a chance of defeating the CPP. Reports started reaching Phnom Penh that tens of thousands of Khmer Rouge and their supporters were emerging from their jungle encampments, clutching legitimate registration cards and voting en bloc for FUNCINPEC or BLDP candidates in their desperation to ensure that the CPP did not win.

On May 28, the polling stations closed and all of the votes were counted under U.N. auspices. Even if many people were angered by the cavalier manner in which the U.N. had run the country, everybody waited with baited breath for the results, and there were no queries over the fairness of the counting procedures. When the results were announced, they showed that FUNCINPEC had won 45.47 percent of the vote, compared to 38.23 percent for the CPP. This meant that FUNCINPEC had 58 seats to 51 for the CPP. The BLDP managed to obtain 3.81 percent of the vote, the LDP received 1.56 percent, and Molinaka achieved 1.37 percent. This gave the BLDP 10 seats in the Constituent Assembly, and Molinaka 1 seat. None of the other, smaller parties received any seats.

Hun Sen was never a democrat, and he and the CPP leadership refused to accept defeat. They started a prolonged negotiation over any possible handover and tried to get FUNCINPEC to agree to a coalition government. Strictly speaking, this was not necessary, as FUNCINPEC, the BLDP, and Molinaka together held 69 of the 120 seats in the Constituent Assembly. This meant that Hun Sen and his supporters had to set up a situation that would achieve their desired result. Prince Norodom Chakrapong, a younger brother of Ranariddh, joined with the CPP Defense Minister Sin Song, and the two announced the secession of the provinces in eastern Cambodia, which had supported the CPP in the elections. The United Nations was hamstrung. They had not prepared for the fact that a major political party would refuse to accept the results of an election that was clearly free and fair—free at least as far as the voting was concerned. It has been estimated that the U.N. operations in Cambodia cost some $4 billion, and it was all looking like a waste in June 1993.

Prince Norodom Ranariddh did not want to see the country breakup, and following his father's intervention, he finally agreed to a coalition government, with himself as the First Prime Minister, and Hun Sen as the Second Prime Minister, as Sen did not like the title of "Deputy Prime Minister." Akashi, the Japanese U.N. official who had presided over the whole process, was later made chief U.N. envoy to the former Yugoslavia, but had to be replaced in October 1995, after the Srebrenica massacre.

On September 21, the new Constitution was approved by the Constituent Assembly, and on September 23, the constitutional monarchy was restored with Prince Sihanouk as King. His wife, Princess Monique, assumed the title "Queen Norodom Monineath Sihanouk." It was not until the end of the year that the country's postage stamps reflected this change, proclaiming them to be from "Royaume du Cambodge." The Constituent Assembly then transformed itself into a National Assembly—a unicameral parliament.

POWER-SHARING

The process toward democratic government in Cambodia was awkward. It began with the division of the spoils, as FUNCINPEC and CPP leaders met to discuss how to divide the cabinet positions. FUNCINPEC received the key portfolios controlling the Foreign and Finance ministries, with the CPP obtaining the Defense and Interior ministries. For FUNCINPEC, Prince Norodom Sirivudh, the half-brother of King Sihanouk, became Minister of Foreign Affairs. He was a party loyalist of an impeccable pedigree, which reinforced the party's status as one of the Royalist elite. Supporting him was the new finance minister, a former banker, Sam Rainsy, who had also been an exile in France. His grandfather, Sam Nhean, had been an important politician in the late 1940s and early 1950s, with his mantle then falling to his son Sam Sary, who was a favorite of Prince Sihanouk, although the two fell out badly in 1959. Sam Rainsy had remained in Phnom Penh while his father was on the run and then murdered, after which Sam Rainsy went to school in France, growing up there and attending the Institute of Political Studies in Paris. During the Khmer Republic era, he made a brief foray into politics on the side of the Republic, writing a letter to U.S. Secretary of State Henry Kissinger in the early 1970s—Kissinger's staff noted that "he seems friendly." Then, he had been involved in politics among the Cambodian exiles in Paris. There, he met and married Saumara Tioulong, daughter of Nhiek Tioulong, who was also keenly interested in politics, and she was seen by some as the driving force of the couple. Prince Ranariddh later described her as having "the power of a jet engine."

To bolster Hun Sen, the CPP made Tea Banh his Defense Minister and Sar Kheng his Interior Minister. They were both early members of the UFNSK, and their appointments ensured that the CPP would retain control of the country's security. The ambassadorial positions had also been divided between FUNCINPEC and the CPP. FUNCINPEC managed to obtain the ambassadorships of the United States/United Nations (Prince Sisowath Sirirath, son of Prince Sisowath Sirik Matak), and Thailand (Roland Eng, brother-in-law of

Prince Ranariddh). In return, the CPP obtained the France/European Union (Hor Nam Hong), Vietnam (Pep Phen), and Australia (Chheam Vun) ambassadorships.

King Sihanouk reserved the right to appoint the ambassadors to China (Khek Sysoda) and North Korea (Oum Mannorine), ensuring a direct line of communication to his most loyal foreign backers. What all parties were eager for was possession of the Cambodian Embassy in Tokyo, which, owing to property price increases in the Japanese capital, was believed to be worth some $440 million. There were queries over whether the Cambodian ambassador's residence in Paris was still haunted, and the embassy building in Australia was not without controversy regarding who specifically had the right to sell it.

While Ranariddh, Sirivudh, and Rainsy were all consummate politicians, they were keen to play a full part in Cambodian society, and Ranariddh would often be found on the golf course, or riding his horse. By contrast, Hun Sen lived and breathed politics all day, scheming and intriguing to try to take over the government from his Royal rival. By this time, the Khmer Rouge had become, militarily, nothing more than an annoyance. Khieu Samphan announced that he had formed a Provisional Government of National Unity and Well-Being of Kampuchea, and the Khmer Rouge did manage one minor success, managing to kidnap three tourists from Australia, France, and the United Kingdom on July 26, 1994. The three unfortunate men were not targeted for any real reason other than that they were foreigners in the wrong place at the wrong time. The Cambodian government launched an abortive attempt to rescue them from the Khmer Rouge jungle base, which they surrounded and shelled, seemingly in the hope of killing the kidnappers and the victims to end the problem, which was becoming an irritant. Allegations were later made that there was an attempt to pay a ransom demand and the money was embezzled. The Khmer Rouge finally killed the three men and managed to evade attempts at capture, although the Australian government managed to push for the two leading Khmer Rouge kidnappers to be brought to trial. In the meantime, there was confusion in Phnom Penh, as rumors spread of another coup attempt in which the names of Prince Norodom Chakrapong and Sin Song were mentioned. Prince Chakrapong went into exile, publishing an open letter announcing his withdrawal from politics. Sin Song was jailed.

By this time, there were large numbers of tourists flooding into the country, and the economy was growing considerably as backpackers and rich tourists alike came to see Angkor Wat and the other nearby temples, as well as many of the other sites, such as the old beach resort at Kep. Some enjoyed soaking up the hot weather and escaping the European or Australian winters. Marijuana and other narcotics were sold openly throughout the country, providing another attraction for some tourists, along with the opportunity to solicit prostitutes—both female and male—many of whom were underage. In his account of the history of Cambodia, John Tully notes that some 70 percent of children living near Siem Reap had been propositioned by foreigners. Some governments acted on their diplomatic staff, and one senior diplomat found unwanted publicity in the newspapers after he was accused of having affairs with two boys, although the legal case collapsed. The main problem was proving the ages of many of the prostitutes, and that case, and many others, showed both the difficulties of prosecution and the real possibility of a miscarriage of justice. One of the most popular emerging tourist attractions in Phnom Penh was an artillery park, where visitors could dress up as soldiers wrapped in bandoliers for five dollars or, for a larger fee, they could fire AK47s, M16s, grenade launchers, or bazookas. Cardboard targets were provided for free, but for $100, the organizers would provide a cow. The tourist dollars were flooding into the country, but there were serious queries about what was happening to Cambodian society. There were occasional crackdowns, but these were conducted as much to elicit bribes from hoteliers and night club owners who had forgotten to pay the police as to stop the misdemeanors.

THE EMERGENCE OF SAM RAINSY

Sam Rainsy, the new finance minister, did a great deal to clean up corruption in the government—perhaps a little too much. *Asiamoney* magazine, published in Hong Kong, cited him as the Finance Minister of the Year. Yet, he was under attack by politicians who were either jealous of the reputation that he had earned, or supported the people who were targets of his anti-corruption probes. On October 20, 1994, Sam Rainsy resigned as Finance Minister after losing a vote of no confidence in the National Assembly. Two months later, Prince Norodom Ranariddh made a remark about Sam Rainsy's impending fate, and on May 13, 1995, he was formally expelled from FUNCINPEC and then from the National Assembly. Sam Rainsy's closest supporter, Prince Norodom Sirivudh, resigned as Foreign Minister. This resignation was not submitted solely in protest of Sam Rainsy's removal, but had more to do with the general malaise in the government. In one fell swoop, FUNCINPEC had lost two of its best Parliamentary performers. Sam Rainsy was replaced by Keat Chhon, and Sirivudh by Ung Huot.

The next elections were to be held in 1998, and Hun Sen had been planning his moves since the day after the last one. His main aim was to divide FUNCINPEC. He had achieved this by splitting Sam Rainsy from Ranariddh, and in November 1995, Sam Rainsy formed the Khmer Nation Party, a liberal democratic party that sought to oppose corruption in government and society, and have a pro-Western foreign policy. It seemed as though Prince Norodom Sirivudh would support him, but soldiers loyal to Hun Sen surrounded Sirivudh's house later in November 1995, and hounded him from the country. Prince Sirivudh had been recorded making a joke about the assassination of Hun Sen. While the entire context of the conversation showed that Sirivudh was not seriously involved in any plotting, Hun Sen used it as an excuse to threaten to have him arrested and jailed—Hun Sen claimed that he now feared his life. In March 1996, FUNCINPEC announced that it would not form an alliance with the CPP in the 1998 elections, and in January of 1997, the party formed a National United Front to fight the CPP in the elections scheduled for mid-1998.

Hardliners in the CPP were by now becoming so annoyed by Sam Rainsy that it appeared that some of them were behind the incident on March 30, 1997 when an assassination attempt was made on him. While addressing supporters outside the National Assembly, he was cheered by poor factory workers after arguing their case, namely that they were being underpaid and exploited. He urged for better pay for workers in the garment industry, and safer working conditions. At that point, a few men in the crowd started throwing hand grenades at Sam Rainsy. Sixteen people—mainly poor factory workers—were killed, and many more were injured. A U.S. citizen standing near Sam Rainsy was also injured as the would-be assassins fled, pursued by an angry crowd. The police then intervened to help the hand grenade throwers escape in a nearby car—the police chasing away Sam Rainsy's supporters. A French restaurateur who told friends that he had seen what happened was later found dead. With a U.S. citizen injured in what was clearly a terrorist action, the FBI was sent in to investigate the case. Their report was never published in full, but parts of it were leaked and these excerpts clearly blamed people in the CPP for the attack.

This was the first of many instances where overseas human rights groups would complain about Hun Sen's actions. Indeed, Amnesty International had long campaigned against the holding of prisoners of conscience in Cambodia, and had organized letter-writing campaigns to Hun Sen since the mid-1980s. From 2005 onward, bundles of these letters—including a number of which were still unopened—were sold to stamp collectors on the Internet auction site Ebay by a Vietnamese stamp dealer.

THE SPLIT IN THE KHMER ROUGE

At this stage, the Khmer Rouge seems to have decided to split. They were unsure whether the CPP or FUNCINPEC would triumph in 1998, and were anxious not to have their proverbial eggs all in one basket. They had done this in 1993, and managed to survive, albeit as a totally marginalized entity operating out of three bases: Pailin, Phnom Malai, and Anlong Veng. With people in the world community arguing for a trial of the surviving Khmer Rouge leadership, they were anxious to obtain protection from whichever party triumphed in 1998. To this end, in August 1996, Ieng Sary and the DK army divisions based in Pailin, and Phnom Malai, announced that they had defected to support the CPP, and Ieng Sary formed the Democratic National Union Movement. This left Pol Pot and his more hardline supporters in Anlong Veng to maintain a tacit alliance with FUNCINPEC. Many foreigners rejoiced, claiming that this showed that the Khmer Rouge was now a spent force, and had been split through internal power struggles. There were power struggles going on in the Khmer Rouge, but these were not what was happening. Some Cambodians quickly recognized the whole action as a charade, ahead of the machinations of the 1998 elections.

In his biography of Pol Pot, Philip Short argued that the split was genuine, and that Pol Pot then suspected Son Sen of preparing to defect to Hun Sen, as well. The relationship between Pol Pot and Son Sen was certainly not as good as it had been in the mid-1970s. Pol Pot had considered purging Son Sen in late 1978, with the Vietnamese invasion, as it turned out, saving Son Sen's life, for a while. It was when King Sihanouk spoke on June 9, and held out the prospect of an amnesty for Son Sen, that Pol Pot became worried. But Sihanouk's actions might have been designed to trigger the Khmer Rouge's self-destruction, which certainly occurred. On June 10, 1997, Son Sen, his wife, Yun Yat, and some of their family members, including small children, were murdered in Anlong Veng on the orders of Pol Pot. The Khmer Rouge then announced that Pol Pot had been arrested by Ta Mok.

Significant questions remain regarding whether Pol Pot was genuinely arrested or not. There was no doubt that Son Sen and Yun Yat, a political figure in her own right, were both dead, but the reason they were killed was a mystery. Perhaps their murders were based on the rumor that went around when Son Sen was found with a mobile telephone, namely that he had been in communication with Hun Sen. If this was the case, then perhaps the former Khmer Rouge security chief was genuinely preparing to defect, and was killed because of this. If he had managed to defect, he would have shown Ieng Sary's defection and the party's split as the charade that it really was.

A top secret meeting of the FUNCINPEC leadership had taken place in the previous year, when it was decided that in the 1998 election, the Royalists would seek a political alliance with both Sam Rainsy and the Khmer Rouge. The only problem was the continued existence of Pol Pot, whose name was synonymous around the world with the mindless mass murder of both political opponents and innocent people alike. Royalist General Nhek Bun Chhay planned for the capture of Pol Pot in the form of whisking him away on a helicopter to a U.S. ship in the Gulf of Thailand, and putting him on trial somewhere. This would leave a less tarnished Khmer Rouge capable of supporting FUNCINPEC. The Khmer Rouge was not desperate to distance themselves from Pol Pot. Announcements had been made of Pol Pot's retirement and even of his death many times. But this had never yet come to pass. The Khmer Rouge in Anlong Veng announced that they had put Pol Pot on trial, with some of the proceedings being broadcast on the radio to a largely disbelieving public. It was not long before whatever was really happening in Anlong Veng became irrelevant, as a coup d'état broke was launched in Phnom Penh.

10

Cambodia under Hun Sen (1997 onwards)

On July 5, 1997, with Prince Norodom Ranariddh having just left for France—
and in mid-flight between Bangkok and Paris—fighting broke out in Phnom
Penh. Soldiers were quickly deployed and tanks rumbled through the streets.
Hun Sen was making a bold bid for power. He accused FUNCINPEC of ille-
gally importing arms for its military intelligence apparatus. Arms were certainly being imported by FUNCINPEC (and also, incidentally, by the CPP),
but Hun Sen never really accepted that FUNCINPEC had won the 1993 elections and hence, were the elected government of the country. He saw them as
an annoyance, and an increasingly marginalized member of the coalition. He
viewed himself as Cambodia's man of destiny, the man who should run the
country in the interests of his supporters, feeling that only he could genuinely
help the people in the country.

When Prince Ranariddh was born, his father had been the King of Cambodia, and once again, Sihanouk was the King. Ranariddh and the Royalists
saw it as their duty to lead the people, and certainly had a sense of noblesse
oblige, which Hun Sen never appreciated. For Hun Sen and some of his supporters, it was an anathema that poor peasants could flock in large numbers and vote for a wealthy prince who made relatively rare appearances in
the provinces, and who spent considerable portions of his time overseas.

Ranariddh had dual Cambodian-French nationality, and it had emerged that he also held a valid Malaysian passport. Hun Sen, who was learning English, was from a peasant background and hated the way that, from his perspective, the Royal Family had paraded over the poor. While Son Ngoc Thanh and his supporters argued against Sihanouk on policy matters, Hun Sen's hatred of the Royal Family ran deep. Although he had officially renounced Communism in 1991, many argued that he was still strongly Communist in terms of his convictions. He was, however, one of the shrewdest rulers that Cambodia had, and was able to tolerate Sihanouk when he needed to. But he certainly had no time for Ranariddh, and although the feeling was mutual, Ranariddh's view of Hun Sen was more dismissive. Ranariddh saw Hun Sen as ill-educated and ridiculed Hun Sen's manner of speech. Royalists undoubtedly saw Hun Sen as an upstart peasant who was pushing his luck too far. They joked derisively about the fact that Hun Sen had lost one of his eyes in the first civil war in 1975. But this time they chose the wrong target.

Hun Sen's soldiers—several thousand—stormed through Phnom Penh on July 5, and sought out FUNCINPEC officials. Hun Sen was at Vungtao in Vietnam with his family. He immediately rushed back to Phnom Penh as things started to turn in his favor. At FUNCINPEC headquarters, there was a firefight as Royalist bodyguards tried to hold off the attackers, while party officials smashed a hole in the wall of their compound to escape. Ho Sok, a former colonel in the Royalist Army in the Second Civil War, and Secretary of State at the Ministry of the Interior, was a particular target for Hun Sen loyalists. He had been heavily involved in attempts to root out corruption and the narcotics trade. Ho Sok sought refuge in the embassy of an ASEAN country and while trying to escape from it the following day, he was seized and taken off to the Interior Ministry, where he was shot dead at point-blank range. It was the only killing that transpired during the coup d'état that Hun Sen acknowledged, but nobody was ever charged or tried for the murder, which was undoubtedly witnessed by many people.

Elsewhere in Phnom Penh, other people connected with the FUNCINPEC security apparatus were hunted down. General Nhek Bun Chhay, one of the FUNCINPEC military commanders, was surrounded at his base near Pochentong Airport. He escaped in a shoot-out, and managed to get to the Thai border on a motorcycle, where the Royalists regrouped at the base at O'Smach. General Serei Kosal also managed to escape, along with some other leading Royalists.

As shoot-outs took place around Phnom Penh, looters trashed a large number of Royalist officials' houses, as well as many shops, including those at the airport, making off with goods that were seen being openly sold in markets for weeks afterwards. For exiles who had returned to Cambodia with such high hopes in 1991, seeing their houses trashed by police and rioters, and their treasured possessions handed over to their enemies, was heartbreaking. But they were the lucky ones. Many were murdered. The Thai government, anxious to safeguard their citizens, sent in paratroopers, who briefly took control of Pochentong Airport and oversaw the evacuation of Thai nationals, those of allied countries, and also a number of BLDP politicians, who had long had close ties with Bangkok. Cambodia's richest businessman, Teng Bunma, a close friend of Hun Sen, later boasted on Australian television that he had financed the coup by providing Hun Sen with $1 million, and in return, Hun Sen protected his hotel. During the same interview for Australia's Channel 7, he also said that he had paid some MPs to support Hun Sen.

After the coup, Hun Sen had Ranariddh on the run, and now he needed somebody in the FUNCINPEC to lead their party as a junior member of the coalition. Ung Huot was in Singapore, returning to Phnom Penh when the coup took place. He headed back and the remainder of the FUNCINPEC elected him as their leader, and he became the First Prime Minister, taking over from Ranariddh who, in a press conference, blamed the coup on unnamed people involved in the sale of narcotics, who were worried about the U.S. anti-narcotics Drugs Enforcement Administration. The Royalists started to gather their forces at O'Smach, but they quickly recognized that neither they nor the country was ready for another civil war. By that time, the focus of Cambodia had shifted back to Pol Pot.

THE END OF THE KHMER ROUGE

The U.S. journalist Nate Thayer had long been involved in reporting on Cambodian politics for the Hong Kong-based *Far Eastern Economic Review*. On July 25, he managed the scoop of his life by being invited to Anlong Veng to film the trial of Pol Pot. Because most people were unconvinced by the radio broadcasts of Pol Pot on trial, the Khmer Rouge decided to invite Thayer to watch and film the proceedings—they had either not concluded, resumed again for Thayer, or were totally separate from the trial, which had been broadcast from the first week of July. They provided the first public images of Pol Pot since 1979. As a much older man, he remained seated, while he and some younger lieutenants were denounced. The crowd sat quietly and occasionally joined an organized but lackluster chanting. It was certainly no denunciation in the style of the Red Guards during the Cultural Revolution in China. Pol Pot seemed to shed a tear as he sat and listened to everything. It seemed that he was wishing that the proceedings would end. At the close of his trial, he was sentenced to life imprisonment and was politely and gently led away to an SUV and driven off. The Khmer Rouge felt that they had exorcised the ghosts of the past. The problem was that many of the relatives of those killed during the Democratic Kampuchea were not satisfied. They demanded that

Pol Pot be put on a public trial in Phnom Penh or somewhere else where his accusers could actually face him. In addition, the charges against Pol Pot seemed to have to do with the killing of Son Sen, and many of the victims of Democratic Kampuchea would no more shed a tear over his death than that of Pol Pot.

Pol Pot did allow Nate Thayer to return to Anlong Veng and interview him. In the historical context, it was an interesting interview, but Pol Pot had little to add, politically speaking. He was able to establish that he was born in January 1925, in the year of the Ox—there had long been debate over his date of birth—although he could not remember the exact day. In 1925, the year of the Ox began on January 25, so the information he provided has helped to narrow down his date of birth. He also denied involvement in the death of Tou Samouth, but by this time, few people seriously felt that he was involved. On April 15, 1998, it was announced that Pol Pot had died. Thai authorities checked the body by taking his fingerprints—which implied that they already had his fingerprints on file somewhere—and his body was duly cremated. He left his second wife and a young daughter. There may also have been a son.

THE 1998 ELECTIONS

With the 1998 elections scheduled for mid-year, by the middle of March, the nation was in a stalemate. Prince Norodom Ranariddh was overseas and he was allowed to return on March 30, with the elections eventually scheduled for July 26. These elections differed from those fought over in 1993; Hun Sen did not leave anything to chance. The Vietnamese settlers who had fled or been disenfranchised by the U.N. five years earlier were allowed to vote. Furthermore, although the actual voting might have been fair, the campaign was certainly not, and the vote counting triggered accusations of outright fraud.

In this election, there were a number of new parties contesting seats in the National Assembly. The CPP wanted to win enough seats to rule in its own right, and FUNCINPEC had the same objective. Sam Rainsy's Khmer Nation Party had been restructured into the Sam Rainsy Party (after a supporter of the CPP registered the name "Khmer Nation Party" ahead of him in the run-up to the elections). Son Sann faced the same problem, and his party became known as the "Grandfather Son Sann Party." Ung Huot, now ejected from FUNCINPEC by Ranariddh loyalists, but still the First Prime Minister, formed his Reastr Niyum Party, whose election posters were spread over walls, trees, and pavements throughout the country. It was to no avail—they did not win any seats in the Assembly.

When the results were declared, the CPP won 64 seats, the FUNCINPEC obtained 43 seats, and the Sam Rainsy Party won 15 seats. Many people did not find this credible. Before the election, Sam Rainsy's rallies had attracted tens of thousands of voters, and in the one constituency—Pailin—where vote-counting was not in the hands of Hun Sen, they registered 51 percent of the vote. Some international election observers pronounced the election free and fair before the votes were counted. The counting procedure consisted of large numbers of government employees and their friends counting ballot papers, with FUNCINPEC and the Sam Rainsy Party only allowed one scrutineer each, who was incapable of observing the count, which was often going on in several different rooms at the same time. That the FUNCINPEC and the Sam Rainsy Party managed to get as many votes as they did under these conditions said a lot about their level of support. At one polling booth, dozens of Ung Huot supporters turned up with banners flying from their cars and their motorcycles emblazoned with his party symbol. Yet when the votes from that booth were counted, government officials counting the vote claimed that Reastr Niyum had not received a single vote there. Few could seriously be expected to believe these results.

As the election results were published, Sam Rainsy's supporters took to the streets, demanding an independent count of the ballot papers. Hun Sen refused to grant this request and he gained support from many quarters. In a speech he later gave in Melbourne, Tony Kevin, then the Australian Ambassador, claimed that the demonstration organized by Sam Rainsy was an unprecedented attempt to bring down an elected government by public protests. When asked about the precedent set by Cory Aquino's People's Power Revolution in the Philippines in 1986, which brought down Marcos, who had rigged the election there, he astounded the audience by saying that he had never heard of it. It seemed that the international community did not want to take on Hun Sen, and certainly did not want another civil war in Cambodia. They were prepared to go along with his regime, however fraudulent the election, in the hope that it would provide stability for the country, and provide many people an opportunity to escape from the grinding poverty in which they were living.

Hun Sen was never happy with half-victories and sought to erode the influence of his rivals. On September 7, 1998, somebody had thrown a hand grenade into Hun Sen's former residence in Phnom Penh, reinforcing Hun Sen's stated fear for his own life. Hun Sen was actually in Siem Reap at the time—195 miles (314 km.) away—and had not lived in the building for several years, and the assassin had also forgotten to pull the pin out from the hand grenade, a fairly elementary mistake. Nevertheless, this attack allowed Hun Sen to rage about some of his opponents resorting to violence to achieve their aims, and that he feared for his life. He certainly had several thousand bodyguards, and it was revealed in the press in January 2009, that Chea Sim, Hun Sen's deputy, had 600 bodyguards, including two brigadier generals, all paid for by funds that the government borrowed, as the country had little in the way of a tax base.

Faced with the possibility of political oblivion, FUNCINPEC finally caved in to CPP demands and on November 30, 1998, entered into a coalition with Hun Sen. The compromise was that the Cambodian Parliament would add an additional chamber, the Senate. Its members were initially nominated by political parties (and later voted in by town and city councilors). This allowed FUNCINPEC to reward some of its loyal supporters with positions. The establishment of the Senate was formally agreed upon on March 4, with the King able to nominate two members. Three days later, Nhek Bun Chhay was able to return to Phnom Penh, and received an official government amnesty. As a result of this power-sharing agreement, Cambodia was able to move to a position of acceptance in the wider international community and on April 30, 1999, it finally became a member of the Association of Southeast Asian Nations (ASEAN).

The Khmer Rouge finally accepted that their struggle for a Communist Cambodia had come to an end and on December 4, their members from Anlong Veng surrendered, and on December 25, Khieu Samphan and Nuon Chea surrendered. Four days later, Khieu Samphan expressed his sorrow for the deaths that had taken place during the period of Democratic Kampuchea. On February 9, 1999, the Khmer Rouge soldiers were integrated into the Royal Cambodian Army, and on March 6, the last major Khmer Rouge leader on the run, Ta Mok, was captured. However, for them, the international press was eager to track down all of the former members. On April 28, the Security Chief, Deuch, who had controlled S-21 (Tuol Sleng) was located by the *Far Eastern Economic Review,* and promptly arrested. His claim that he had converted to Christianity, like Paul after "seeing the light" on the road to Damascus in the *Book of Acts*, was ridiculed by the foreign press and many Cambodians. Ta Mok was charged with genocide on September 7, 1999, and Duch also charged with genocide three days later.

By 1999, it had been 20 years since the end of Democratic Kampuchea, and many Cambodians had been born or grown up after that time. For them, the crucial event of the year was the murder of the beautiful Cambodian actress Piseth Pilica. She had emerged as one of the country's great actresses after her role in the 1988 film *Sramol Anthaka* ("Shadow of Darkness") about life in the harsh environment of Democratic Kampuchea. Pilica was also involved in the Royal Ballet, and had been romantically linked by the press to Hun Sen. On July 6, 1999, she was shot by a hired assassin on a crowded street in Phnom Penh, and died in hospital seven days later. More than 10,000 people, led by Sihanouk's eldest daughter, Princess Norodom Bopha Devi, the Minister of Culture and Fine Arts, mourned her at her cremation. It seems extremely unlikely that Hun Sen was involved in her death, but because nobody was ever arrested or charged with her killing, people spoke of a political system of lawlessness that was sweeping the country. She was the most famous person to be killed, but she was not the only one. Businessmen, farmers, and peasants were being murdered with impunity, albeit on a much smaller scale than several years earlier.

Given the serious queries about the state of law and order in the country, there were continued attempts to try to set up an international tribunal to judge the surviving Khmer Rouge leaders. As previously mentioned, it was hard to charge many of them with either war crimes or genocide. There was also the problem of many people wanting to restrict any tribunal's terms of reference to what happened in Cambodia between April 17, 1975, and December 25, 1978. If the tribunal went any further back, some U.S. lawmakers were worried that Henry Kissinger might be arraigned. Any later, and Hun Sen might find himself in the dock. In July 2000, Chhouk Rin, a Khmer Rouge commander involved in the death of three foreigners, one of whom was an Australian, walked free from court amidst cries of protest from the Australian government and press. Finally, on August 10, 2001, the Khmer Rouge tribunal law was enacted, but on February 8, 2002, the United Nations announced that they would withdraw from the trials system, as these hearings were clearly not going to be impartial.

THE 2003 ELECTIONS

As these legal battles raged, the ransacking of the Cambodian countryside continued apace. Fishermen using hand grenades or landmines had been active during the 1980s, wreaking havoc on the fish stocks. Logging companies acting with impunity started destroying much of Cambodia's rainforest. Vast areas of the countryside were clear-felled in violation of Cambodian laws and international treaties. Trucks carrying these logs regularly plied highways in full view of the public. Wild animals in the countryside were tracked down and shot by local and foreign hunters. Pimps toured poor villages, persuading parents to part with their daughters or sons for cash payments. Diseases, including HIV/AIDS, continued to take a toll on the population. There was also an instance when a Taiwanese company was involved in dumping contaminated waste near a Cambodian port, after which many poor people started suffering from illnesses connected with radiation.

But with the vast influx of tourist money into the country, a new middle-class emerged, comprised of tour guides, shop-keepers, and artisans making objects to sell to tourists. Cambodians overseas started to return to settle in their country, with many doing quite well in an increasingly cosmopolitan Phnom Penh. Many mourned the desecration of the countryside, but felt powerless to do anything as the society (and the government) became more and more rapaciously capitalist. King Norodom Sihanouk, who was increasingly unwell, started to play less and less of a role in politics.

There were some successes. Since the 1980s, and some would say since the 1880s, there had been pillaging of statues and parts of monuments at Angkor Wat. These pillages had taken off during the second civil war, and continued through the 1990s. In 1999, the U.S. Department of State had agreed to prevent the importing of stone artifacts from Cambodia, and in 2003, extended this ban to include metal and ceramic objects. The minefield clearance groups that had set about trying to clear much of the country of landmines, after many years of painstaking work, were able to enable the opening up of more farmland. In October 2001, at the insistence of foreign donor countries, some 30,000 soldiers were demobilized. However, in communal elections in February 2002, the ruling Cambodian People's Party managed to win control of 1,600 of the 1,621 communes, with the Sam Rainsy Party (SRP) emerging as the major opposition to Hun Sen. The CPP's victory in the communal elections followed the murder of some 20 SRP candidates and activists. Allegations of intimidation were clear for all to see. With the run-up to the July 2003 elections, rumors spread in early 2003 that a Thai singer had performed a song that included the comment that Thais had built Angkor Wat. She denied saying this, but nationalist mobs went on the rampage in Phnom Penh on January 29, 2003, with Thai businesses attacked and Thai women working in Phnom Penh being raped and humiliated. The government of Thailand withdrew its Ambassador, ordered the Cambodian Ambassador to leave Bangkok, and closed its borders, preventing many tourists from reaching Angkor Wat. The situation was finally resolved on April 10, when Cambodia paid $5.9 million in compensation, and 14 days later, Chatchavet Chartsuwan, the Thai Ambassador, returned to the Cambodian capital. In May, the Cambodian and Thai governments held a joint meeting of cabinet ministers, and they signed off on agreements to prevent the trafficking of women and children, and the repayment of loans to Thailand.

Targeted political assassinations continued with a leading adviser of Prince Ranariddh, Om Radsady, who was shot as he left a restaurant in Phnom Penh on February 18, 2003, dying later the same day. On April 23, Sok Sethamony, a senior judge, was gunned down by an assassin on a motorcycle. He had been involved in the trial, in absentia, of Chhun Yasith, a member of the Cambodian Freedom Fighters. On October 18, Chou Chetharith, a newspaper editor associated with the FUNCINPEC was murdered. Three days later, Touch Sunnich, a pop music star who also connected with the FUNCINPEC, was gunned down as he left a flower shop. His mother, who was with him, was also killed. On January 22, 2004, the president of the Free Trade Union of Workers of the Kingdom of Cambodia, Chea Vichea, an ally of Sam Rainsy, was murdered.

In the run-up to the elections, in June 2003, Colin Powell, the U.S. Secretary of State, arrived in Phnom Penh to show his support for Sam Rainsy, citing his (Powell's) hope for a "free, fair, open election." When the elections were held on July 27, 2003, they occurred in a climate of fear. The CPP won 73 of the 123 seats in the National Assembly, with the FUNCINPEC getting 26 seats (down from 43), and the SRP increasing their representation from 15 to 24 seats, winning nearly all the urban seats. According to official returns, the CPP had gained 2,447,259 votes (47.35 percent), with the Sam Rainsy Party obtaining 1,130,423 (21.87 percent), and the FUNCINPEC winning 1,072,313 (20.75 percent). It was the first time the SRP had outpolled FUNCINPEC. Then, after the results were published, both the FUNCINPEC and the SRP united to form the Alliance of Democrats, demanding that Hun Sen resign, and that there be a recount for two of the seats that the CPP claimed to have won. Furthermore, the FUNCINPEC and the SRP refused to take part in the opening of the National Assembly, citing massive intimidation in the election campaign. King Norodom Sihanouk also decided not to preside at the opening of the National Assembly on September 27. There was a long period of uncertainty until, on November 5, an agreement was reached between the three parties, which left Hun Sen in control. Hun Sen then launched a lawsuit against Prince Ranariddh whom, he claimed, had implicated the prime minister in the murder of Chou Chetharith. Ranariddh then stated that he would not attend any meetings until Hun Sen stopped using these legal ruses. On January 10, 2004, at the behest of the Chairman of the Senate, Chea Sim, a close ally of Hun Sen, King Sihanouk announced that he would extend the Senate's term of office until the stalemate had ended and a constitutional crisis was averted.

In June 2004, 11 months after the election, Hun Sen was able to form a new government with the CPP and FUNCINPEC in coalition—the Royalists had finally broken with the SRP. The new National Assembly and Senate quickly passed a law by which they could confirm all of the government ministers and legislative officials in a single vote to prevent some from being elected and others rejected. The new government had a staggering 26 cabinet ministers and 160 other ministers—there were only 123 seats in the entire National Assembly. The period in which Lon Nol wanted to embrace the political nation in a "warm hug" had returned. Many Cambodians were outraged by the government's extravagance when the per capita GDP in the country was $459 per year, with three-quarters of all Cambodians still living on the land.

By this time, Sihanouk was worried about the position of the Crown. The Throne Council was invested with the authority of choosing a successor, and since the restoration of the monarchy in 1993, there had been many people mooted as possible successors. Prince Norodom Yuvaneath, Sihanouk's eldest son, was never a contender, but for many years, Prince Norodom Ranariddh certainly was, with Hun Sen helping to raise the profile of Prince Norodom Chakrapong. Some people suggested some of the most unlikely of contenders, such as Prince Sisowath Sirivudh Panhara, who had spent several years in a French prison for shooting a fellow student dead during a Lon Nol-GRUNK dispute in the 1970s. Prince Norodom Norindrapong, the youngest son of Sihanouk, died in 2003, and finally, Sihanouk decided to make his second-youngest son, Prince Norodom Sihamoni, the new King. King Sihanouk formally abdicated on October 7, and a week later, the Throne Council gathered and unanimously elected Sihamoni. He was enthroned on October 29, 2004, with pictures of him going up around Cambodia.

Sihamoni, the first son of Sihanouk and Monique, had long been one of his father's favorites. He had been educated in Prague in the 1960s, and also in Pyongyang, becoming an accomplished ballet dancer in Cambodia and then in France, teaching Western Classical Ballet in the French capital during the 1990s. He was unmarried, and some people felt that his appointment only delayed the possibility of Cambodia returning to Republic status, but in the relatively short time he has been King, he has managed to enhance the prestige of the throne in Cambodia and overseas. His visits to Beijing, Pyongyang, and other foreign capitals were notable successes. He has also benefited from the advice of his uncle, Oum Mannorine, who returned to Phnom Penh soon afterwards, after 13 years as Ambassador to Pyongyang.

HUN SEN V. SAM RAINSY

On February 3, 2005, Hun Sen launched another lawsuit, this time against Sam Rainsy, who had accused the Prime Minister of being behind the March 1997 hand grenade attack on him (Rainsy). The suit was clearly political—the allegation had been made by many journalists and authors, with Philip Short stating in his biography of Pol Pot that that attack "was ordered by Hun Sen." Hun Sen could have challenged these accusations by Short and others in foreign courts (Foreign Minister Hor Nam Hong had done so successfully against accusations made against him), but he chose the Cambodian courts for his litigation. Once again, Sam Rainsy was forced to flee the country and go into exile in France with a Cambodian court sentencing him to 18 months in prison *in absentia* for criminal defamation on December 22.

In this atmosphere, the elections for the Senate were held, with the voters being village and town councilors. Hun Sen carried the day with 45 of the 57 contested seats. On February 5, 2006, Rainsy was pardoned, and five days later, he returned to Phnom Penh, several weeks before the Consultative Group on Cambodia—Western donor nations—met to discuss aid to Cambodia. On February 14, Hun Sen managed to get a new law passed by which the National Assembly could decide on any legislation by a simple majority, casting aside the need for a two-thirds majority, which had twice forced him into an alliance with the FUNCINPEC.

In late 2005, Hun Sen again found a way of getting at his opponents with, on September 1, a new law passed by the National Assembly and the Senate that would strip parliamentarians of their immunity from prosecution if they expressed any opinions deemed harmful to an individual's dignity, social customs, or law and order, or the national security of the country. They also passed a law that criminalized adultery, polygamy, and incest. This was clearly aimed at Prince Ranariddh, who had taken a new partner, Ouk Phalla, and was openly seen with her in public. This led to the FUNCINPEC ousting Ranariddh and appointing Keo Puth Rasmey, the former ambassador to Malaysia and then Germany, as the new leader of FUNCINPEC on October 18, 2005, and on October 24, he became the new Deputy Prime Minister. Keo Puth Rasmey had worked in the office of Sihanouk for many years, and had married Princess Arun Rasmey, Sihanouk's sixth and youngest daughter. He was also a relative of Nhiek Tioulong, the father-in-law of Sam Rainsy.

While politicians were arguing, finally, on May 4, 2005, 13 international jurists and 17 Cambodian ones convened to oversee the trial of the Khmer Rouge leaders. Most of them had already died and Khieu Samphan, Ieng Sary, and Nuon Chea had received government pardons for some of their "misdeeds." Duch, the commandant of Tuol Sleng, was still in custody, as were some others, and eventually, Khieu Samphan, Ieng Sary, and Nuon Chea were arraigned and charged. The trials began with Khieu Samphan hiring controversial French lawyer Jacques Vèrges, the man who, nearly 60 years earlier, had befriended the student Saloth Sar (Pol Pot) in France, and, some sources claim, encouraged him to join the Communist Party of France. Court costs quickly climbed to $60 million, and then to $100 million, with some seriously beginning to challenge the price of the process. Prince Ranariddh, whose family had suffered heavily under the Khmer Rouge, openly queried whether—given the death of Pol Pot and many of the other senior Communist leaders—further justice could be achieved by handing out thousands of dollars to the victims (and considerably transforming their lives for the better), rather than paying millions to foreign jurists.

On May 29, 2005, after an interval of 18 years, Cambodian and Vietnamese officials started their work on delineating the Cambodia-Vietnam border, allowing a number of border gates to be opened and staffed to help local people, traders, and tourists. Although it appeared that the border disputes with Vietnam had been sorted out, an old one with Thailand resurfaced. Cambodia sought U.N. World Heritage listing for the Preah Vihear Temple, which the International Court of Justice had awarded to Cambodia in 1962, after hearing legal disputes from both sides. However, some Thai nationalists disputed this ruling and in July 2008, they started trying to take over the Temple complex, and Thailand sent in soldiers on July 15, to try to stop the protestors, as Cambodia sent in its army. Hun Sen was able to portray these actions as his defense of Cambodian honor, just as the country headed to the polls.

Beginning in the 1990s, there has been a proliferation of books on Cambodia, most of which were written by non-Cambodians. The few Cambodian accounts were either written largely by Sihanouk, or in the form of harrowing autobiographical stories about survival amidst the most horrendous conditions. The early 2000s saw many Cambodians starting to research and write about the 20th-century history of their country, and some of their books have been controversial, as they have sought to reinterpret events. In his 1971 book *My War with the CIA*, Sihanouk had poured scorn on Dap Chhuon, whose reputation had not fared much better in the works of foreign scholars. However, in 2008, a publisher, Men Narong, sought to rehabilitate Dap Chhuon, his greatuncle, in his book *Who's Who 2007–2008*, which was rapidly suppressed in Phnom Penh, showing that some historical events could still hit a raw nerve in Cambodia. It was in this climate of growing awareness of their past that the Cambodians headed to the polls again in 2008.

On July 27, 2008, the National Assembly elections were held. This time, the scenario was very different. The CPP had been in effective control of much of the country since January 1979, even after losing the 1993 elections, and, almost certainly, those held in 1998 and 2003. But the opposition remained hopelessly divided. While most serious opposition figures had long since flocked to Sam Rainsy, some splinter parties had formed, and Hun Sen relished seeing his opposition divided. A new party, the Human Rights Party, had been founded in on July 22, 2007, by Kem Sokha, the former head of the Cambodian Center for Human Rights, and Keat Sukun, the adopted son of 1960s Parliamentarian Prince Sovannareth, and an activist in the KPNLF during the 1980s and 1990s.

The CPP managed to get 3,492,374 votes, securing 90 seats, with the SRP getting 1,316,714 votes and 26 seats. The Human Rights Party took 397,816 votes with 3 seats, the Norodom Ranariddh Party gained 337,943 votes, with 2 seats, and the FUNCINPEC won 303,764 votes and 2 seats. The League for Democracy Party, the Khmer Democratic Party, and the Hang Dara Democratic Movement Party did not win any seats. Hun Sen finally had his overwhelming majority in the National Assembly, although many observers were very critical of the election, the hindrance of opposition candidates, and the intimidation of opposition voters. It was certainly neither free nor fair, and the Chinese *People's Daily* reported that nongovernmental organizations (NGOs) and supervising bodies put the distribution of seats closer to about 70 for the CPP and 50 for the SRP. At the end of the day, however, the opposition only had themselves to blame, especially for the proliferation of new parties, which served to split the vote of Hun Sen's opponents. Had they united before the election, instead of while they were lodging complaints about it, they might have been able to dislodge Hun Sen. The results were, however, interesting in a few other ways. They did show that Sam Rainsy's popularity as the leader of the opposition made him the only candidate capable of defeating Hun Sen in the next elections. But they also showed that Prince Norodom Ranariddh's continued popularity was so great that even without the FUNCINPEC party structure, he could form a party that could outpoll the whole of the FUNCINPEC.

Hun Sen's reaction to the results was one of caution. He rejected calls to recount the votes, but did surprise everybody when the CPP announced that it would remain in coalition with FUNCINPEC, but did not want Keo Puth Rasmey to lead the Royalists, preferring Nhek Bun Chhay for the role, which would make the General the first non-Royal to lead the Royalist Party. However, it is also worth noting that one of the victors in the election was Hun Manet, the son of Hun Sen, who was elected for Siem Reap province. A graduate of West Point—in fact, the first Cambodian graduate from West Point—it has been suggested by some newspapers that he is being groomed as his father's successor. This certainly seemed more likely after the death of CPP strongman Hok Lundi from a helicopter accident on November 9, 2008; Lundi was a man whose name struck fear in many Cambodians.

In January 2009, King Sihamoni announced that he was appointing his older brother, Prince Ranariddh, as the President of the Supreme Privy Council to His Majesty the King of Cambodia, with the rank of Prime Minister, effectively reviving a title that had first been established by his ancestor King Jayavarman V in the 970s. This has essentially given Cambodia both a Parliamentary Prime Minister, Hun Sen, and its Royal Prime Minister, Prince Ranariddh—the latter in an apolitical role that the prince said he would use to unite the country. His plan is to give his and, by implication, the Palace's support for worthwhile grassroots projects to help ordinary people. To this end, he has started becoming involved in building projects in poor villages near Phnom Penh, and encouraging Cambodians to take a greater role in this work, which had previously been so heavily run by foreign NGOs. Later the same month, the funeral of Chau Sen Cocsal at the age of 104, which occurred on January 26, 2009, symbolized the transition of Cambodia from the French colonial period through the Sangkum era and the period of Communism to democracy, prosperity, and rule by its new strongman.

As Cambodia proceeds forward, the political nation is now effectively divided into two camps: the rural power base of Hun Sen, relying on coercion and local patronage links, and the urban supporters of Sam Rainsy, who are hopeful of an end to corruption, and a change in government. Hun Sen has continued to maintain the support of many of the people in the countryside, a certain number of which were certainly cajoled by commune officials into acquiescence in the actions of the government that they may not like, but have learned to accept. But if the opposition groups could finally put aside their differences and unite, Sam Rainsy, with the overwhelming support of the people in the cities and towns, and with a high profile overseas, should be able to win the next election. But Hun Sen has managed to divide the opposition so many times before, and he has claimed that he will be able to do so again. If he does, he will remain in power. If the opposition unites, as they did in 1993, he will once again face defeat at the polls.

Notable People in Cambodia

Chan Si (1932–1984). The Prime Minister of the PRK from 1982 until 1984, Chan Si was born on May 7, 1932, in Kompong Chhnang, joining the Communist movement at the age of 17. He fought alongside the Viet Minh and after 1954, moved to Hanoi, where he was active in the Khmer People's Revolutionary Party. It seems that he returned to Cambodia between 1970 and 1972, and in 1978, became a founding member of the pro-Vietnamese United Front for the National Salvation of Kampuchea. He took part in the Vietnamese invasion of Cambodia in December 1978, and in May 1981, was appointed to the Politburo of the People's Revolutionary Party of Kampuchea as Deputy Prime Minister and Minister of Defense. Following the purging of Pen Sovan in December 1981, he became Prime Minister of the PRK, remaining in that position until his death on December 24, 1984, from a heart attack.

Chea Sim (b. 1932). The Chairman of the CPP and President of the Senate from its formation in 1999, Chea Sim was born on November 15, 1932, at Romeas Hek, Svay Rieng, and in 1952, he joined the Khmer Issarak and served under Son Ngoc Minh, becoming a member of the KPRP in 1959. He remained in the jungle and fought during the first civil war, ending up as a military commander within Democratic Kampuchea from April 1975 until mid-1978, when he fled to Vietnam and became a founding member of the pro-Vietnamese

United Front for the National Salvation of Kampuchea. Appointed in charge of the Interior Ministry in the PRK, he served in the politburo of the People's Revolutionary Party of Kampuchea, he was elected chairman of the CPP in 1991, after Hun Sen became the most powerful figure in the CPP. Occasionally, rumors have spread about a possible rift between him and Hun Sen, but Chea Sim has remained loyal to Hun Sen throughout the 1990s and the early 2000s.

Douc Rasy (b. 1925). A Republican politician and later a diplomat, he was born on March 8, 1925, in Phnom Penh, the youngest of ten children of a magistrate, and the brother-in-law of the prominent nationalist Pach Chhoeun. Present at the 1943 demonstration against the French, he studied law in France and gained a doctorate, returning to Cambodia and serving at the United Nations, in Thailand, and at the Foreign Ministry in Phnom Penh. From 1962 until 1972, he was a member of the National Assembly, and was one of the most outspoken right-wing critics of Prince Sihanouk, and an opponent of state corruption in the Khmer Republic. In 1972, he was appointed Ambassador to London and moved to France in 1975, where he taught law until his retirement in 1991.

Heng Samrin (b. 1934). The Head of State of the PRK from 1979 until 1991, he was born on May 25, 1934, at Anlung Krek, Kompong Cham, joining the Khmer People's Revolutionary Party in 1959. Becoming a close friend of Chea Sum, the two served in the first civil war, and he ended up as a senior Khmer Rouge figure in eastern Cambodia in the late 1970s. Defecting to Vietnam, he was involved in the Vietnamese invasion of Cambodia in December 1978, and he was appointed as the Head of State of the PRK on January 7, 1979, a position he retained until 1991. As leader of the PRK during these years, critics of his government often referred to it in public debates as the "Heng Samrin regime." Elected to the National Assembly, he remains an important figure in the CPP.

Hor Nam Hong (b. 1935). The Minister of Foreign Affairs in the PRK from 1990 until 1993, and then again from 1998, he was born in Phnom Penh and was appointed to the Cambodian Embassy in Paris, where he wrote a thesis eulogizing Prince Sihanouk. Joining Sihanouk's GRUNK in the first civil war, he was appointed as ambassador to Cuba, and in 1975, was recalled to Phnom Penh, where he languished in an internment camp. He rallied to the pro-Vietnamese United Front for the National Salvation of Kampuchea and in May 1981, was appointed as Deputy Foreign Minister, serving under Hun Sen. From 1982 until 1990, he was the PRK Ambassador to Moscow, and in 1990, was appointed Minister of Foreign Affairs, a post he held, in effect, for three years, after which he was appointed Ambassador to Paris, returning to Phnom Penh in 1998 as Minister of Foreign Affairs.

Hun Sen (b. 1952). The Prime Minister of the PRK and SOC from 1985 until 1991, and Prime Minister of the Kingdom of Cambodia from 1998, he was born on April 4, 1952, at Peam Koh Snar, Kompong Cham. In 1968, he left school and joined the Communists in the wake of the Samlaut Uprising. He served in the Communist forces until 1975, losing his left eye in a battle near Kompong Cham in April 1975. He was a deputy regimental commander of the Khmer Rouge in Democratic Kampuchea, and fled in 1977 to Vietnam, where he joined the United Front for the National Salvation of Kampuchea. With the proclamation of the PRK in January 1979, he was appointed in charge of foreign affairs, and remained Foreign Minister until 1985 when, on January 14, he was appointed as Prime Minister. He transformed the PRK, renaming it the State of Cambodia (SOC) in 1989 and changing the People's Revolutionary Party of Kampuchea into the Cambodian People's Party two years later. He remained Prime Minister of the SOC until June 1993, and although the CPP lost the election in May 1993, he managed to persuade the winners, FUNCINPEC, to form a coalition government, assuming the position of Second Prime Minister. After his coup d'état in July 1997, he was accused of involvement in the deaths of Royalists, and after the 1998 elections, he has been the Prime Minister in charge of a government that has been alleged to be involved in massive election rigging and widespread corruption, as well as doing little to stop the ecological damage to the country.

Ieng Mouly (b. 1959). A prominent Republican, he was born on November 2, 1950, at Snaypol Village, Prey Veng, his father being an active member of the Democrat Party. He trained as an accountant and moved to France in 1973, where he worked for several French companies. In 1982, he moved to Thailand and became active in the KPNLF, advancing to Secretary-General and remaining loyal to Son Sann in factional disputes. He was a member of the Supreme National Council, and a leading figure in the Buddhist Liberal Democratic Party.

Ieng Sary (b. 1925). The Foreign Minister of Democratic Kampuchea from 1975 until 1979, he was born on October 25, 1925, in southern Vietnam, moving to Cambodia as a boy and going to school in Phnom Penh. A friend of Saloth Sar, the two campaigned for the Democrat Party and Ieng Sary went to France on a government scholarship and became a member of the Communist Party of France. Returning to Cambodia, he taught history and was active in the underground Communist movement, fleeing to the jungle in 1963. He became active in the Sihanoukist Royal Government of National Union of Kampuchea, and in 1975, was appointed Minister of Foreign Affairs of Democratic Kampuchea, a post he held until the invasion of Cambodia by Vietnam. He then remained one of the leaders of the Party of Democratic Kampuchea, and lived in Pailin, on the Cambodian-Thai border, taking part in the split in 1996. In 1999, he moved to Phnom Penh, and has been arraigned before the International Cambodia Tribunal for war crimes and crimes against humanity.

In Tam (1922–2006). A longtime political activist and Prime Minister in 1973, In Tam was born on September 23, 1922, at Prek Kak, Kompong Cham, and joined the government service in the realm of provincial administration and was a member of the National Assembly from 1966 until 1972. One of the major figures involved in the overthrow of Prince Sihanouk in March 1970, he urged the proclamation of the Khmer Republic, which took place in October 1970. Gradually, he began to have major policy differences with Lon Nol and contested the 1972 presidential elections, which he may well have won had it not been for ballot-rigging by Lon Nol's supporters. On May 15, 1973, In Tam was appointed Prime Minister, and was reappointed on October 22, remaining in that position until December 26, 1973. He then returned to farming, but left the country in April 1975, becoming active in resistance groups along the Cambodian-Thai border, and serving in the Sihanoukist army. His Democratic Party failed to win any seats in the 1993 elections, and retired to the United States.

Khieu Samphan (b. 1931). The President of the State Presidium of Democratic Kampuchea from 1976 until 1979, he was born on July 27, 1931, and won a scholarship to France, where he studied law and wrote a thesis on Cambodia's economy. Returning to Phnom Penh, he became a teacher of Mathematics, and founded a newspaper *L'Observateur,* going into politics as a member of the National Assembly from 1958 until 1967, when he was worried about his safety and fled Phnom Penh for the jungle, where he joined the Communists. In 1970, he rallied in support of Prince Norodom Sihanouk and became a major figure in the Royal Government of National Union of Kampuchea. With the proclamation of Democratic Kampuchea, he became one of the most powerful people in the country and the head of state until the overthrow of the government with the Vietnamese invasion in December 1978. He was the leader of the Party of Democratic Kampuchea and Foreign Minister of the Co-alition Government of Democratic Kampuchea. Surviving his near-lynching when he returned to Phnom Penh in 1993, he remained in charge of the Communists and in recent years, he has been arraigned before International Cambodia Tribunal for war crimes and crimes against humanity.

Kong Korm (b. 1941). The Foreign Minister of the PRK from 1986 to 1987, he was a schoolteacher in Prey Veng, and worked in the fields in Democratic Kampuchea, fleeing to Vietnam in 1978. He became an adviser to Hun Sen, the Foreign Minister of the PRK, and was Minister of Foreign Affairs himself from December 1986 until December 1987. Marginalized by Hun Sen's CPP, he joined the Khmer Nation Party as vice president, and has been a Sam Rainsy Party member of the Senate.

Lon Nol (1913–1985). The Prime Minister of Cambodia from 1966 to 1967, and Prime Minister of Cambodia and then the Khmer Republic from 1969 until 1972, he was President from 1972 until 1975. Born on November 13, 1913, at Prey Chraing, Prey Veng, he joined the Cambodian police, rising to the position of Police Chief, and in 1947, formed the Khmer Renewal Party with Nhiek Tioulong. In 1955, the party was disbanded and the members joined Sangkum, with Lon Nol serving as Minister of Defense in many of the governments from 1955 until 1966, when he became Prime Minister. However, his government collapsed after a year, although he returned as Prime Minister in 1969. In March 1970, he took part in the overthrow of Prince Sihanouk and ran the country, leading it during the first civil war. Winning a rigged presidential election in 1972, he remained in charge of the Khmer Republic until April 1975, when he left for exile in Hawaii, later moving to California, where he died on November 17, 1985.

Nhek Bun Chhay (b. 1958). Deputy Prime Minister from 2004, he was born on February 7, 1958, in Battambang. He escaped from Democratic Kampuchea in January 1976, and on the Thai-Cambodian border helped organize the *Khmer Sar* (White Scarves) guerilla group, which formed a part of the Royalist forces when these were merged into the Armée Nationale Sihanoukienne (ANS). As the ANS deputy commander for technical operations, he became an important figure in FUNCINPEC working under Prince Norodom Ranariddh. He was one of the main targets of CPP forces in the July 1997 coup, and managed to escape to O'Smach on the Thai-Cambodian border, later returning to Phnom Penh and becoming Second Vice President of FUNCINPEC, and then its Secretary-General. He was appointed Deputy Prime Minister in 2004, a post he retained after the 2008 elections.

Nhiek Tioulong (1908–1996). Power broker and Prime Minister in 1962, Nhiek Tioulong was born on August 23, 1908, in Phnom Penh, and became a provincial administrator and governor of Battambang. In 1947, he and Lon Nol formed the Khmer Renewal Party and he formed a close friendship with Sihanouk, being appointed as Prime Minister of Cambodia from February 13 until August 6, 1962. He had been in charge of reorganizing the Cambodian army and was involved in facilitating the Vietnamese Communists by using the Ho Chi Minh Trail through Cambodia, a decision made by Prince Sihanouk. In 1969, he retired to France, later becoming active in politics with the formation of FUNCINPEC in 1981. He died on June 9, 1996. One of his daughters, Saumara, married Sam Rainsy.

Norodom Ranariddh (b. 1944). The First Prime Minister from 1993 until 1997, Prince Ranariddh was the second son of Norodom Sihanouk. In the 1970s, he moved to France, where he became a professor of political science and law, specializing in maritime law at the University of Aix-en-Provence.

In 1983, he was appointed his father's personal representative in Cambodia and Thailand, and then as Commander-in-Chief of the Sihanoukist Army. From 1986 forward, he was President of FUNCINPEC, and was a member of the Supreme National Council from 1990–1993. When FUNCINPEC won the largest share of votes in the May 1993 elections, he was appointed as Prime Minister of Cambodia, continuing to build on his international profile, gained from the years he spent in exile. He helped with the country's rebuilding process and the expansion of its economy. However, he was unable to deal with abuses of power by Hun Sen, who staged a coup in 1997, while Ranariddh was en route to France. He returned in July 1998 to fight the elections, losing amid allegations of widespread fraud. Appointed President of the Senate, he continued to lead FUNCINPEC until 2005, when he was ousted. He formed the Norodom Ranariddh Party, which won two seats in the 2008 elections; and after retiring from politics, in January 2009 Ranariddh was appointed as President of the Supreme Privy Council, with the rank of Prime Minister.

Norodom Sihamoni (b. 1953). The King of Cambodia from 2004, following the abdication of his father King Norodom Sihanouk, Prince Sihamoni was born on May 14, 1953, in Phnom Penh, the second-youngest son of Sihanouk and Princess Monique. Educated in Prague, he became interested in cinematography, which he studied in North Korea, and from 1981 forward, he taught classical dance in Paris. From February 1992 until November 1993, he was the Permanent Representative of the Supreme National Council at the United Nations, and was then appointed as Ambassador to UNESCO. On October 14, 2004, following the abdication of his father, he was elected by the Throne Council as King of Cambodia. In that role, he has continued to earn respect for the monarchy, and has made many international visits, which have helped to give him a wider international profile.

Norodom Sihanouk (b. 1922). The major figure in Cambodian politics in the 20th century, Prince Norodom Sihanouk was King of Cambodia from 1941 until 1955, and from 1993 until 2004. He was also leader of the country from 1955 until 1970, and leader of a government-in-exile from 1970 until 1975. The only son of Prince Norodom Suramarit and Princess Sisowath Kossomak, Norodom Sihanouk was educated in Phnom Penh and at the Lycée Chasseloup-Laubat in Saigon. On April 25, 1941, he was summoned back to Phnom Penh and appointed as King. Four years later, in March 1945, the Japanese induced him to declare Cambodia independent. He kept a low profile during the next few months, and when the French returned, he remained out of day-to-day political developments. In May 1950, however, because of a constitutional crisis, he became Prime Minister, and held that position again from June 1952 until January 1953, following his overthrow of the Huy Kanthoul government. He then embarked on the Royal Crusade for Independence and after Cambodia became independent in November 1953, he initiated plans for his own political movement, which was launched in 1955, as Sangkum Reastr Niyum—Sihanouk abdicated in favor of his father on March 2, 1955. The party won all of the seats in the 1955 National Assembly elections and went on to dominate the country during the rest of the 1950s and the 1960s. Sihanouk then presided over an increasingly prosperous country. However, as the Vietnam War intruded into Cambodia, and with economic problems, the governments became increasingly unpopular, and in 1970, he was overthrown as the leader of the country, the role he had served in since the death of his father ten years earlier. In exile, Sihanouk formed an opposition group which, aided by the Communists and China (and quickly dominated by the Communists), came to power in 1975 and quickly sidelined him. Sihanouk made a political comeback in 1979, and in 1981, formed FUNCINPEC, leading them in a war against the People's Republic of Kampuchea/State of Cambodia until the Paris Peace Agreement of 1991. He then returned to Phnom Penh and was reinstated as King on September 24, 1993. He tried to help establish some unity of purpose in the country and on October 7, 2004, in increasingly ill health, he abdicated and the Throne Council chose his youngest surviving son, Prince Norodom Suramarit.

Norodom Sirivudh (b. 1951). The Foreign Minister of Cambodia from 1993 until 1994, he was the son of Norodom Suramarit, but his last wife, Kim-An Yeap, making him a half-brother of Norodom Sihanouk. Living in Paris and then New York, he was active in FUNCINPEC, and in 1992–1993, was heavily involved in campaigning that saw FUNCINPEC win the 1993 elections, and Sirivudh became Minister for Foreign Affairs and International Cooperation. He resigned in October 1994, and in the following year, was hounded from the country by Hun Sen, who accused the Prince of threatening an assassination attempt. Closely allied to Sam Rainsy, Prince Sirivudh remains one of the major Royalists on the Cambodian political scene.

Norodom Suramarit (1896–1960). The King of Cambodia from 1955 until 1960, Prince Norodom Suramarit was the second child of Prince Norodom Sutharot, a son of King Norodom. He was born on March 6, 1896, in Phnom Penh, and educated in Phnom Penh and in Saigon. In 1918, he joined the French colonial service and two years later, married Princess Sisowath Kossomak. Their only child, Prince Norodom Sihanouk, was born two years later. Suramarit was Chancellor at the Royal Palace in 1929, and then Minister of Marine. Interested in Cambodian nationalism, he supported the *Nagara Vatta* newspaper of Son Ngoc Thanh in the late 1930s. A respected member of the Royal Family, although slightly estranged from his son, he was proclaimed King on March 2, 1955, after the abdication of Sihanouk. Doing much to enhance the prestige of the throne in his five-year reign, King Norodom Surmarit died on April 3, 1960.

Pen Sovan (b. 1936). Prime Minister of the People's Republic of Kampuchea in 1981, Pen Sovan was born on April 15, 1936, in the Takeo province. As a youth, he joined the Khmer Issarak and spent the late 1950s and 1960s in Hanoi. He came to support the Sihanoukists and the Communists in 1970, but soon came into conflict with Pol Pot and went to Vietnam in January 1974, where he remained until the Vietnamese invasion of Cambodia in December 1978. Pen Sovan was appointed as the first secretary of the People's Revolutionary Party of Kampuchea in 1979, and in May 1981, was appointed Prime Minister of the Vietnamese-backed government. However, in December 1981, he was critical of the continued Vietnamese presence in the country, and was arrested and jailed in Hanoi. Released in 1992, he tried to make a political comeback, but was unsuccessful.

Penn Nouth (1906–1985). Prime Minister of Cambodia on ten occasions between 1948 and 1976, he was born on April 1, 1906, in Phnom Penh and served in the French colonial service, ending up in the Ministry of Finance. Initially a member of the Democrat Party, he soon became a close adviser of King Norodom Sihanouk, and during the Sangkum years of the late 1950s and the 1960s, was an important and respected figure in many Cambodian governments. He was overseas when Sihanouk was dismissed in 1970, and helped with the formation of the Sihanoukist government-in-exile. He returned to Phnom Penh in 1975, and was nominal Prime Minister for a year, then moved to France where he died on May 18, 1985.

Pol Pot (1925–1998). The leader of the Cambodian Communists—Khmer Rouge—and the Prime Minister of Democratic Kampuchea from 1976 until 1979, Pol Pot was born in January 1925, according to his own account. His name at birth was Saloth Sar, and he was the son of a relatively prosperous farmer in Kompong Thom. He went to Ecole Miche in Phnom Penh, and then Collège Preah Sihanouk in Kompong Cham, then attended a technical school in the Cambodian capital before obtaining a scholarship to study in France after having supported the Democrat Party in the 1947 elections. He was in Paris for two years, and there, joined the French Communist Party, returning to Cambodia a convinced Marxist and—after the 1955 elections—he was dedicated to bringing down the Sihanouk government as the principal secretary of the Khmer People's Revolutionary Party. Elected secretary after the capture of Tou Samouth, in 1963, he left Phnom Penh for the jungles, and there worked for the overthrow of the Cambodian government. In 1970, he rallied to support Sihanouk and fight Lon Nol, and gradually, Pol Pot and his colleagues took over the Royalist government-in-exile, so that when the civil war ended in April 1975, they were in charge of the country. Pol Pot and his close supporters ordered the evacuation of Phnom Penh on the day of victory, and imposed their will on the population, being the leader of Democratic

Kampuchea, although he only held the position of Prime Minister from 1976. A hardline Communist, Pol Pot fled Phnom Penh following the Vietnamese invasion in December 1978/January 1979, and with the support of China, he rebuilt his party base. This time, he was able to rally peasants who objected to the rule of a pro-Vietnamese government run by Heng Samrin, and with support from China and also from Thailand, Pol Pot's soldiers were involved in a vicious border war along the Thai-Cambodian border. With the formation of the Coalition Government of Democratic Kampuchea in 1982, the Khmer Rouge gained some international respectability, and they participated in the Paris Peace Agreement of 1991. However, they decided not to contest the 1993 elections, with Pol Pot still being their actual leader, even though his resignation, retirement, and even death had been reported many times—the Khmer Rouge having recognized the international notoriety of his name. He was planning another war, and then, in 1997, the Khmer Rouge split. He was arrested by other Communists and in a trial in July 1997, he was found guilty of high treason and sentence to life imprisonment. He died on April 15, 1998, near his former base at Anlong Veng, on the Thai-Cambodian border.

Sak Suthsakhan (1928–1994). The Head of State of the Khmer Republic from April 12–17, 1975, Sak Suthsakhan was born on February 8, 1928, in Battambang and after World War II, joined the Cambodian military, training in France. He rose through the ranks of the Cambodian army and was at the Geneva Conference in 1954, having minor government posts alongside senior military ones. A supporter of Lon Nol, he backed the dismissal of Sihanouk in 1970, and rose through the ranks of the Cambodian army, becoming Minister of National Defense. When the acting Head of State, Saukham Khoy, left the country on April 12, 1975, he appointed himself Supreme Commander in a desperate attempt to stop the Communists from capturing Cambodia's capital. Fleeing to Thailand and then living in exile in the United States, he was encouraged to help form the KPNLF on the Thai-Cambodian border to oppose Communist (and pro-Vietnamese) rule in Cambodia. He formed the Liberal Democratic Party, which was unsuccessful in the 1993 elections. He died on April 29, 1994, from a heart attack.

Sam Rainsy (b. 1949). The Opposition Leader in Cambodia, Sam Rainsy was born on March 10, 1949, in Phnom Penh, son of Sam Sary, an associate of King Norodom Sihanouk. After his father's disgrace and murder, Sam Rainsy grew up in France, and married Saumara Tioulong, the daughter of Nhiek Tioulong. A founding member of FUNCINPEC, he was one of the organizers of the Royalist election victory in 1993, and was appointed Minister of the Economy and Finances, receiving many plaudits for his efforts to root out corruption. However, he was forced from the government and expelled from FUNCINPEC. He then formed the Khmer Nation Party, and after that name was subsumed by an opponent, he formed the Sam Rainsy Party. He survived an assassination attempt in March 1997, and ran a spirited opposition to Hun Sen, winning many seats in the elections in spite of electoral malpractice. His party is now the largest opposition party in the National Assembly.

Sisowath Monivong (1875–1941). The King of Cambodia from 1927 until 1941, Sisowath Monivong was the sixth son of King Sisowath. He was born on December 27, 1875, in Phnom Penh, and was educated at the Ecole Coloniale in Paris. Serving in the French army, and then as secretary to his father, he succeeded his father as King in 1927. During his reign, Cambodia prospered, with better-educated Cambodians securing work in the expanding civil service, and the French gradually building up the infrastructure of the country. However, King Monivong was angered by the Franco-Siamese War of 1940–1941, and died on April 24, 1941, at Bokor.

Sisowath Sirik Matak (1914–1975). Acting Prime Minister of the Khmer Republic from 1971 to 1972, Prince Sisowath Sirik Matak was born on January 24, 1914, in Phnom Penh, and was educated in Saigon, and then entered the Cambodian provincial service. He joined the Democrat Party and later was a member of the Khmer Renewal Party and, later still, Sangkum. He held numerous minor cabinet positions and was Ambassador to China and then to Japan. One of the organizers of the overthrow of Sihanouk in March 1970, he was a major political figure throughout the Khmer Republic and was Acting Prime Minister from February 1971 until March 1972, when he was Prime Minister for three days. His Republican Party was gradually sidelined from politics, and he remained in Phnom Penh and was killed by the Communists on April 21, 1975.

Sisowath Youtévong (1913–1947). Prime Minister from 1946–1947, Prince Sisowath Youtévong was from a minor branch of the Royal Family. He studied in Phnom Penh, Saigon, and Paris, where he remained during the Nazi Occupation. Much influenced by the French Socialist Party, he returned to Phnom Penh in mid-1946 to organize the Democrat Party and became Prime Minister of the country in December 1946, after the Democrats won the elections to the National Assembly. However, he was overworked and died on July 18, 1947.

Son Ngoc Thanh (1908–1977). A leading Cambodian nationalist, Son Ngoc Thanh was born on December 7, 1908, in Cochinchina (southern Vietnam), and studied in Saigon and then in France, taking up a position as a librarian in Phnom Penh, where he rapidly became active in nationalist circles. In 1936, he founded *Nagara Vatta,* the first Cambodian-language newspaper in the country, but in 1942, fled Phnom Penh for Tokyo, where he remained until May 1945. He then returned to the country and in August, he became Prime Minister.

Deposed and arrested by the British in October, he was sent to France, where he remained in exile for the next six years. Returning in triumph in October 1951, he hoped to rally his supporters for independence. However, he was unsuccessful and led a guerilla resistance against Sihanouk until 1970. He then returned to Phnom Penh and in 1972, was Prime Minister again. Toward the end of the Khmer Republic, he left Cambodia for Vietnam and was captured there and died on July 8, 1977, in a Vietnamese prison camp.

Son Sann (1911–2001). Prime Minister of Cambodia from 1967–1968, Son Sann was born on October 5, 1911, in Phnom Penh, his family being Khmer Krom. Educated in Phnom Penh, Paris, and London, he worked in the Cambodian provincial service, and joined the Democrat Party in 1946. He held a range of ministerial positions in the late 1940s and throughout the 1950s, becoming Director of the National Bank of Cambodia from 1964 until 1967. In the early 1970s, he tried to broker a peace agreement between Sihanouk and the Khmer Republic, but this failed. As one of the acknowledged leaders of the Cambodian exiles in Paris, he formed the KPNLF to fight the Communists, and they were involved in the fighting against the People's Republic of Kampuchea. Forming the Buddhist Liberal Democratic Party, and winning some seats in the 1993 elections, he then formed the Grandfather Son Sann Party, and was effectively marginalized. He died on December 19, 2001.

Son Sen (1930–1997). One of the major figures among the Cambodian Communists, he was born on June 12, 1930, in southern Vietnam, and went to school in Phnom Penh, and then to Paris for tertiary studies. Returning to Cambodia, he was a teacher and supported the neutralist policy of Prince Norodom Sihanouk. However, in 1963, he fled to the jungles and became a leading figure in the underground Communist movement, being in control of the security apparatus. As such, he was involved in the purges of many people during the period of Democratic Kampuchea. With the Vietnamese invasion, he fled the Cambodian capital, remaining a powerful figure in the Khmer Rouge. He was murdered on June 10, 1997, in an internal Khmer Rouge power struggle.

Ung Huot (b. 1945). First Prime Minister of Cambodia from 1997 to 1998, he was born on January 1, 1945, in the Kandal province. As a student, he studied accounting and finance, and in 1971, was awarded a scholarship to study in Australia. He remained in Australia after 1975, and worked for the Australian telecommunications conglomerate Telecom Australia (later Telstra), and was active in Cambodian community politics in Australia, becoming president of FUNCINPEC Australia. He returned to Cambodia in 1991, and helped mastermind the FUNCINPEC victory in the 1993 elections, becoming Minister of Posts and Telecommunications. In 1994, he was appointed Minister of Foreign Affairs, and in July 1997, following the coup launched by Hun Sen, Ung Huot became First Prime Minister. He then formed his own political party Reastr Niyum, but failed to win any seats in the 1998 elections. Ung Huot later returned to FUNCINPEC and became one of their Senators.

Selected Bibliography

GENERAL WORKS

Chandler, David P. *Facing the Cambodian Past*. Chiang Mai: Silkworm Books, 1996.
Chandler, David P. *A History of Cambodia*. 3rd edition. Boulder, Colo.: Westview Press 2000.
Corfield, Justin J., and Summers, Laura. *Historical Dictionary of Cambodia*. Lanham, Maryland: Scarecrow Press, 2003.
Mabbett, Ian, and Chandler, David. *The Khmers*. Oxford: Blackwell, 1995.
Men, Narong. *Who's Who: The Most Influential People in Cambodia*. Phnom Penh: MBN International & Promo-Khmer, 2008.
Tully, John. *A Short History of Cambodia: From Empire to Survival*. Crows Nest, N.S.W.: Allen & Unwin, 2005.

CAMBODIA TO 1432

Briggs, Lawrence Palmer. *The Ancient Khmer Empire*. Philadelphia: American Philosophical Society, 1951; Bangkok: White Lotus 1999.
Chakravarti, Adhir. *Royal Succession in Ancient Cambodia*. Calcutta: Asiatic Society, 1982.
Coe, Michael D. *Angkor and the Khmer Civilization*. London: Thames & Hudson, 2003.
Coedès, Georges. *Angkor: An Introduction*. New York: Oxford University Press, 1962.
Coedès, Georges. *The Indianized States of Southeast Asia*. Honolulu: East-West Center, 1968.

Cohen, Joan Lebold. *Angkor: Monuments of the God Kings.* London: Thames & Hudson, 1975.

Dumarcay, Jacques, and Pascal Royere. *Cambodian Architecture: Eighth to Thirteenth Century.* Leiden: Brill Academic, 2001.

Giteau, Madeleine. *Khmer Sculpture and the Angkor Civilization.* Diana Imber (trans.). London: Thames and Hudson, 1965.

Groslier, Bernard-Philippe. *Angkor: Art and Civilization.* New York: Praeger, 1966.

Higham, Charles. *The Archaeology of Mainland Southeast Asia.* Cambridge: Cambridge University Press, 1989.

Higham, Charles. *The Civilisation of Angkor.* London: Weidenfeld & Nicolson, 2001.

Jacques, Claude. *Angkor.* Cologne: Könemann, 1990.

Jacques, Claude. *Angkor: Cities and Temples.* London: Thames & Hudson, 2000.

Mabbett, Ian "Devaraja." *Journal of Southeast Asian History*, Vol. 10/2 (1969), p. 202–23.

Myrdal, Jan, and Gun Kessle. *Angkor: An Essay in Art and Imperialism.* New York: Pantheon, 1970.

Pym, Christopher. *The Ancient Civilization of Angkor.* New York: Mentor Books, 1968.

Vickery, Michael. *Society, Economics and Politics in Pre-Angkor Cambodia.* Tokyo: Toyo Bunko, 1998.

Yung, Peter. *The Khmers in Ancient Chinese Annals.* Oxford: University Press, 2000.

CAMBODIA FROM 1432 TO 1945

Bassett, David K. "The Trade of the English East India Company in Cambodia 1651–1656." *Journal of the Royal Asiatic Society* (1962), p. 35–62.

Boxer, C. R. "Spaniards in Cambodia." *History Today*, Vol. 21 (April 1971), p. 280–87.

Brodrick, Alan. *Little Vehicle: Cambodia and Laos.* London: Hutchinson, 1949.

Edwards, Penny. *Cambodge: The Cultivation of a Nation 1860–1945.* Honolulu: University of Hawai'i Press, 2007.

Franck, Harry A. *East of Siam: Ramblings in the Five Divisions of French Indo-China.* London: T. Fisher Unwin, 1939.

Khin Sok. *Le Cambodge entre le Siam et le Vietnam de 1775 à 1868* [Cambodia between Siam and Vietnam, 1775–1868]. Paris: EFEO, 1991.

Lancaster, Donald. *The Emancipation of French Indo-China.* Oxford: Oxford University Press, 1961.

Mouhot, Henri. *Travels in the Central Parts of Indo-China During the Years 1856, 1859, and 1860.* London: John Murray, 1864; *Travels in Siam, Cambodia and Laos 1858–1860.* Singapore: Oxford University Press 1992.

Muller, Gregor. *Colonial Cambodia's "Bad Frenchmen": The Rise of French Rule and the Life of Thomas Caraman 1840–87.* London: Routledge, 2006.

Osborne, Milton E. *River Road to China.* London: Allen & Unwin 1975; Sydney: Allen & Unwin 1997.

Osborne, Milton E. *The French Presence in Cochinchina and Cambodia.* Ithaca, N.Y.: Cornell University Press, 1969.

Pym, Christopher (ed.). *Henry Mouhot's Diary.* Kuala Lumpur: Oxford University Press, 1966.

Theam, Bunsrun. *Cambodia in the Mid-Nineteenth Century: A Quest for Survival, 1840–1863.* MA Thesis, Australian National University, 1981.

Tully, John. *Cambodia under the Tricolour: King Sisowath and the "Mission Civilisatrice," 1904–1927.* Clayton, Vic.: Monash University, 1995.

Tully, John. *France on the Mekong: A History of the Protectorate in Cambodia, 1863–1953.* Lanham, Md.: University Press of America, 2002.

CAMBODIA FROM 1945

Ablin, David, and Marlowe Hood (eds.). *The Cambodian Agony*. Armonk, N.Y.: M.E. Sharpe, 1987.

Ashley, David. *Pol Pot, Peasants and Peace: Continuity and Change in Khmer Rouge Political Thinking 1985–1991*. Bangkok: Chulalongkorn University, 1991.

Barron, John, and Anthony Paul. *Murder in a Gentle Land: The Untold Story of Communist Genocide in Cambodia*. New York: Crowell, 1977.

Bartu, Peter. *The Fifth Factor: The United Nations Interest in Cambodia, 1991–1993*. PhD Thesis, Monash University 1998.

Becker, Elizabeth. *When the War Was Over: The Voices of Cambodia's Revolution and Its People*. New York, Simon & Schuster, 1986.

Bizot, François. *The Gate*. New York: Knopf, 2003.

Burchett, Wilfred. *Second Indochina War: Cambodia and Laos Today*. London: Lorrimer Publishing, 1970.

Burchett, Wilfred. *The China-Cambodia-Vietnam Triangle,* Chicago: Vanguard Press, 1981.

Chanda, Nayan. *Brother Enemy: The War after the War*. New York: Harcourt Brace, 1986.

Chandler, David P. *The Tragedy of Cambodian History: Politics, War, and Revolution Since 1945*. New Haven, Conn.: Yale University Press, 1991.

Chandler, David P., and Ben Kiernan (eds.). *Revolution and its Aftermath in Kampuchea: Eight Essays*. New Haven, Conn.: Yale University Press, 1983.

Chandler, David P.; Ben Kiernan and Chanthou Boua (eds.). *Pol Pot Plans for the Future: Confidential Leadership Documents from Democratic Kampuchea, 1976–1977*. New Haven, Conn.: Yale University Press, 1988.

Chomsky, Noam, and Edward Hermann. *After the Cataclysm*. London: South End Press, 1979.

Conboy, Kenneth, and Kenneth Bowra. *The War in Cambodia 1970–1975*. London: Osprey, 1989.

Corfield, Justin J. *A History of the Cambodian Non-Communist Resistance 1975–1983*. Clayton, Vic.: Monash University, 1991.

Corfield, Justin J. *Khmers Stand Up! A History of the Cambodian Government 1970–1975*. Clayton, Vic.: Monash University, 1994.

Corfield, Justin J. *The Royal Family of Cambodia*. Melbourne: Khmer Language & Culture Centre, 1993.

Deac, Wilfred P., and Summers, Harry. *Road to the Killing Fields: The Cambodian War of 1970–1975*. College Station: Texas A&M University Press, 1997.

Dumarcay, Jacques. *The Palaces of South-East Asia*. Singapore: Oxford University Press, 1991.

Etcheson, Craig, *The Rise and Demise of Democratic Kampuchea*. Boulder, Colo.: Westview Press, 1984.

Evans, Grant, and Kelvin Rowley. *Red Brotherhood at War: Vietnam, Cambodia, and Laos Since 1975*. London: Verso, 1984; rev. ed. 1990.

Igout, Michael. *Phnom Penh: Then and Now*. Bangkok: White Lotus, 1993.

Jeldres, Julio, and Somkid Chaijitvanij. *The Royal Palaces of Phnom Penh and Cambodia Royal Life*. Bangkok: Post Books 1999.

Jeldres, Julio. *The Royal House of Cambodia*. Phnom Penh: Monumental Books, 2003.

Kamm, Henry. *Cambodia: Report from a Stricken Land*. New York: Arcade, 1998.

Khieu Samphan. *Cambodia's Economy and Industrial Development,* trans. and with an introduction by Laura Summers. Ithaca, N.Y.: Cornell University Southeast Asia Program Data Paper 111, 1979.

Kiernan, Ben (ed.). *Democracy and Genocide in Cambodia*. New Haven, Conn.: Yale University Press, 1994.

Kiernan, Ben (ed.). *Genocide and Democracy in Cambodia: The Khmer Rouge, the United Nations, and the International Community.* New Haven, Conn.: Yale University Press, 1993.

Kiernan, Ben, and Boua Chanthou (eds). *Peasants and Politics in Kampuchea, 1942–1981.* London: Zed Press 1982.

Kiernan, Ben. *Cambodia: The Eastern Zone Massacres.* New York: Columbia University Press, 1988.

Kiernan, Ben. *The Pol Pot Regime: Politics, Racism and Genocide.* New Haven, Conn.: Yale University Press, 1996.

Martin, Marie-Alexandrine. *Vietnamised Cambodia: A Silent Ethnocide.* Singapore: Indochina Report, 1986.

Mehta, Harish C. *Cambodia Silenced: The Press Under Six Regimes.* Bangkok: White Lotus 1997.

Mehta, Harish C. *Warrior Prince: Norodom Ranariddh, Son of King Sihanouk of Cambodia.* Singapore: Graham Brash Pte. Ltd., 2001.

Mehta, Harish C., and Julie B. Mehta. *Hun Sen: Strongman of Cambodia.* Singapore: Graham Brash, 1999.

Norodom Sihanouk, and Wilfred Burchett. *My War with the CIA.* Harmondsworth: Penguin Books, 1971. Reprinted with revisions, 1974.

Norodom Sihanouk. *Prisonnier des khmers rouges* [Prisoner of the Khmer Rouge]. Paris: Hachette, 1986.

Norodom Sihanouk. *Souvenirs doux et amers* [Bitter-sweet memories]. Paris: Hachette, 1981.

Norodom Sihanouk. *War and Hope: The Case for Cambodia.* New York: Pantheon Books, 1980.

Osborne, Milton. *Sihanouk: Prince of Light, Prince of Darkness.* Honolulu, University of Hawai'i Press, 1994.

Picq, Laurence. *Beyond the Horizon.* New York: Hill and Wang, 1989

Pin Yathay. *Stay Alive, My Son.* London: Bloomsbury, 1987.

Ponchaud, François. *Cambodia: Year Zero.* New York: Holt, Rinehart & Winston, 1977.

Sak Sutsakhan. *The Khmer Republic at War and the Final Collapse.* Washington D.C.: U.S. Army Center of Military History, 1980.

Schanberg, Sydney. *The Death and Life of Dith Pran.* New York: Penguin, 1980.

Seng, Theary C. *Daughter of the Killing Fields: Asrei's Story.* London: Fusion Press, 2005.

Shawcross, William. *Sideshow: Nixon, Kissinger and the Destruction of Cambodia.* New York: Simon & Schuster, 1979.

Shawcross, William. *The Quality of Mercy: Cambodia, Holocaust and Modern Conscience.* London: Simon & Schuster, 1985.

Short, Philip. *Pol Pot: The History of a Nightmare.* London: John Murray, 2004.

Steinberg, David J. *Cambodia: Its People, Its Society, Its Culture.* New Haven, Conn.: HRAF Press, 1959.

Stuart-Fox, Martin, and Ung Bunheang. *The Murderous Revolution: Life and Death in Pol Pot's Kampuchea.* Chippendale, N.S.W.: Alternative Publishing Company, 1985.

Summers, Laura. "The Sources of Economic Grievance in Sihanouk's Cambodia." *Southeast Asian Journal of Social Science* Vol. 14, No. 1 (1986), p. 16–34.

Swain, Jon. *River of Time.* London: Heinemann, 1995.

Szymusiak, Molyda. *The Stones Cry Out: A Cambodian Childhood.* New York: Hill and Wang, 1986.

Thion, Serge. *Watching Cambodia.* Bangkok: White Lotus, 1993.

Vickery, Michael. *Cambodia, 1975–1982.* London: South End Press, 1984.

Vickery, Michael. *Kampuchea: Politics, Economics and Society.* London: Lynn Reinner 1986.

Widyono, Benny. *Dancing in Shadows: Sihanouk, the Khmer Rouge, and the United Nations in Cambodia.* Lanham, Maryland: Rowman & Littlefield, 2008.

BIBLIOGRAPHIES

Burns, R. D., and Milton Leitenberg. *The Wars in Vietnam, Cambodia and Laos, 1945–1982.* Santa Barbara, Calif.: Clio, 1984.
Jarvis, Helen. *Cambodia.* Oxford: Clio, 1998.

Index

About the Author

JUSTIN CORFIELD was born in London, U.K., completed his doctorate on the Cambodian government 1970–1975, at Monash University in Australia, and has been teaching History and International Relations at Geelong Grammar School since 1993. The school is heavily involved in charity work in Cambodia, and in January 2009 he and some of his students travelled to Cambodia to start a program of building houses for the poor in a settlement near Phnom Penh. As well as books on Australian history, he has written extensively on Southeast Asia, including *The History of Vietnam* in this same series, and he has travelled and researched throughout the region.

Other Titles in the Greenwood Histories of the Modern Nations
Frank W. Thackeray and John E. Findling, Series Editors

The History of Afghanistan
Meredith L. Runion

The History of Argentina
Daniel K. Lewis

The History of Australia
Frank G. Clarke

The History of the Baltic States
Kevin O'Connor

The History of Brazil
Robert M. Levine

The History of Canada
Scott W. See

The History of Central America
Thomas Pearcy

The History of Chile
John L. Rector

The History of China
David C. Wright

The History of Congo
Didier Gondola

The History of Cuba
Clifford L. Staten

The History of Egypt
Glenn E. Perry

The History of El Salvador
Christopher M. White

The History of Ethiopia
Saheed Adejumobi

The History of Finland
Jason Lavery

The History of France
W. Scott Haine

The History of Germany
Eleanor L. Turk

The History of Ghana
Roger S. Gocking

The History of Great Britain
Anne Baltz Rodrick

The History of Haiti
Steeve Coupeau

The History of Holland
Mark T. Hooker

The History of India
John McLeod

The History of Indonesia
Steven Drakeley

The History of Iran
Elton L. Daniel

The History of Iraq
Courtney Hunt

The History of Ireland
Daniel Webster Hollis III

The History of Israel
Arnold Blumberg

The History of Italy
Charles L. Killinger

The History of Japan, Second Edition
Louis G. Perez

The History of Korea
Djun Kil Kim